THE GRAY DETECTIVE

BOOKS BY STEPHEN BURDICK

Deemer's Inlet
The Gray Detective

STEPHEN BURDICK

THE GRAY DETECTIVE

Three Novellas

Down & Out Books
3959 Van Dyke Road, Suite 265
Lutz, FL 33558
DownAndOutBooks.com

Cover design by Zach McCain

ISBN: 1-64396-281-7
ISBN-13: 978-1-64396-281-8

TABLE OF CONTENTS

THE GRAY DETECTIVE

Chapter 1

Joe Hampton had seen quite a few sunsets since he'd retired. The balcony of his condominium on Island Estates in Clearwater Beach, Florida, was the perfect vantage point. Those living around him shared equally advantageous roosts. But they never appeared to be grateful for the sun slowly sinking into the blue-green waters of the Gulf of Mexico, or the many colors refracting off the cumulous clouds hovering above the horizon. Maybe they'd grown accustomed to the magnificence or were too busy to notice. Maybe they flat out didn't care. Joe's deep-seated appreciation of his new surroundings had a lot to do with the uplifting mood he often experienced. Thirty-five years of police work in Philadelphia behind him was a major reason he looked forward to living a quiet life. Another reason, and the most important, was his lovely wife Joyce. Before she passed away, they had shared a number of sunsets all over the country. She liked to travel, and was all for moving to the inviting Gulf Coast community after a visit. He wasn't so sure. But he loved her, and loved making her happy.

Joe sighed and reached for the glass of whiskey sitting on the TV table next to his blue chaise. Whiskey on the rocks was his traditional after-dinner beverage. This time of year, though, the humidity was climbing, and the "rocks" melted quickly. He took a long drink and sighed a second time. "I'm doing it again, Joyce," he whispered to himself. "Beautiful sunsets always make me wish you were here." As he finished the whiskey, he heard the annoying tone of his cell phone. He shook his head and set the glass on the table. He knew who was calling.

"Joe, you're not going to miss Bingo Night, are you?"

"I don't know, Shirl. I'm feeling awfully lazy right now."

Shirley Lyon was an acquaintance who'd latched onto him shortly after he'd arrived at the Crimson Conch Condominiums. She was friendly and attractive for a woman of seventy. Her once-blond hair was now white as the sand dunes, and her lively blue eyes were pale and failing. Her verbose and perky nature struck him as annoying at times.

"Oh, Joe, it won't be the same without you. Tony and Emma are coming. So are Tom and Doris. They'll be disappointed if you don't join us."

Joe rolled his eyes. "Okay. Let me grab a—"

"I'll stop by in ten minutes. Is that okay?"

"Shirl, I need to shower first. I'll meet you in the Rec Room."

"Don't be too long or I'll come after you."

He heard her giggle before he ended the call. *Just what I need*, he thought, *a giggling old woman*. He'd already showered. What he really wanted was another drink. The extra boost to help him face the horde of bingo maniacs was an absolute necessity. *Why do I do this, Joyce*? He chuckled at the question. *Who am I kidding*? *We'd be going to bingo if you were here.*

Fifteen minutes and another drink later, he left his condo.

The Rec Room was filled with lines of tables and buzzing with white-haired women and bald-headed men. Joe still had a full head of hair, albeit gray, and was one of the youngest occupants in the complex. The median age was seventy-five, and being sixty-eight made him a prime target for all the widows and divorcees. He felt like a show dog on display as he strolled about the room.

"Over here, Joe!" Shirley shrieked.

Joe stopped and slowly scanned the crowd until he saw her.

Wonderful, he thought, *right in the middle of everyone. There's plenty of room in the back*. He forced a smile as he worked his way to where she and the others were seated.

"I saved you a spot. Here's five cards and the chips to mark your numbers."

"What would I do without you, Shirl?"

"Probably be home watching the ballgame," Tom groused. "The Rays are playing Baltimore."

"Oh, hush up, Tom!" Doris scolded. "You can watch the baseball game tomorrow night."

Tom was a heavyset man, six feet tall with silver hair, who'd spent his working years as a telephone installer and lineman. Doris was barely five-five and a brunette. Like her husband, she'd worked for the phone company in a switching station before retiring. Together they were quite a pair. He was personable and outgoing while she was shy and conservative.

"Tomorrow night is Bridge Night," Tony reminded them. "How could you even think of missing a hot night of bridge?"

"Thanks, Tony. You're a real pal," Tom said.

Tony laughed. Doris and Emma laughed. Shirley leaned against Joe as she straightened his cards.

"I feel lucky tonight. How about you, Joe?"

Joe caught her drift and winked. "You never know, Shirl. How much do I owe you for the cards?"

A mischievous smile settled on Shirley's face. "We can discuss that later."

"All right, people, let's get under way," the caller announced. "The prize for the winner of the first game is five dollars. That's five dollars for the winner."

Tony rubbed his hands together. "You folks might as well relax. I've got this game in the bag."

"Good," Tom said, and started to stand up. "I can catch the first inning."

"Sit down, Tom!" Doris ordered.

Tom returned to his chair, muttering.

"The first number is I-forty-two," the caller declared. "That's I-forty-two."

Joe took a breath, looked over his cards, and resigned himself to a long, boring night.

A little after ten o'clock, Bingo Night came to an end. The winners had received their prizes, and most everyone was ready to return home and go to bed.

"Now that was a lot of fun," Tony said.

"For you, maybe," Tom grumbled. "If I'd won six games, I'd be happy, too."

"Now, Tom, we come here to play for fun and relaxation," Emma said.

"Winning is fun. There's no fun in losing."

"Oh, hush up, you old grump," Doris said.

The group blended into the rest of the residents making their way out of the room. Once outside, they paused on a grassy plot close to the seawall as the others filled the sidewalk.

Emma looked up at the black canvas of night dotted with endless specks of light, some twinkling, some simply glowing. "Isn't it beautiful?" She nestled against Tony as he put his arm around her.

"One of the nicer things about living down here," Tom said. He winked as he gently nudged Doris.

Doris smiled. "You old grump."

Shirley walked to the seawall, transfixed by the lights reflected in the water from a condominium across the channel. She slowly lowered her gaze. "Joe, come here, will you?"

Joe walked up beside her.

"What is that?"

"Where?"

"Down there," she said, raising her right hand and pointing.

In the shallow water a dark object about five feet long bumped against the concrete barrier. With the nearest source of light being the lamps surrounding the Rec Room, identifying the buoyant object was next to impossible. Joe strained to look. A second later, stark realization hit him.

"Tony, call nine-one-one."

"What?"

"Call nine-one-one and tell them there's a disturbance," Joe said, taking hold of Shirley's arm.

"Come with me."

"Why, Joe? What's wrong"

"Shirley, please come with me," he said, attempting to draw her away from the seawall.

She removed his hand and peered over the wall again. "Oh, my god! It's a body!"

Joe latched onto her arm and led her away, intercepting the others coming toward them. "Hold on, everybody. We shouldn't go tramping around before the police get here."

"Yes, that's right, operator," Tony said. "The Crimson Conch Condominiums on Island Estates. I'll be waiting out front in the parking lot." He lowered his cell phone. "The police are on the way, Joe."

"Doris, Emma, I think Shirley needs to sit down. Would you take her home?"

"Sure, Joe," Emma said.

They each took an arm and escorted Shirley, still wide-eyed and shaken, to the rear entrance of the main building.

"Tony?" Joe said.

"Right! The parking lot." Tony hurried after the women.

"Tom, you stay with me in case somebody gets nosey."

"Good idea, Joe." Tom leveled his gaze on the channel. "You think it's someone who lives here?"

"Hard to tell. The body could have been floating for awhile. You know, carried by the current. Perhaps someone got drunk and fell off a boat or a dock."

"Sure. A drowning. That makes sense."

Joe nodded. A drowning was what he wanted his friend to

believe. No need to upset him. He knew that the incoming tide wasn't due for another two hours. And the way the body was situated in the shallow water, perpendicular and not adjacent to the seawall, almost guaranteed it had been dumped. A fact not needed to be made public—especially when keeping bystanders at bay.

"I guess you've seen your fair share of bodies," Tom said. "How many years were you in Homicide?"

"Eighteen," Joe said."

"You've pretty much seen it all, I bet."

"I've seen enough." *Enough for this lifetime, anyway.*

A siren wailed in the distance and immediately was joined by a second.

"You've lived here longer than I have, Tom. Has anything like this ever happened before?"

"Not that I recall." Tom pinched up his face. "Anything like what?"

"A body in the channel."

"Oh. No. The only thing I remember seeing is dead fish. You know, during a red tide invasion. That doesn't happen too often, though."

The sirens grew louder.

"I sure hope it isn't someone we know. That would be terrible."

"Try not to think about it, Tom."

"Yeah. Right. But if it is someone we know, Doris will take it hard. She always cries at funerals."

Simultaneously hitting their highest pitch, the sirens abruptly ended. Fifteen seconds later, Tony led two Clearwater Police officers through the rear door of the building. They were followed by a small group of curious residents. Tony stopped and pointed to Joe and Tom, who were standing twenty feet from the seawall.

"Over there," he said.

"Where's the disturbance?" the shorter officer said.

"The fellow on the right. Talk to him."

The officers were looking around as they approached the pair. Joe motioned with his head. "There may be a body in the water."

The officers switched on their flashlights and moved forward, taking calculated steps while searching the grass in front of them.

"What's going on?" someone in the group asked.

"Something happened by the seawall," another answered.

A chorus of murmurs followed.

Carefully training their LED beams into the water, the officers peered over the seawall.

"We'd better call Homicide and the Criminal Analysis Unit," the short one said.

They cautiously backtracked to Joe and the others.

"Which one of you discovered the body?" he asked.

"I did," Joe said.

Chapter 2

Joe's conversation with the police officer was short and riddled with the usual questions. "When did you discover the body?" "What were you doing before the discovery?" "Did you notice anyone acting suspicious?"

Another siren announced the arrival of an ambulance and the EMTs.

The Criminal Analysis Unit appeared next, and set about cordoning off the immediate area, erecting temporary lighting before initiating a search for evidence.

Joe and the other residents stood quietly by and watched the small army tackle the task at hand. Some in the group were fascinated by the activities, periodically whispering their observations to one another. Others drifted back to their condos. The former detective remained silent, noting the team's actions with an educated eye and questioning little about how they went about their work. Experience had taught him to let professionals do what they were trained to do; ask, not demand, and locate the most trustworthy crime scene technician when first beginning to piece everything together. An involuntary reflex whisked him back to the days when chasing murderers was a way of life. The transition brought with it a tingling sensation. The "old itch" had returned.

"Where's Charlie?" someone bellowed.

Joe and the remaining residents turned in the direction of the voice to discover a woman with a raven pixie haircut, wearing a midnight blue blouse and matching slacks. Her forcefulness and unpleasant scowl left no doubt about who was in charge. A female criminal analysis technician walked over to her, and they huddled. After a few seconds, the technician turned around and both women stared at Joe.

Raven Hair left the technician and headed in his direction. As she passed by, she gave him the once-over with her piercing green eyes.

At the seawall, she barked, "Get it up here and let's have a look!"

Two male technicians wearing rubber boots hopped into the shallows and hoisted the body. Two more technicians grabbed hold and pulled it into the grass. Raven Hair knelt down and began an examination.

"Excuse me, sir."

Joe turned to find a young man with steel-blue eyes holding a wallet bearing a badge and identification. He was a few inches taller than Joe, wore a beige polo shirt and blue jeans. The blond military-cut suggested he held a position of authority. That and the automatic strapped to his right side.

"I'm Detective Sizemore, Clearwater Police Department," he said. "I'm told that you discovered the body."

"That's right," Joe said.

Sizemore shoved the wallet into his back pocket and brought out a note pad and pen.

"Your name, sir."

"Joseph Hampton." Joe could feel Tom, Tony, and the others hanging on his every word.

"And you live here?"

"Unit four-oh-five."

"When did you discover the body?"

"About a half-hour, forty-five minutes ago, I guess. We'd finished our bingo games and were out here talking."

Sizemore grinned. "Was anyone with you?"

"I was," Tony said, "Anthony Dunham...and my wife Emma, Unit two-thirty-nine." Tony brushed his silver moustache with his right forefinger.

"And me and my wife," Tom said. "Tom and Doris Vernon. We live in Unit one-seventeen."

"Shirley Lyon, an acquaintance of mine, was also with us. She lives in unit three-fourteen," Joe added.

"And where is she?"

"Doris and Emma took her to her condo. She's very upset," Tom said.

"Did you notice anyone in the area when you came out of the building?" Sizemore continued.

"It was quiet," Joe said.

Tom and Tony nodded.

"Why were you standing by the seawall, Mr. Hampton?"

"Shirley was admiring the reflection of the lights in the channel. She saw the body, didn't know what it was, and asked me to come take a look."

Noticing that Tom and Tony were staring at him, Joe looked to his left and came face to face with Raven Hair.

"Is this the one who found the body?" she asked.

"Detective Sergeant Truffant, this is Joseph Hampton," Sizemore said.

Joe and Truffant locked eyes.

"Have you lived here long, Mr. Hampton?"

"Going on four years, I guess."

"Where are you from?"

"Philadelphia."

"Know many people in the condo?"

"Five or six, maybe."

"In four years you only know a half-dozen people?"

"I have some acquaintances. Wouldn't say I really know them."

"What did you do before you retired, Mr. Hampton?"

"I was with the Philadelphia Police Department."

"I see. And, of course, you did register your weapon when you moved to Florida, correct?"

"I don't own a weapon."

Truffant studied him. "That's a first. What did you do with the police department?"

"I was a beat cop in the beginning. Then I was a detective."

"Wouldn't be Homicide, would it?"

"It would."

Truffant's face held no expression. "Would you follow me, please?" She looked at her partner. "Sizemore."

Joe followed a step behind her. Sizemore said something to Tom and Tony, then hurried after them. The threesome walked to the seawall and stood over the body.

"Do you recognize this woman, Mr. Hampton?" Truffant asked.

Joe knelt down slowly. Under the temporary lighting he estimated the woman to be in her middle seventies. Her wrinkled face was drawn tautly over her high cheekbones. Her pale lips were encircled by copious wrinkles, suggesting she might have been a smoker. Wet, scraggly brown hair plastered her head to slightly below her jaw line. A gaping gash on the left side of her neck marred her aged elegance.

"She's a resident, but I don't know her name." Joe said.

"Would your friends know?"

"It's possible. They've lived here longer than I."

The detective faced her partner and nodded toward Tom and Tony.

Sizemore left quietly.

Joe returned his gaze to the woman. "She hasn't been dead long. No rigor mortis." He leaned closer. "Pupils are exploded. Has Crime Scene found anything yet?"

"They discovered a lot of blood out there."

A few feet away from them a small wooden dock jutted out from the seawall.

"No weapon, though. The killer either tossed it in the water or took it with him."

Joe picked up the woman's left arm and examined it closely. He repeated the procedure with her right arm. "No defense wounds. No bruising on her face. Are you certain she was murdered, Detective?"

Truffant narrowed her green eyes. "Is that your idea of a joke?"

Joe wasn't smiling. "She either knew her assailant or she was surprised, but she wasn't overpowered."

Sizemore appeared with Tom and Tony. Joe stood up and backed out of the light.

"Gentlemen, does either of you know, or have you ever seen this woman before?" Truffant asked.

"Oh, no!" Tony gasped, and turned his head.

Tom stood stunned, eyes wide and mouth agape, frozen for several seconds. "That's Beth Randolph. She was playing bingo with us. I don't believe it."

"Was she with your group?" Truffant asked.

"Yes. I mean, no. I mean, she came into the Rec Room with us."

"Did you see her leave?"

"We took two or three breaks. I really wasn't paying attention. There were a lot of players tonight."

"What's your name, sir?"

"Vernon, Tom Vernon."

"Mr. Vernon, are you absolutely certain you saw her inside the Rec Room?"

"She was sitting at the table in front of us. To our left, I think."

"Does any of you know her unit number?"

"The building manager could tell you," Tony said.

"Sizemore, go find the manager's office. Ask him..." She glanced at Joe. "...or *her* where our victim lived."

Sizemore started to leave.

"Mac's not home," Joe said.

Sizemore stopped immediately.

"Where is he?" Truffant asked. "Mac *is* a he, right?"

"Michael McDougal. He visits his daughter on Tuesday nights."

"Is there an emergency number?"

"It's on the wall above the mailboxes in the lobby."

Sizemore left without saying a word.

Truffant looked again at the water-soaked body of Beth Randolph, then back to the elderly trio. "Have you seen any strangers around your building lately? Other than utility or repair people, I mean?"

None of the men answered.

"Then, in the future, I suggest you keep your eyes and ears open."

Chapter 3

A germ of uneasiness was growing inside Joe as he entered his condo and turned on a table lamp. Although he hadn't known her, he felt a kinship with Beth Randolph. At the end of his career in homicide he'd noticed the onset of empathy tugging at his conscience. Part of being human, his partner had told him, but a condition a good detective could ill-afford to harbor. Personal involvement blinded objectivity, skewed the details of statements, and sometimes lured an investigator from a truth staring him in the face.

Joe sighed as he dropped into his brown leather recliner. *I'm starting to get the itch again*, he thought. The itch he'd always felt at the beginning of a case when he was younger. *Ridiculous. The game has passed me by. Best I leave it to the young stalwarts who understand the modern criminal mind. I'd look like a fool compared to them.*

He closed his eyes and lay back, knowing he should prepare for bed, but lacking the will to do so. The image of Shirley Lyon crept into his head. *I should be with her*, he thought. Being interviewed by the police was likely a new experience for his outgoing friend. Witnessing Shirley's reaction to the discovery of Beth Randolph, he figured she would welcome a strong shoulder of support—especially if being questioned by the insensitive Detective Truffant.

As Joe got to his feet, he heard both knees pop.

I hate being old, he thought.

Ambling slowly to the door, he promised himself he would not stick his nose into the investigation. Detectives Truffant and Sizemore seemed to be competent investigators.

Making certain the door was locked, he stepped into the hallway. Drawing up his face in disgust like he always did when seeing the pink carnation walls and maroon carpet, he began the now familiar walk to the elevator.

After a brief descent to the third floor, he stepped out of the elevator and gazed in the direction of Unit 314, Shirley's condo. Tom and Tony were standing in the hall by her door. Both were unable to hide their displeasure as he reached them.

"That detective threw us out!" Tom grumbled.

"Yeah! We come up to check on Shirley and she gives us the boot," Tony added.

"Where are Doris and Emma?" Joe asked.

"Inside with Shirley," Tom said. "It's okay for them to be with her. That detective's a real bitch."

Joe scowled at his friend and rapped lightly on the door. A few seconds passed before the door opened.

With his steel-blue eyes leveled, Detective Sizemore filled the doorway, a less than inviting expression on his face. "Mr. Hampton, we're in the middle of an interview."

"I know, and I apologize for the interruption. Would you please let Shirley know if she needs anything I'll be glad to help."

"I will."

"Who is it, Sizemore?" Truffant growled from inside.

Sizemore looked over his shoulder. "Mr. Hampton."

Joe heard a muffled female voice.

"Let him in," Truffant said.

Sizemore stepped aside and allowed Joe to enter.

Shirley was sitting in the middle of her buttercup yellow sofa flanked by Doris and Emma. A pine coffee table covered with magazines separated them from Detective Truffant. Doris got up and moved to an overstuffed chair nearby. When Joe sat down in the vacated space, Shirley immediately took hold of his right hand.

Detective Truffant glared at him before she resumed the interview. "Now, Mrs. Lyon, you said you remembered seeing Beth Randolph enter the Rec Room. What time was this?"

"Let me see, I think it was shortly before Joe came in." She glanced sideways at him. "So that would have been right about seven-thirty, I suppose."

"Did you see her leave?"

"Yes, around the time we took our first break. When was that, Joe?"

"Eight-fifteen."

"On my way to the restroom I saw her in the hall talking to one of the maintenance men. I can never remember his name. You know, Joe, the one with the shaved head."

"You mean Gary?"

"Yes, that's right, Gary."

"And his last name?" Truffant asked.

"I don't believe I know his last name. Do you, Joe?"

"Burgess," Doris said.

All eyes settled on her.

"I heard Mac mention it one time."

Truffant focused on her partner. "Got that, Sizemore?"

The blond detective nodded while scribbling in his notepad.

"Mrs. Lyon, did you see this Gary Burgess again after he talked to Beth Randolph?"

"No, I didn't." She paused. "I'm sure I didn't."

Truffant glanced at the others. "Did any of you see him later in the evening?"

No one spoke.

"Okay, I believe we're done here. Sizemore, what about McDougal?"

"He's on his way."

"Let's go downstairs and wait for him." Truffant looked at Joe. "Thanks for your help, Mr. Hampton."

"My pleasure."

Doris, Emma, and the detectives left Shirley and Joe on the sofa. Once he heard the door close, Joe started to get up.

"Please don't leave, Joe. Not just yet."

"Okay, Shirl, I'll stay for a little while. How are you holding up?"

Shirley squeezed her eyes shut and shook her head. "I don't think I'll sleep a wink tonight. I keep seeing poor Beth lying in that dark water."

"It's not something I'd wish on anyone. Maybe a glass of wine would help?"

She didn't answer.

"Is anything wrong, Shirl?"

Shirley opened her eyes. "I'd prefer something stronger. Can you keep a secret, Joe?"

"Sure."

"In the kitchen cabinet above and to the right of the sink is a bottle of Scotch."

Joe chose not to comment.

"Pour yourself one."

He patted her hand and got up, making the short walk to the kitchen. Pulling open the cabinet door, he immediately saw a half-full bottle of Dewar's and two tumblers. A tight grin formed on his face. *She's probably been waiting for the right occasion to invite me to join her*, he thought. He grabbed the glasses and the bottle by the neck. Two large ice cubes went into the tumblers along with three fingers of Scotch. He returned to the sofa, sat down beside Shirley, and handed her one of the drinks.

"Joe, please don't tell anyone about this. Sometimes I like a little nightcap before I go to bed. You understand, don't you?"

"Your secret is safe with me." As he brought the Scotch to his lips, Joe thought of the bottle of Evan Williams in his own kitchen cabinet. *We could all use a little nightcap tonight.*

Shirley sipped her drink then sat back. "I should have listened to you before."

"About what?"

"You tried to keep me from looking into the water. You didn't want me to see her, but I can be so stubborn at times."

"It's only natural to be curious, Shirl. Sometimes curiosity isn't a good thing, though."

Shirley offered a brief smile and sipped more Scotch. "Curiosity killed the cat."

"That's not what I meant."

"I know. You're a good man, Joe. You're kind and considerate and you care about other people. That's one of the things I admire about you."

Joe lowered his eyes. *Comes with old age*, he thought.

"What?" Shirley asked.

"I was just thinking. If Joyce was sitting here with us, she would take issue."

"You miss your wife, don't you?"

"More than I ever imagined possible."

"I miss Lenny, too. He was so much fun. Oh, we had our disagreements. What couple doesn't? But we laughed a lot, too. He was quite the jokester."

Joe tilted his glass and finished his drink. "I should be going."

Shirley sat up and set her drink on the coffee table. "Please, Joe, not yet." She let go a short sigh. "Would you think poorly of me if I asked you to stay? Stay the night, I mean."

"I can't."

"But why?"

"Shirl, I just wouldn't feel right."

"Joe, Joyce has been gone more than four years now. Don't you think she would want you to get on with your life?"

"Shirl, I'm really sorry, but I can't."

"Please, Joe. It would mean a lot to me."

Chapter 4

Joe awoke before morning slid its slender sunlit fingers through the half-drawn curtains. He eased out of bed, slipped on his clothes, and quietly left Shirley's darkened condo.

The day's first cup of coffee brought Joe no satisfaction. His night spent with Shirley left him feeling off-balance and wounded by pangs of regret. He'd stayed with her out of sympathy—always a bad idea—and callously departed without waking her. They hadn't made love. He couldn't. And though he'd sensed her willingness, guilt whispered strongly in his ear. The image of his wife began to fill his mind as it had when he lay in Shirley's bed.

"Damn!" he muttered and drank more coffee. "I miss you so much, Joyce."

He got up from the dining table and went into the kitchen, pouring another cup of coffee. He stared into the steaming French roast, still thinking of his wife, and made a snap decision. He would apologize to Shirley and make clear his feelings toward her. Then he would disappear for three days to get back on track. A motel room in Sanibel or Captiva was his first choice—somewhere on the beach where he could be alone with his thoughts. Decisions needed to be made and now was the time to act.

The hour was early, and the coffee was starting to work its magic. Joe decided to take his cup to the rear of the building and study the crime scene—from a respectful distance, of course. The old itch was back and stronger than ever. Surrendering was easier than putting up a fight.

He locked the door and quietly walked to the elevator. While waiting, a feeling of release came over him. A wonderful sense of knowing the course to be taken was the correct one—no doubt or hesitation to impede his progress.

A surprise waited when the door finally opened. Shirley stood alone in the elevator car, eyes wide at the initial sight of him, fading to concern a second later.

"Are you all right, Joe?"

"I'm okay. I was going to call you later and—"

"When I woke up and saw you were gone, I thought maybe you were ill."

"I didn't want to wake you."

"Well, you should have!" Her eyes narrowed. "I was worried about you."

Joe pushed the button for the ground floor. "Shirl, we need to talk."

"We can talk over breakfast. I'll make you whatever you want. I'm a good cook."

"That's what we need to talk about."

"My cooking?"

"No, about you and me and what happened last night."

"Oh. But *nothing* happened last night."

The elevator door opened, and a couple started inside. They hesitated before offering smiles and greetings. Joe and Shirley exited into the hall, eventually passing through the glass door in the rear of the building. Joe took Shirley by the arm and positioned her so that neither of them was looking into the sun.

"Shirl, I'd appreciate your hearing me out."

"Sure, Joe." Fear began to creep into her eyes.

"I like you, Shirl. You're a wonderful woman. And I'm lucky to have you as a friend. But that's how I would prefer it to stay between us...as a friendship."

"But what about—?"

Joe held up his hand, palm forward. "I know you were shaken last night, but I shouldn't have agreed to...well, I shouldn't have. I believe you want something more than a friendship. I'm not able to give you what you want. You're right, Shirl, I miss my wife very much. And when you and I are together...I can't, Shirl, I just can't. Believe me, it's not you or anything you've done. It's me."

A single tear then another trailed down Shirley's cheek. "I understand, Joe. I was hoping we could..." She lowered her head and brought a hand to her mouth. Saying no more, she left him and walked inside the building.

Joe took a deep breath then moved to a bench near the seawall and the small wooden dock. He sat down, setting his coffee cup beside him. He hated that he'd hurt Shirley. Not being honest with her now would have hurt her more at a later time. He hoped she understood.

The sight of the black and yellow police tape fastened to the dock and stretching to where Beth Randolph's body had been hoisted onto the grass brought with it a flood of memories. He'd seen too many miles of the dreaded barricade ribbon. Taking a sip of coffee, he visualized the woman's final moments.

Beth leaves the Rec Room and wanders onto the dock for a breath of fresh air. The assailant, man or woman, approaches her. They talk. Or embrace. Beth says something her assailant doesn't care to hear. Or the assailant says something to Beth. With no expectation of an attack, Beth neither defends herself nor tries to escape. The assailant strikes.

Another sip of coffee prompted the primary question: who? Yet another sip encouraged an equally important question: why? Not knowing Beth Randolph made it difficult for Joe to list her enemies. Everyone had enemies. Or, at the very least, people who didn't like them. Perhaps it was a homeless person who'd wandered onto the property. Joe shook his head. The police were good about keeping the island free of vagrants.

Besides, the homeless might steal but they seldom murdered. He studied the dock a few seconds. The specter of Gary Burgess looming over the diminutive woman took shape. Gary would know the time allotted for breaks during the bingo games. And he would know her. At least, he would know of her.

"Working on your tan, Joe?"

Lost in thought, Joe hadn't heard Tom arrive. He eased his head around as his friend sat down. "No, just thinking."

"About last night?"

"How does a murder occur a few yards away from a building full of people, and no one sees or hears anything?"

Tom shrugged. "You're the detective. You tell me."

Joe sipped more coffee.

"I ran into Shirley in the hall. She was really upset."

"I know."

"You two have a spat?"

"We had a discussion."

"I guess she wasn't happy with the outcome."

Joe remained silent.

"Doris and I are going to have lunch at the *Sloppy Seagull* on the beach. We were thinking of asking you and Shirley to go with us."

"I'll take a raincheck."

"No chance of reconciliation by noon?"

Joe shifted his body so he could face his friend. "Tom, first of all there's nothing to reconcile. And second, it's really none of your business."

Tom threw his hands up. "Okay! Okay! I didn't mean to tread on sacred ground."

Joe sighed and set his coffee cup in the grass beside the bench. "Shirley wants to be more than friends and I can't right now...maybe not ever."

"She's a good woman."

"I know."

"Doris and I think a lot of her."

A moment of silence lingered between them.

"I'm going to take a vacation," Joe finally said.

"Heading back home?"

"The other direction. Somewhere on a beach where it's quiet. Somewhere I can think."

"I would ask you where, but it's none of my business."

Joe grinned and shook his head.

Footsteps dragging along the sidewalk caused both men to look over their shoulders.

A rotund, balding man with a sprinkling of brown hair on his upper lip came plodding toward them. His green Hawaiian shirt adorned with palm trees, baggy khaki cargo shorts, and the worn leather moccasins covering his huge feet suggested he was a transplant from the north. His thick, snow-white legs confirmed it.

"Mac McDougal," Tom said. "To what do we owe the pleasure of your company?"

Mac drew a couple of deep breaths after he reached them. "Joe, that detective who was here last night, the bitch with the attitude, she wants you to call her."

"Why did she call you?" Joe asked.

"Because you weren't answering your phone."

Joe grabbed both of his pants pockets. "Sorry, Mac, guess I left it upstairs."

"No worries. I can use the exercise."

"I wonder what she wants."

Tom winked at Mac. "She probably wants a date, you handsome devil."

"Or to ask you more questions," Mac said. "She kept my ass up 'til midnight."

"How come?" Joe asked.

"She wanted to know all about Gary."

Joe paused, thinking. "May I use your phone, Mac?"

"Sure, Joe, let's go to the office. I left her business card on my desk."

Joe picked up his coffee cup, rose from the bench, and joined the hefty building manager in a slow and deliberate trek.

"Think about lunch," Tom called out.

"Raincheck," Joe said over his shoulder.

Mac's office was on the first floor next to the lobby, the door clearly marked. Joe followed him inside. After Mac handed him the business card, Joe picked up the receiver, punched in the number, and waited.

"Homicide. Truffant."

"Detective Truffant, this is Joe Hampton. I received a message you were trying to reach me."

"Yes, Mr. Hampton, we brought Gary Burgess in for questioning this morning. He tells a very interesting story about his conversation with Beth Randolph."

Brought him in? Joe thought. "I'm a bit confused, Detective. Why are you calling me?"

"Because he's changed his story three times, and now he's refusing to say another word until he talks to you."

"I don't know why he wants to talk to me. I don't know him that well. He didn't ask for a lawyer?"

"No, Mr. Hampton, he specifically asked for you."

Chapter 5

Joe was familiar with the location of the Clearwater Police Department building on Pierce Street. After taking the appropriate steps to be properly announced, he experienced an old and well-established feeling. As he walked into the Homicide office, he was home again. The surroundings and faces were different, but the atmosphere was similar to his workplace in Philadelphia. Cops were cops the world over. He recognized someone he'd met before.

"Detective Sizemore."

"Mr. Hampton."

"Detective Truffant called me. Where is she?"

"With Gary Burgess in an interview room."

"I'm curious to know why you brought him in."

"He wasn't thrilled to see us earlier and refused to cooperate. Carly didn't appreciate his attitude."

"Carly? You mean Detective Truffant?"

Sizemore's uneasiness confirmed his error. "Let's keep that between us if you don't mind."

Joe grinned.

"Please follow me."

A short trip to another part of the building brought them to Interview Room 1. Through the one-way glass, Joe could see the raven-haired detective sitting at a table with Burgess.

In his thirties, the maintenance man sported an average

build, his plain white T-shirt, hanging loose, added girth to his appearance. His bald head was of his own doing—a look popular among some men of this millennium. Joe saw no reason for shaving off a perfectly good head of hair.

"Detective Sizemore, I have to tell you again that I have no idea why he wants to see me. I don't know the man."

The detective shrugged and opened the door.

Burgess flinched as Joe and Sizemore entered the room. Truffant didn't move.

"Mr. Hampton," Sizemore announced.

"Have a seat," Truffant said.

Joe pulled out a chair and sat down beside her.

"Okay, he's here, Mr. Burgess."

Burgess's eyes flickered from Joe to Truffant. "I want to speak to him...and only him."

Truffant exhaled sharply and shook her head. "I don't believe this guy. All right. I don't have to do this, you know."

She and Sizemore left the room.

Burgess relaxed and leaned back in his chair. "I appreciate this, Mr. Hampton. I can't talk to her. She gets me all confused."

"Why did you ask for me, Gary?"

"Because you're honest, and I heard that you were a good cop in Massachusetts."

"Pennsylvania."

"Oh. Right."

"What do you want?"

"I didn't kill Mrs. Randolph. No one's going to believe me, but I didn't do it."

"Why won't they believe you?"

Burgess released a nervous chuckle. "If she had told you that I tried to rape her, would you have believed her?"

"Did you?"

"Of course not! I wouldn't do that to someone like Mrs. Randolph."

"An older woman, you mean?"

"Right."

"But you would if she was a younger woman."

"No! That's *not* what I mean."

"Then what, exactly, do you mean?"

"Mr. Hampton, sometimes I get together with a few of the women in the condo and we have...you know."

"You service them?"

"They pay me to do it. I mean, some of them aren't bad looking for being so..."

"Old?"

Burgess nodded.

"You're a prostitute."

"No! I never asked for the money. They offered it."

"So, naturally, being the accommodating fellow you are, you took it."

Burgess shrugged. "It's an easy way to make a few bucks."

"And Beth Randolph? Did she refuse to pay for your *service*?"

"You got it all wrong, Mr. Hampton. I refused her."

Joe arched his right eyebrow. "You refused her?"

"See, I knew you wouldn't believe me."

"Why her and not the others?"

"I don't go to bed with just anyone."

"I see. Go on."

"She'd approached me before. I told her no, but she kept bothering me. Last night she told me if I didn't agree to do her she would tell the police that I tried to rape her."

"Is that what you two were talking about in the Rec Room hallway?"

Burgess acted surprised. "Uh...no, it was after. She asked me to meet her out back on the dock."

"What did you do?"

"I met her on the dock. When she threatened me again, I caved in and told her I'd call her in a couple of days. Then I left."

"You agreed to have relations with her."

"What else could I do? Refuse?"

"No one heard this conversation, I suppose."

"We were alone."

"You said you left after talking to her. Did you go home?"

"I went to JoJo's on Court Street. I needed a few shots to calm my nerves. You can ask the bartender."

"Detective Truffant said you keep changing your story."

"I told you she got me all confused. She wouldn't stop asking me why I killed the old lady."

Joe nodded and got to his feet.

"Can you help me, Mr. Hampton?"

"I didn't come here to offer legal assistance, Gary. You asked for me, remember?"

"Then tell that cop I want a lawyer."

"I think she already knows." Joe opened the door and exited the interview room.

Truffant and Sizemore were standing next to the one-way glass. Truffant switched off the intercom.

"What do you make of his story?" Joe asked.

"He had time to put together a nice little tale while we were waiting for you," Truffant said.

"You don't believe him."

"The blood on the dock belongs to Beth Randolph. Burgess admits to being on the dock with her last night. Of course, no one heard their conversation. We'll get the names of the women he slept with after he talks to his lawyer. But I have a feeling they'll all be too embarrassed to admit to paying for sex. If you were in my shoes and trying to build a case, would you believe him, Mr. Hampton?"

"He doesn't have much going for him, does he?"

"Oh, and there's one more item that may be of interest to you. Tell him, Sizemore."

"Gary Burgess was charged with rape five years ago. The charges were later dropped."

***

Joe could barely remember the drive back to his condo. His exchange with Gary Burgess continued to barrel through his mind like a commuter train with no plan to stop. The inflections and pleading nature in the man's voice, as well as his sincerity in delivering his explanations, was most convincing. A line of horse fertilizer lay down by many a con man was equally compelling. Distinguishing the difference between the two proved to be the challenge.

Something wasn't sitting right with Joe this time, though. Why would Burgess kill Beth Randolph on the dock? People saw them talking in the hall outside the Rec Room. Killing her soon thereafter was a guarantee of guilt.

Joe took his time getting from his car to the front entrance of the condominium, head down and wheels turning. He nodded to a couple he didn't know on his way to the elevator. He pressed the button and waited, still trying to decide whether Burgess was lying. Swiveling his head to the right when he heard someone leave through the rear exit door, he turned from the elevator and exited through the same door. Facing the channel in the shade of the overhang, he thought, *Beth comes out of the Rec Room, goes into the building, and talks to Gary in the hall. They agree to meet on the dock. He follows her*. Joe stared at the dock for several seconds. *Or did he? I have no idea if he followed her right then. They could have met later.* Without more information, like Beth Randolph's time of death, he didn't know much at all. He shook his head and went back inside the building.

Standing in front of the elevator door again, he tried to remember how long Shirley had been gone during the first break.

As the door opened and revealed an empty car, he chuckled. "Why am I doing this? I'm retired."

The elevator took him directly to the fourth floor. When the door opened again, he stepped out and nearly bumped into Emma.

"Joe!"

"Emma. Are you lost?"

"I just came from your place. Could I have a word with you?"

"Certainly." He followed her down the hall.

Joe inserted his key into the lock, opened the door, and gestured Emma inside.

As she entered, she surveyed the living room.

"You keep your place looking very nice, Joe."

"Joyce would yell at me if I didn't."

"What?"

"Never mind. Have a seat. Would you care for something to drink?"

"No, thank you. Joe."

Emma sat down on one end of the sofa. Joe took a seat in the living room chair nearby, and waited to see what she wanted.

"Is anything wrong, Emma?"

"It's none of my business really, but Shirley is very upset. What did you say to her?"

Joe sighed deeply. "To put it simply, she wants to be more than a friend and I..."

"Don't?"

"Can't."

"Why not?"

"Emma, I don't care to discuss it."

"Joe, it's been years since Joyce passed away. You really need to move on."

"I agree. But the simple fact is I would hate to make a commitment only to realize it was a mistake."

"Shirley would be good for you."

Joe sighed again. *She's not listening*. "That may be true, but I might not be good for her."

"I don't believe that for one minute. You're a fine man, Joe Hampton. Everybody says so."

"And you're a good friend, Emma."

Momentary silence spawned awkwardness.

"I guess I should be going," she said.

"Emma, I'd like to ask you something, if you don't mind?"

"What is it?"

"This is difficult, so bear with me." Joe could feel himself slipping into *cop mode*. He had to be gentle. "Has word gotten back to you that some of the women in our building might be socializing with the staff?"

"What?"

"You know, getting friendlier than usual?"

Emma's mouth fell open. "You mean going to bed?"

Joe's stare was icy.

"Well, there has been talk of...I mean I don't want to believe that..." She couldn't free herself of his gaze. "Yes."

"How many women?"

"Well, I believe I heard of five or six. Maybe."

"Are they all widowed?"

"All but one."

"Who is the—?"

"Oh, please don't ask me, Joe! She would absolutely die if people found out."

Joe was unfazed. "Who is the staff member providing the service?" He noticed Emma breathing easier.

"From what I've heard, it's Gary Burgess."

Chapter 6

Opposing trains of thought tugged at Joe after Emma left. He spent the rest of the afternoon divided between the cloud of suspicion hovering over Gary Burgess, and the pending drama most certain to unfold when he crossed paths with Shirley again. And he would cross paths with her again.

That's the problem with telling the truth, he thought. *Explaining the reasons over and over until an understanding is reached. It's so much easier to lie.*

But he wouldn't lie to her. He couldn't. He liked Shirley. But love her? He loved Joyce. Still.

Joe rose from his sofa and went to the kitchen, removing a bottle of water from the refrigerator. He cracked the seal on the cap and was about to take a healthy pull when his cell phone sang out. He set the bottle on the counter, pulled the phone from his pants pocket, and checked the caller ID. The number wasn't listed.

"Mr. Hampton, this is Detective David Sizemore."

"Detective, what can I do for you?"

"I thought you should know that we didn't hold Gary Burgess." There was a slight echo behind his voice.

"I didn't think you could. Most of what I heard was circumstantial."

"Carly is really pissed. She's positive that he killed Beth Randolph."

"Frankly, I'm surprised. I would think she'd be more open-minded so early in the case."

"Me, too. She normally doesn't act this way."

"Something get under her skin?"

"She has a soft spot for little old...for elderly women."

"I see."

"Anyway, we're heading back to your condo to interview the women Burgess mentioned when he talked to you."

"You got their names?"

"The lawyer didn't object."

"David, if I may call you David, does Detective Truffant know you called me?"

"Uh, no, sir."

"Then why did you?"

Dead air filled Joe's ear.

"Carly's an outstanding detective, Mr. Hampton. One of the best in the department. But lately she hasn't been acting like herself."

"Did you ask her why?"

"In the time I've been working with her I've learned that Carly is Carly. She's a very private person. Some things you don't question."

"If her behavior is affecting the case, though, shouldn't you, at least, ask if something is wrong?"

"I know what's wrong. She doesn't like Burgess."

"I see. So why are you telling me this, David?"

"I would like you to help us. Unofficially, of course."

"Of course."

"I did some digging and found out you were quite successful in Philadelphia. Practically a legend."

"I wouldn't go that far."

"Would you think it over, Mr. Hampton? At least until Carly gets back on track?"

"Only if you agree to call me Joe."

"Would you think it over, Joe?"

"I will."

"Thank you. I'd better get going."

"Say, David, where are you calling from? I keep hearing an echo."

"I'm calling from a stall inside the Men's Room. It's one of the few places Carly isn't allowed...yet."

Joe chuckled and ended the call. He picked up the bottle of water from the counter and returned to the sofa. David Sizemore's request that he assist with the investigation struck him as ironic. He'd automatically begun to investigate on his own.

Old habits die hard, he thought, and took a drink.

Emma's confirmation of Gary Burgess being the "Condo Casanova" set him to wondering if the maintenance man had told him the truth. Joe didn't know Beth Randolph. But he *did* know what desperation could drive a person to do. Add loneliness, and there was no telling how low someone might stoop to attain satisfaction. But if Burgess didn't kill her then who did? And why? Joe took another drink and decided to wait until he heard from Sizemore again. With more information, the pieces of the puzzle might fall into place.

Shirley, he thought. *I'd better go talk to her. If she'll talk to me.*

With his water bottle in hand, he locked the door and strolled down the hall to the elevator, again making a face at the pink carnation walls and maroon carpeting. One floor later the elevator door opened. As he stepped into the hall, he spied Shirley, Doris, and Tom standing by the door to Shirley's condo.

Guess they just got back from lunch, he thought.

His friends didn't notice him until he was a few feet away. Tom grinned, but Doris's big blue eyes grew wide. Shirley's expression was stern and unforgiving.

"Thank you for taking me to lunch," she said.

"Let's do it again," Doris said, cutting glances at Joe.

Tom nodded and Doris smiled as they moved away down the hall.

"Shirl, I'd like a moment of your time if it's convenient," Joe said.

"And if it isn't?"

"Shirl, look, I'm sorry if I hurt your feelings. I didn't want to lie to you."

"Thank you for that, at least."

"I'm not ready to enter into a—"

"You made that perfectly clear!"

"I hope we can continue to be friends."

"Fine, friend, now if you don't mind, I have some things I need to do."

"Shirl, there's something else. It'll only take a minute."

Shirley released a sigh of disgust and glowered at him.

"Could we go inside?"

"I don't think so. And stop calling me Shirl! I hate it!"

Joe hesitated, unsure if another time might not be better. "How well did you know Beth Randolph?"

"Well enough to speak. I got the feeling she wanted to keep me at a distance...like some other people I know."

"This next question may sound a bit unusual."

"Go ahead. Nothing surprises me anymore."

"Have you heard of any staff members getting friendly with some of the residents? Female residents, I mean?"

"I don't pay attention to gossip. It can give people the wrong impression."

Sensing her hostility mounting, Joe decided to discontinue his inquiry. "Thank you, Shirley."

He looked on as she entered her condo, slamming the door as a message he understood well.

"Joyce, this isn't my fault," he mumbled to himself. The heaviness in his chest began to grow.

After supper, Joe settled in to watch some television from his generation. The new millennium offerings were silly and stupid and simply not funny. Not funny to him, anyway. He was fully engrossed in a show about a small-town sheriff and the antics of his overly-eager deputy when he heard the doorbell. Somewhat miffed, but not entirely because he'd seen the episode before, he turned off the TV. Setting the remote on the coffee table, he got to his feet and made his way to the door, taking a second to peer through the peephole.

"Sorry to bother you, Mr. Hampton."

"Detective Truffant. And Detective Sizemore. What can I do for you?"

"We've been interviewing some of your neighbors," Truffant said. "May we come in?"

"Certainly." Joe stepped back and allowed them to enter. "Please have a seat. Care for some iced tea or water?"

Sizemore started to speak.

Truffant cut him off. "We're fine, thank you."

She sat down on the sofa with Joe. Sizemore chose the living room chair.

"Mr. Hampton, we've verified what Gary Burgess told you earlier today to be true. He was bedding some of the women who live here," Truffant said.

"They freely admitted it?"

"A couple did. The rest were too embarrassed at first. They finally caved in."

"Were they able to tell you anything about Beth Randolph?"

"Yes, as a matter of fact, and that's why we're here."

Joe noticed Sizemore shift in his seat.

"Have you been interfering with this investigation, Mr. Hampton?"

"Interfering?"

"Talking to others about who was involved with Gary Burgess?"

Joe knew better than to lie. "I may have wondered aloud to an acquaintance or two. Is there a problem?"

"I don't like people getting in my way. Not even former

detectives."

"I didn't mean to cause any—"

"I would appreciate it if you would stop nosing around."

"I understand."

"Have you seen him today?"

"Gary Burgess? No, I haven't seen him." Joe desperately wanted to ask her why but didn't.

"Thank you for your time, Mr. Hampton."

The three rose and walked to the door.

"Detective Truffant, you're well aware that someone other than a resident or staff member could have killed Beth Randolph. We have quite a few visitors come by here every day. Relatives, vendors, repairman, you name it."

Truffant shook her head. "You don't know when to quit, do you?"

"Old habits die hard, I guess."

"Yes, Mr. Hampton, I *am* well aware. It's also possible that Gary Burgess had been harassing Beth Randolph and it came to a head last night. You remember he admitted to being on the dock with her. And not that it's any of your business, but the autopsy report says her death occurred around the same time. So for now that's what I'm going with. Anything else on your mind?"

Joe had nothing to say.

"Good evening, Mr. Hampton."

Truffant and Sizemore left.

Walking slowly back to the sofa, Joe sat down and allowed the words of the detective to linger in his mind. More and more it appeared as though Gary Burgess was the killer. Regardless of what he'd said, the evidence against him was solid.

Joe started to lean forward and grab the remote off the coffee table then hesitated. Television no longer interested him.

Chapter 7

A soft glow from the light in the kitchen painted a portion of the living room. The rest, what Joe saw upon waking, was a collage of dark shapes and shadows. The half-full bottle of water sat on the coffee table where he'd left it. Still not clear of mind, he picked up the bottle, removed the cap, and took a drink. Although room temperature, the water washed away the dryness inhabiting his mouth. No sounds distracted him as he lingered on the sofa. No people walking the hall or sirens wailing on Memorial Causeway. He figured the hour to be late.

An unexpected surge of energy persuaded him to rise, and then urged him onto the balcony. As he leaned against the railing, a warm breeze off the Gulf of Mexico caressed his face, a seductive sensation. A cluster of stars sat above the horizon across the ebony sky.

Maybe I'll sleep out here on the chaise lounge, he thought, wistful and dreamy-eyed—until he looked down.

Someone was lying next to the pool. At least the figure looked like a person. The pool lights were dark and the scant illumination from a half-moon high overhead was of little help. Neither were the LED lamp posts bordering the perimeter of the pool deck.

Joe leaned farther over the railing, unable to make a positive identification. He hurried inside, grabbed his keys, and quietly exited his condo, the maroon carpeting silencing his footsteps to the elevator. The elevator door opened immediately.

Quick-stepping from the elevator on the first floor, Joe rounded the corner and breezed through the glass door at the rear of the building. He slowed only to unlatch the gate to the aluminum fence surrounding the pool deck. Once inside he focused on the far side of the deck. The closer he got to the figure the more he became convinced it was a body. Stopping ten feet away, he was certain. A halo of dark liquid had settled around the torso. Cautiously taking a few more steps, he endeavored to look for evidence, careful not to disturb the scene. Closer still, he took a final look around before he knelt down.

Joe was astonished when the pale moonlight revealed the victim's face, and leaned closer to make certain his eyes were not deceiving him.

"Gary Burgess," he whispered and straightened up.

He remained focused on the man while his mind overflowed with questions: *who*, *what*, *where* and *why*, questions familiar to all detectives—even those retired. He surveyed the immediate area one last time and got to his feet. Stuffing his right hand into his pants pocket, he felt his keys and nothing else. His left pocket was empty.

"Damn! I forgot my cell phone again."

Careful to retrace his steps, Joe quietly returned to the building and headed for Mac McDougal's condo.

The third series of rapping's on the door brought the building manager to face him—and he was not happy.

"Joe! What the hell are you doin'? It's three o'clock in the damn mornin'!"

"Sorry, Mac, I wouldn't have bothered you if I hadn't forgotten my phone. We need to call nine-one-one."

"What! Why?"

"Gary Burgess is dead. He's out by the pool."

Mac's eyes widened and his mouth dropped open. "Oh, my god!"

***

Fifteen minutes later, the Crimson Conch Condominium was again buzzing with police and emergency vehicles.

There were two sides to the way Joe was feeling as he waited to give his statement. One: he hoped that detectives Truffant and Sizemore had been called to handle the case. Two: he hoped they hadn't. Immense dislike of Detective Truffant was beginning to build inside him and the reason was obvious. She reminded him of another detective he'd known many years ago—the cocky young cop he used to see in his bathroom mirror every morning.

"Joe," Tom said as he walked up.

Leaning against the aluminum fence, Joe turned to address his friend. "Hey, Tom."

"Is it really Gary Burgess?"

"I'm afraid so."

"What happened?"

"I don't know. I walked out on my balcony and happened to look down. That's when I saw him."

"You saw him from up there?"

"I didn't know it was a person until I came down to the pool."

"Two murders in two days. This is getting kind of scary."

Joe started to ask his friend how he knew the maintenance man had been murdered. They were distracted by the sound of the door opening at the rear of the building.

"Uh-oh," Tom said. "The bitch is back. I'll catch you later."

As Tom escaped and joined a small group of onlookers, detectives Truffant and Sizemore approached Joe. Truffant wore an expression similar to the one worn by Shirley the last time he'd seen her. Joe took a deep breath.

"Mr. Hampton, we meet again."

"Detective Truffant." Joe nodded to Sizemore.

"Do I need to ask who found the body?"

"I did."

"Of course. Out for a stroll in the dark, were you?"

"I was standing on my balcony."

"As I recall you live on the fourth floor. You could see the body from way up there?"

"I wasn't sure what it was at first, so I decided to come down and—"

"Do you wear glasses, Mr. Hampton?"

"Only for reading."

"So you took it upon yourself to nose around. I asked you not to do that."

"Would you have preferred I ignored it?"

Truffant's unpleasant expression deepened. "You didn't touch anything, did you?"

Sizemore stepped forward. "Carly, I think Mr. Hampton knows better than to compromise a crime scene."

Truffant's head snapped around. "If I want your opinion, Detective Sizemore, I'll ask for it!"

Sizemore wilted.

"I didn't touch anything," Joe said.

"Is the victim a man or woman?"

"It's Gary Burgess."

Surprise replaced discontent on Truffant's face. "Well, I guess what I've heard is true. What goes around comes around."

"I wouldn't know."

"Some might call it justice."

"Would you?"

"Since you know the victim's identity, any theories on how he was killed?'

"I couldn't tell in the dark."

"But you recognized him."

"I see him almost every day. He's one of the youngest around the building."

Truffant focused on the pool, and then the lights running around the deck. "You must be slipping, Mr. Hampton. With all these lights on you couldn't tell how he was killed?"

Joe scowled. "Detective, I'm finding it increasingly difficult to like you, not that it's a major item on my Bucket List. I don't understand or appreciate your animosity. Are you jealous, or is it simply that you don't like men?"

Truffant's green eyes flamed. "Sizemore, take his statement! I'm going to look at the body!" She stormed through the gate in the aluminum fence and barked for a criminal analysis technician.

Sizemore pulled a pen and notepad from the pocket inside his coat. "Joe, you really shouldn't aggravate her. She's not a bad person."

"David, that woman begs to be aggravated."

"Between you and me, I found out what's been bothering her."

"Besides a soft spot for little old ladies and a dislike for nosy retired detectives?"

"Word around the department has it her husband wants a divorce."

"Oh. How long have they been married?"

"Nine years, I think."

"That's a shame."

"So, Joe, tell me what happened."

Joe recounted his observations and movements leading up to his discovery of Gary Burgess.

"And you didn't see anyone in the building or by the pool?" Sizemore asked.

"It was quiet outside. And dark. There was no one on the first floor when I got out of the elevator."

"How about on your floor?"

"Not a soul." Joe pinched up his face.

"Did you remember something?"

"The elevator. I didn't have to wait for it."

Sizemore gave him a puzzled look.

"What I mean is, our elevator isn't the fastest around unless it stops on or near your floor."

"Does it normally return to the first floor after someone uses it?"

"I don't know, David." Joe thought some more. "Even if it doesn't, the car could have been sitting on the fourth floor, fifth floor or third floor for hours."

"I'll make a note of it, anyway, and check it out."

Joe continued to ponder his observation.

Sizemore did a double-take. "Looks like Carly wants me." He reached inside his coat and pulled out a business card. "If you think of anything else, Joe, call me."

Joe watched him hustle off to join his partner, and thought, *I wonder if Gary was shot or stabbed. Probably stabbed. A gunshot would have awakened people.*

He continued to study the detectives and criminal analysis technicians as they milled about.

A half-hour later he returned to his condo and made a pot of coffee.

Chapter 8

Joe was sitting at the dining table finishing the last of the freshly brewed coffee. He hadn't bothered with breakfast because his back was bothering him.

I must have slept wrong, he thought.

He smiled, remembering that he had sometimes suffered similar physical ailments when working a difficult case.

Here we go again, Joyce. Will I ever get used to retirement?

He hoped his appetite would return by lunch time. If not, well, he'd suffered through starvation before. A soft rapping on the door drove him from his thoughts.

Tony stood in the hall looking uneasy, his thinning silver hair perfectly combed as usual.

"Joe, I was hoping you were awake. I, uh…would you like to go fishing?"

"Fishing?" Joe chuckled. "I didn't know you were a fisherman, Tony."

"I don't go often. I don't really…we can go to Pier 60 and rent some rods. My treat. What do you say?"

Joe studied his friend. Tony didn't appear to be himself. Being nervous was not a part of his normally upbeat behavior.

"Is there something you want to tell me?"

"Uh, yes, but…"

"Then why don't you come in. I'll make some more coffee."

"Joe, I'd prefer that we talked somewhere else." Tony looked to his left and then to his right.

"Okay, let's go fishing."

After changing into a faded blue work shirt, khaki trousers, and his favorite black running shoes, Joe slipped on his red Phillies baseball cap. Following Tony to the elevator and, eventually, the parking lot, he climbed into his friend's silver Honda Pilot, and they drove to Memorial Causeway. There was no discussion during the trip to Clearwater Beach. *Odd*, Joe thought. Tony was as friendly and outgoing as anyone he'd ever known. Not today.

Pier 60 sat on Clearwater Beach not very far from their Island Estates condominium. When they arrived at the beach parking lot, they circled it a few times before finding a space. Leaving the SUV, they casually strolled to the pier's entrance, slowed to a halt, and gazed at the one thousand-eighty-foot-long structure with its bait house, six pavilions, and mounted telescopes for inquisitive tourists.

"I don't *really* want to go fishing," Tony said.

"I gathered," Joe replied.

The Beach Walk, a meandering promenade running parallel to the beach and dotted with people on this day, looked inviting.

"Are you up for taking a walk, Joe?"

"Sure. I can always use the exercise."

The men headed south on the concrete walkway at a relaxed pace.

Joe could sense his friend's anxiety, but decided to allow him to open up when he was ready. No point in adding more stress to an apparently stressful situation. They passed a couple who looked several years their junior, a happy group of Asians sporting cameras, and a young woman on her way to work or some unpleasant rendezvous, judging from the scowl etched upon her face. When she was well past them, Tony cleared his throat.

"I apologize for acting so secretive, Joe. It's just..." He released a sigh. "Emma told me about your conversation. You know, about Gary Burgess."

"I figured she would."

"Part of what she said wasn't true. The part about one of the women being married, I mean."

That's interesting, Joe thought. *The police verified what I was told by her and Gary.*

Tony glanced at the Gulf before turning back to him. "Emma was trying to protect Shirley."

Shock silenced Joe for a moment. "Shirley and Burgess were—"

"Emma was afraid that if you found out then you might not want to continue your friendship with Shirley. I feel terrible telling you this, Joe."

"Why *are* you telling me, Tony?"

Tony stopped walking. His blue eyes looked burdened with guilt.

"During the first break on Bingo Night, Emma went back to our condo to get a sweater."

"I remember. She was uncomfortable because the Rec Room was so cold."

"On her way back, she saw Gary Burgess leave through the main entrance as she was getting out of the elevator. When she reached the door to the Rec Room, she saw Shirley heading toward the dock."

"Was Shirley alone?"

"Yes, but someone was waiting for her. Emma didn't recognize the person because the lights on the dock aren't very bright."

Joe looked away, thinking.

Shirley said she was going to the restroom. And she admitted seeing Gary Burgess talking to Beth Randolph. Another thought, most unpleasant, filtered into his mind. *She lied to the police by pretending she couldn't remember his name.* "Did Emma say anything else?"

Hurt displaced the guilt in Tony's eyes. "In light of what happened last night, she thinks it was Beth Randolph she saw on the dock. And Shirley killed her." He took a deep breath. "She may have killed Gary, too."

"But why kill him?" Joe countered. Before Tony could answer, he added, "Why kill either of them?"

"I don't know. Maybe it had something to do with what Gary was doing. Emma feels terrible."

"She has to go to the police."

"She won't do that."

"Tony, she has to tell them!"

"You know how stubborn Emma can be, Joe. Her mind is made up."

Joe cocked his head to the right. "And that's why you came to me."

"You can tell the police you got an anonymous tip."

"Lie to them in other words."

"Joe, Emma doesn't want to get involved!"

"She's already involved! And you're putting me in a difficult situation, Tony. Detective Truffant is not one of my biggest fans. Lying to her will only make the situation worse."

"I know, and I'm sorry."

The men continued walking until they reached the Hyatt Regency. Tony had said all he was going to say, so they turned around and headed back to his SUV.

Joe's cell phone sounded as they left the parking lot and entered the roundabout leading to Memorial Causeway.

I wonder who needs a favor now, he thought, and stuffed his hand into his pants pocket.

"Mr. Hampton, this is Detective Truffant."

"Oh!" Joe cleared his throat. "What can I do for you, Detective?"

"I'd like to talk to you if it's convenient. I can be at your condo in five minutes."

"Make it fifteen. I'm not at home right now." Joe ended the call and shoved the phone back into his pocket. "Seems I'm popular today. I have a date for brunch."

***

Detective Truffant was true to their agreement, knocking on Joe's door exactly fifteen minutes after she had called. Having prepared himself for another round of her discourteous behavior, he was caught unaware upon seeing her smile. He responded with a cordial invitation.

"Would you care for something to drink?"

"No, thank you, Mr. Hampton, I...I'll get right to the point."

"Then please sit down."

Truffant claimed one end of the sofa. He sat down on the other.

"Mr. Hampton, we got off to a bad start, and I'm to blame. We have another case that's pending. A double homicide. And our lack of progress is frustrating. Getting this case on top of the others hit me the wrong way. And I've allowed my personal life to...what I'm trying to say is I'd like to start again."

"That's fine by me, Detective. I understand how the demands of the job can affect the home front."

"I hoped you would...and please call me Carly."

"If you'll call me Joe."

He could see the woman's smile was heartfelt—a smile that reminded him of Joyce.

"So there's no misunderstanding, Joe, David and I had it out earlier. Whew! Boy did we have it out. He unloaded both barrels."

"Was it because of me?"

"Partly, and my attitude, and the way I've been approaching the job."

"I noticed you called him by his first name."

"I'm working on that, too."

"Does he know that you came here?"

"I'm going to tell him as soon as we're done."

"Good. But, Carly, I think you're being a little hard on yourself. I've seen how you work a crime scene. I'd have no problem partnering with you."

"Thank you, Joe. I feel much better."

"As do I."

"And if you'd care to lend a hand, any help will be greatly appreciated."

"Now that you mention it, there has been a development I should pass along."

Carly raised her left hand. "Hold on." She fished through the pocket of her gray slacks and pulled out her iPhone. "Let's get David over here."

The conversation with her partner was brief. Joe could see a noticeable change of behavior in the young woman.

"It may take him a while to get here," Carly said. "He'll need some time for the shock to wear off."

Joe chuckled. "I feel I must come clean, Carly. David and I had a few discussions about you. In case you don't know it, he would follow you to Hell and back."

"That's good to hear. Lately, I've put *him* through hell. And I know about your discussions. He told me in no uncertain terms when he ripped my head off."

"I hope you're not angry."

"Not now. Sometimes it's difficult for the truth to sink into this hard head."

Joe chuckled again, amazed at how alike they were.

Chapter 9

Joe noticed immediately that David seemed pleasantly surprised at the relaxed demeanor between he and Carly. The atmosphere was definitely more civil.

Once he'd settled into the dark blue chair nearest the sofa, the conversation began.

"I've come to know that the night Beth Randolph was killed, Shirley Lyon was in the immediate vicinity," Joe said. "By that I mean she was seen heading toward the dock."

"Was this around the time that Beth Randolph met with Gary Burgess?" Carly asked.

"I understand it to be after they met. Someone *was* on the dock, though. Who it might have been, exactly, was not known."

"Who saw Lyon, Joe?"

"Emma Dunham."

Carly turned her attention to David. "Did we interview her?"

"Indirectly. She was one of the two women present when we interviewed Mrs. Lyon."

"Do you know why she didn't tell us this earlier, Joe?"

Joe grimaced. "This is where it gets personal."

"Personal or not, you have to tell us. You've been in my shoes before."

"I know."

Joe explained Emma's reasoning down to the smallest detail, including his own beliefs.

David finished scribbling in his notepad and sat back when the retired detective finished his statement.

"Joe, the Dunhams aren't exactly cooperating with this investigation," Carly said. "One lied to us, and they both withheld important information."

"I know."

David looked up from his notepad. "Joe, I'm sorry, but I have to ask."

"Ask him what?" Carly interrupted.

"Did *you* kill Gary Burgess?"

Joe felt the sting of being on the other side of a question he'd asked many times before. "No, David, I did not kill Gary Burgess. I didn't find out that Shirley was a part of his harem until this morning."

"When Tony Dunham told you."

"Right."

"And he'll confirm that he told you."

Joe shrugged.

"Why wouldn't he?" Carly asked.

"I don't think Emma knows he spoke to me. He may be reluctant."

Awkward silence hung among them.

"We *have* to talk to the Dunhams," Carly said.

"I know."

"Sounds like it might cause some hard feelings," David said.

"Wouldn't be the first time."

"Well, we'd better get to it," Carly said. "Thanks for your help, Joe, and thanks for understanding."

"Glad to be of service, and I'm glad we sorted it out."

"Me, too," David said, "but I would expect no less from someone as well respected as The Gray Detective."

Carly's mouth dropped open. "You just had to bring it up, didn't you?"

"The Gray Detective?" Joe asked.

Carly sighed and shook her head. "The first night...when we

were heading back to the station...I was really mad at you. I went on a tirade about how you were a monumental pain in the ass."

The beginning of a grin formed on Joe's face.

"And?" David said.

"And last night, after we talked to you, I was *really* pissed," Carly continued. "Among other things, I called you The Gray Detective, a nosey old goat whose time had come and gone."

"And she said she would step on you if you got in the way again."

"You're enjoying this, aren't you?"

David laughed.

Joe's grin became a smile. "Well, Carly, since we're being honest, I presumed that you were another hard-driving...feminist out to bulldoze everyone in your way to prove your worth. I now know that I was mistaken."

Joe felt better after they left. He was even hungry. Figuring he should eat while in the mood, and knowing the ton of grief sure to come his way later, he decided to indulge in his favorite noontime meal: a ham and Swiss on whole wheat lathered with mustard.

Sorry, Joyce, I don't feel like lettuce and tomato today.

He went to the kitchen, lifted in spirit. His back had stopped hurting as well. He gathered the ingredients necessary and readied himself. With two slices of bread laid out on a paper towel and a squeeze bottle of yellow mustard aimed and ready, he was about to begin building his masterpiece when his cell phone rang.

"Aw, wouldn't you know it."

He set the bottle on the kitchen counter and pulled the phone out of his pocket.

"Joe, I'd like to talk...if you want to."

There was no mistaking Shirley's voice.

"All right. How are you?"

"I don't mean on the phone. How about I treat you to lunch?"

Joe's stomach tightened. He might be accepting a date with a murderer. "What do you have in mind?"

"I'd like to try that new place on North Fort Harrison, Simply Salad."

Joe rolled his eyes.

So much for real food. "Sounds good."

"Would you mind driving?"

"Not at all. How much time do you need?"

"I'm ready now."

"Great! I'm starved. I'll be right down."

Joe put away the fixings for his lunch except for a slice of ham and a slice of cheese, which he rolled into a cylinder and ate quickly. At least he could enjoy a sampling of real food. Grazing was not his idea of a meal.

Making certain he had his cell phone, he locked the door and walked to the elevator, making a face at the carpet and walls like he always did.

Shirley was all smiles when she invited him into her condo. Joe silently breathed a sigh of relief. Facing him as they stood in the doorway, her pale blue eyes were hopeful.

"Joe, I want to apologize. I shouldn't have treated you the way I did."

"Shirley, it's okay, I understand. And I hope you understand."

"You were just being honest, and I...well, we can still be friends, can't we?"

"Of course."

"Good. Shall we go?"

Joe knew at once that all was right between them again. What he couldn't figure out was why. When a woman's feelings were hurt, recovery was slow in coming—if at all. That was his experience anyway.

Shirley started talking, rehashing all the events of the previous two evenings. She shared her feelings and, every so often, inquired of his. He offered only the expected answers. She continued the one-sided conversation until they got into his Camry. Before they left the parking lot, Shirley pulled his right hand from the steering wheel and held it.

"There's something you should know, and I want you to hear it from me."

"Is that what you wanted to talk about?"

"Partly." Shirley sighed deeply. "The police came to see me again last night."

"Oh?"

"About Gary Burgess."

Joe said nothing.

"On occasion, Gary and I have been intimate and...actually, it was often more than occasionally."

"I see."

"No, Joe, you don't. I was so lonely I couldn't stand it anymore. I really wanted to be with you. Anyway, I heard that Gary was, uh, helping others, so I called him. I hope you don't think poorly of me for what I did."

"No, I can see where...you say there were other women?"

"The police talked to all of us, I guess."

"When was the last time you saw Gary?"

"I wanted you to know before you heard it from the gossip mill."

Too late. Your secret's out. "I appreciate your telling me, Shirley."

"And I'd appreciate your keeping it under your hat."

"I don't wear a hat."

Shirley laughed.

Joe gave her his best smile. "Let's go have a nice Caprese salad."

"Who are you trying to kid, Joe Hampton? You're going to get a chef's salad. With double the meat, most likely."

"All right, you got me."

Joe started the car and slowly pulled out of the parking lot, wondering what else was on Shirley's mind.

Chapter 10

Simply Salad was a cafeteria-style restaurant located a block south of Cleveland Street. Joe and Shirley had no problem parking, with available spaces on the sides and in the rear of the free-standing building. When time came to select their meals, Shirley acted her old self again, laughing when Joe chose the chef's salad as she had predicted. He only smiled when she opted for a Caprese salad.

Cordial best described the exchange between them after they were seated, but uneasiness slowly built a path inside Joe. His friend had endured a great deal in the past two days, yet she appeared unfazed for the most part. Was this a show of strength she'd never permitted him to see? Or the confidence displayed by a murderer who believed herself above reproach? Joe had witnessed this self-assurance in killers before, but not in such a retiring and inoffensive person as Shirley. In light of Emma's unsubstantiated accusation, though, a shadow of doubt was emerging.

"Joe, I respect your feelings about us. Wanting to be friends, I mean. But I enjoyed your staying with me the other night."

Joe attempted to chew and swallow the raw vegetables and slice of turkey he'd shoved into his mouth. "Shirley...you must understand...Joyce and I...were married a long time."

"Couldn't we enjoy the intimacy without officially having a permanent relationship? You know, no strings attached?"

What she was suggesting would have set well with most men.

Joe's suspicious nature wouldn't allow him to consent to such an agreement without wondering if there was a catch. He finally cleared his mouth of food.

"Shirley, I've never told anyone this, but I'm a notorious foot-dragger. I always have been. It used to infuriate Joyce. I take my time and consider all the possibilities before making a decision. Especially an important decision. That's not going to change."

Shirley batted her pale blue eyes. "I'm not Joyce. I can wait. You don't know what you're missing, though."

Nothing more was said—or needed saying. In Joe's mind, this was either an invitation to spend his winter years in a blissful, uncomplicated union, or the song of the spider to the fly. An error in judgment could prove to be deadly.

They had finished their meals and were about to leave when they heard the muffled tone of Joe's cell phone.

"Must be one of your other girlfriends," Shirley said with a smile.

"Oh, no doubt," Joe replied. He pulled the phone out of his pants pocket and didn't bother to check the caller I.D.

"Joe, it's Carly."

Frigid shards iced his insides. He glanced at Shirley. "Well, it's been a long time. How are you?"

"What do you mean? I just left your...you're not alone are you?"

"That's right. Funny how time slips away."

"We went to see Shirley Lyon. She wasn't home."

"Really? That's too bad. Maybe you should try again some other time."

"Is she with you?"

"Truer words were never spoken, but you shouldn't give up."

"Are you coming home soon?"

"Now that's hard to say. Truth is, I really don't know."

"We need to talk to her."

"Okay, I'll see what I can do."

"We'll wait fifteen minutes, and Joe, be careful. Emma

Dunham broke down and told us a lot about your friend Shirley. She very well may be the killer."

"Wonderful. Good talking to you, too." Joe ended the call, grinned, and shook his head.

"One of your old police friends needs your help, Joe?" Shirley asked.

Joe's insides grew colder. "You were right before. It was one of my other girlfriends." He paused to see her reaction. "I'm kidding. You know what they say: once a cop, always a cop."

"Can't it wait? I have a craving for ice cream. Do we have time to go to the Barefoot Beach House?"

"I'm sorry, Shirley, the matter needs to be addressed immediately."

"Sounds like it could be serious."

"That's the concern of my friend. How about a rain check?"

"I'm going to hold you to it."

They left the restaurant for Joe's Camry.

Joe was preparing for the backlash coming his way once they got home. Shirley was oblivious, talking non-stop about Tom and Doris and Tony and Emma. When the real reason for them not going for ice cream became known, she might never speak to him again. Hurting her was unacceptable. Deceiving her was inexcusable.

The truth of the matter came when they pulled into the parking lot—after a bout of anxiety for Joe. Shirley hesitated before unlatching her seatbelt and stuck her hand inside her purse. Joe's eyes darted to her lap thinking the worst. He quietly exhaled when she pulled out a tissue to dab her forehead.

After leaving his car, they were several steps from the building's entrance when someone called out.

"Mrs. Lyon, may we have a word?"

Shirley turned and faced the man and woman. Joe looked away.

"Detective Truffant, what brings you..." Shirley snapped her head around and glared at Joe. "So this is what the call was about. You lied to me."

"Mrs. Lyon, if we could speak to you in private."

"Most certainly. I don't want to spend another moment with this man."

Joe remained anchored in place as the trio entered the building, his eyes never leaving the sidewalk.

It's funny, Joyce. I feel bad for what I did to Shirley, and yet, she could be the killer.

He shook his head and walked to the entrance, paying no attention to the swooshing sound of the automatic glass doors as they slid open.

His guilt was growing as he reached the elevator, but soon disappeared when the bell announced its arrival.

He and Tony stood face to face.

Joe knew at once that more turmoil was headed his way. The expression on his friend's face made it abundantly clear.

Chapter 11

Tony stepped back as Joe entered the elevator. Expecting his friend to begin the conversation, Joe reached out to press the button for his floor. He was mildly surprised when Tony chose not to speak, looking in every direction but his.

Something is definitely wrong, he thought.

When the elevator door opened, he exited with Tony following close behind. Arriving at his condo, they paused to face each other.

"Tony, would you like to join me for a glass of iced tea?"

"Uh, sure. I need to talk to you anyway."

This ought to be good.

Once inside, Tony went straight to the green and blue striped sofa.

"I don't want anything to drink, Joe."

Anxiety slithered through the insides of the retired detective as he sat down in his brown leather recliner. He leaned back, folded his hands across his stomach, and leveled his eyes.

"Joe, Emma knows I talked to you." Tony chuckled nervously. "Pretty obvious, huh? She's really mad at me. I...I should have kept my mouth shut."

"Is that what's really bothering you, Tony?"

The man's expression said otherwise.

"I saw you and Shirley and those two detectives in the parking lot. I knew they were going to question her."

"Whatever gave you that idea?"

"I told them what I told you...earlier when they came to see Emma."

Pretty much confirms what Carly said.

"Emma had already figured out what I'd done." Fear crept into Tony's eyes. "And now I'm afraid of what she..."

"You're afraid of Emma?"

Tony shook his head. "I'm afraid of Shirley. All of us are afraid of her."

"Who is all of us?"

"Tom, Doris, Emma, and me."

"Why does Shirley frighten you?"

"Shirley has lived at the Crimson Conch longer than most of the people here. And she's been the president of the condo association for quite some time."

Joe nodded.

"The association keeps a close watch on the various activities involving the residents. They also ensure that a certain standard of living is maintained, basically keeping out the undesirables."

"For the betterment of all, so they say," Joe added.

Tony took a deep breath. "It's my understanding that another committee was formed before the rest of us moved here. Over time the members of this select group have come and gone. But their sole purpose is to *weed the garden*, as it was explained to me."

Joe arched his right eyebrow. "Weed the garden?"

"If a resident ignores or breaks the rules, goes against the wishes of the condo association, or basically becomes a pain in the ass, the committee votes on their removal. If the majority agrees, the resident is asked to leave."

"I'm not sure the condo association has the legal right to do that."

"Legalities aside, if the resident refuses, then steps are taken to guarantee removal."

"What sort of steps?"

The fear in Tony's eyes grew deeper. "Beth Randolph was voted out a month ago."

Joe sat up straight. "The committee had her killed?"

"For the betterment of all."

"How is it you know so much about this committee?"

"Emma and I are part of it."

Joe fell back in his chair. "Who else is on this committee?"

"Tom and Doris. Shirley is the chairperson."

"I don't believe it! The five of you are responsible for issuing a permanent eviction notice?"

"Most people just leave. Some have sued. The lawyers for the association are top-notch and tie them up in court. Eventually the lawsuits are dropped."

"And some end up like Beth Randolph."

"Sadly, yes."

"How many?"

"How many what?"

"How many have ended up like Beth Randolph?"

"Three others to my knowledge. While Emma and I have lived here, anyway."

"I can't believe that you, Emma, Tom, and Doris just sit by and let this happen. It's inconceivable."

"That's why I'm here, Joe. When we agreed to become part of the committee, we didn't know anyone was going to be murdered. We just figured there would be lawsuits."

"Why didn't you report it?"

"Shirley threatened us. We thought she was joking. That is, until Millie was killed."

"Who is Millie?"

"Millie Barclay. She lived on the sixth floor. One night she fell off her balcony."

"How did it happen?"

"Millie drank a lot. And when she drank, she became obnoxious. One of the reasons she was asked to leave. Everyone figured she got drunk and lost her balance."

"Is that what the police determined?"

Tony nodded.

"When was this?"

"Six or seven years ago."

"And Shirley ordered this accident?"

"Once the gavel drops, the decision is final."

Joe paused to think. Could it be true? Could Shirley Lyon, the grandmotherly one so full of energy, be the Crimson Conch's judge, jury, and executioner?

Unbelievable! He cocked his head to the right. "Knowing this about Shirley, why were the four of you so gung-ho about she and I becoming a couple?"

"It's what Shirley wanted. She took a shine to you the minute you moved in."

"Don't I know it. The woman was constantly at my door after she found out I was a widower. I can't tell you how many plates of cookies I threw in the garbage."

"There's another reason."

"Other than the obvious?"

"You know what they say about keeping your friends close and your enemies closer."

"She considered me an enemy?"

"You're a cop."

"And it would be easier to keep tabs on me if we were living together."

Tony's sour grin confirmed Joe's belief.

"I'm finding it difficult to buy into Shirley being a killer."

"She isn't. She gives the order to someone else."

"Any idea of who it might be?"

Loud knocking on Joe's door caused Tony to flinch. He glanced at the door then back at Joe. "Are you expecting anyone?"

"Maybe it's Emma."

"I don't think so. I've been getting the silent treatment all day."

Joe slowly rose from the recliner. When he got to the door he peered through the peephole. "It's the police."

"Police!" Tony shouted and quickly jumped to his feet.

Joe opened the door wide.

Carly started to address him when she saw Tony. "Sorry to bother you, Mr. Hampton. We have some more questions."

"I was just leaving," Tony said.

Carly and David separated as Tony scurried between them.

"Why don't you come in," Joe said.

Carly moved without hesitation. David paused before entering and gazed down the hallway after Tony, watching him hurry past the elevator and disappear through the door to the fire escape.

"I guess you already know what Emma Dunham told us," Carly said.

"I got the full report," Joe said.

"And Shirley Lyon is not very happy with you, either."

"You don't know the half of it." Joe gestured to the sofa. "You two better sit down."

In great detail, Joe relayed his entire conversation with Tony. Both detectives scribbled in their notepads without looking up, Carly letting loose with an occasional grunt or "uh-huh." When Joe finished his statement, he sat back in his recliner and allowed them to finish their note-taking.

"So Shirley Lyon deals the death card when she feels the need?" Carly asked.

"It would seem so," Joe replied. "Problem is we have no proof, no witnesses, and we don't know who the executioner is."

He noticed that Carly and David were grinning.

"Did I say something humorous?"

"It appears as though *we* may have to dig deeper," Carly said.

"All right, you got me."

"Millie Barclay. Did Tony Dunham tell you when she had her accident?"

"Six or seven years ago. There should be a police report. I don't remember hearing her name mentioned at all when I moved in, though."

"I'll check it out," David said. "And Dunham told you there were two more besides her?"

"Yes. But he didn't give me their names."

David started to get up. "I'll go talk to him."

"I'm going to ask you not to do that."

"Why not?"

"Tony and Emma live in fear of Shirley. I doubt if you'll get anything out of either of them."

"But Dunham had to know that you would tell us," Carly said. "We need those names to build our case, Joe."

"Let me talk to him again."

Carly and David stared like mannequins.

"Please. Let me work on him."

Chapter 12

Carly and David's initial reluctance to allow him the opportunity to pry more information out of Tony hurt Joe. Hurt his pride was more like it. During his time on the job he was never one to leap into the spotlight and call attention to himself. Unlike many young people today, he had always let his record of success do all the talking without the self-serving fanfare. He realized his time away from the game might be a drawback, but he would be talking to a friend, not some hardened criminal with something to hide. Conversing with Tony would be no different than when they'd strolled the promenade at Clearwater Beach. Nervous as he was, Tony hadn't hesitated to reveal the truth either time they'd spoken. Why would another parlay be different?

Joe decided to wait until after dinner to set up a meeting. Several small lounges and bars came to mind. Thinking it through, he settled on Henry's Hideaway. Located on Laura Street, the quaint little bar was a favorite among the Social Security set, and would ensure a quiet and cozy atmosphere. Not having to look over his shoulder every few seconds guaranteed Tony an easy avenue to giving up the information necessary to end Shirley's committee of death.

Initially, Tony balked at the idea of another meeting. Though Emma being mad at him was the obvious excuse, both of them were drowning in uncertainty. Fear of being exposed followed by the chance of a visit from the faceless executioner clearly had them rattled.

Considering the events of the last few days, their paranoia was certainly justified.

Joe's easy-going persistence and cool approach finally coerced his friend into agreeing to a short evening of drinks and conversation. That was the idea, anyway.

Sitting in the last booth in a far corner, Joe glanced at his watch. He began to wonder why Tony hadn't called if he was going to be delayed. He checked his watch again.

A dozen or more people occupied Henry's on this evening. Even with the closeness of the room, Joe didn't feel crowded or bothered by the murmur of conversation riding on the air.

He took another peek at his watch.

The blond server who greeted him upon his arrival slunk up to his booth. Joe couldn't remember her name. Decidedly younger than her customers, she moved about in a comfortable fashion, fitting the ambience of the establishment.

"Ready for another whiskey on the rocks, sir?"

"I'm fine, thank you." Joe glanced at the entrance. "I really thought my friend would be here by now."

"I don't think I've seen you before. First time?"

"No, but it's been a while."

"I started working here two months ago. I like it. I didn't think I would. Frank's a good boss, though. And the customers are okay for the most part."

"You like waiting on a bunch of senior citizens?"

She laughed. "It's better than having every guy who walks through the door hitting on me."

"That would be irritating, I suppose."

"Oh, every so often some old..." She bit her bottom lip. "Someone tries his luck. I just laugh."

"A good philosophy."

"Excuse me, I gotta go."

Joe watched her navigate the room, focusing on the delightful curves of her blue jeans.

I know, Joyce, but your bottom looked that nice at one time.

Ten minutes later he paid for his drink, generously tipped the server, and walked out of Henry's, annoyed that his friend hadn't called him. A light, salt-tinged breeze embraced him as he neared his car.

I wonder what happened to Tony.

Maybe an emergency prevented him from coming to the meeting. Joe paused a moment, thinking the worst, and considered giving him a call. The possibility of having to deal with Emma persuaded him to scrap the idea. Whatever the reason, he would find out soon enough.

Pulling out of the parking lot, Joe's mind drifted back to the blond server. He smiled.

I wouldn't have been caught dead in a room full of old fogeys when I was her age.

Turning south on Myrtle Avenue, the face of the blond blended into Joyce's.

Sweetheart, what am I going to do? I can't go on without you.

The headlights from the cars racing toward him along Memorial Causeway were blinding, making Joe's trip home most worrisome. In and out of his thoughts about Tony, he couldn't get past an eerie sensation that something terrible had happened.

Slowly pulling into the parking lot of the Crimson Conch, he found the property brimming with the usual vehicles and nothing out of place. A quiet stroll through the well-lit lot ended at the entrance doors and, eventually, the elevator.

Again, curiosity grew inside him. Not only in regard to Tony's absence, but the empty hallway as well. Someone was always roaming the first floor. As the door to the elevator opened, Joe remembered it was Bridge Night.

I'll stick my head inside the Rec Room and have a look around. I'll bet Emma forced Tony to go. The grin on his weathered face lasted only seconds. *Maybe Shirley forced all of them to go.*

Peering through the Rec Room doorway as he stood in the hall, Joe was surprised to discover that none of his friends were seated at the bridge tables.

Not even Tom and Doris. Strange.

He quietly closed the door, leaving the crowd of players to their games.

Outside, he was about to grab the aluminum handle to the door of the main building when a wave of fear paralyzed him.

The Committee! They had a meeting!

Joe hurried to the elevator on ancient legs, his heartbeat doubling. With Bridge Night nearing the halfway point, the executioner could be poised and ready to waylay him—anywhere. He punched the button countless times while looking up and down the hall. "Come on! Come on!" he whispered loudly, and continued to strike the button. A bell sounded, and as the door started to open, terror wrapped its icy fingers around his throat. He backed up in anticipation of an attack by the executioner. As his heart pummeled his chest, he let loose nervous laughter when he discovered the car was empty. Hurling himself inside, he pounded on the button for the fourth floor, doing his best to regain his composure.

Every hallway of the enormous building was straight and free of nooks and pockets, so Joe knew his line of sight in both directions would be unobstructed. Only one foreseeable problem existed: he couldn't outrun the executioner if he emerged from the fire escape or from behind a door to one of the units.

The bell sounded again. The elevator door opened.

Joe cautiously stepped into the hall.

Never had a passage appeared so long or silence so loud.

I wish you hadn't asked me to get rid of my automatic, Joyce.

He took a deep breath, remembering how much he had hated having to search the darkened alleys and buildings when he was on the job.

The job...I've been trained for this type of situation!

He took another deep breath, and began a calculated path to his condo, intermittently looking over his shoulder while fishing through his pocket for his keys. Determination won out when he opened the door and hurried inside. Making certain the lock and deadbolt were engaged, he took a moment to catch his breath—a long moment.

All he saw was a splash of moonlight from the partially-opened curtain shielding the glass door to the balcony. The remainder of the room was as dark as the vision of death he had always believed would veil his eyes upon dying.

"Now I *really* wish I had my automatic," he murmured, imagining the executioner concealed in the shadows.

You're safe now, Joe, he heard Joyce whisper.

He paused, realizing she was right, and let go of the rigid anxiety imprisoning his body. One final deep breath was all he needed to will himself down the narrow hallway to his bedroom.

Chapter 13

Nervous exhaustion overcame Joe. His sleep was troubled and the rest he desired elusive. He dreamed that a jury of his friends passed judgment, condemning him one by one. Shirley, the judge, handed down the sentence. When the gigantic gavel fell, Joe jumped awake. Streams of perspiration rolled down his face. Not having bothered to get undressed, he wiped his brow with the damp sleeve of his shirt. Darkness, thick and gloomy, filled his bedroom. As he wallowed in the silence, the face of the one he loved materialized.

What are you doing, Joe?

Dying without you, my love.

That doesn't sound like the man I married.

I'm not that man anymore.

Fiddlesticks!

I'm afraid, Joyce...oh, god, I am so afraid.

Afraid of what?

You were my reason for living. My reason to go on. Now...

You know I'll always be with you, Joe.

It's not the same.

You were always strong for both of us. Be strong now.

The muffled tone of his cell phone was enough to chase away the vision. Joe fumbled through his pants pocket and retrieved the menace. The caller I.D. was no help.

"Joe, it's Carly. Sorry to wake you."

"That's okay. I needed to talk to you anyway. I was supposed to meet Tony at Henry's Hideaway last night, but he didn't show." An odd thought slipped into his mind. "Wait a minute, why are you calling me?"

"Joe, Tony's dead."

The ride to Sand Key Park took less than ten minutes. Dawn had not yet driven away the night, but a pale blue glow radiated in the eastern sky.

From Gulf Boulevard, Joe turned right into the park and slowly traversed the uninhabited asphalt road. The headlights of his Camry cut through the darkness and uncovered a gradual turn to the left. A branch road to a small parking lot and dock peeled off to the right. Hitting the pine trees and foliage with the high beams, Joe came out of the turn and was immediately bathed in the red and blue strobe lights of Clearwater Police and emergency vehicles. Before he had chosen a place to park, an officer approached his car.

"Sir, you'll have to turn around and leave," she said.

"The victim is my neighbor, Officer. I was notified by Detective Sergeant Carly Truffant."

The young woman studied him a moment. "What's your name, sir?"

"Joe Hampton."

"Wait right here."

She walked across the road and met with a patrol sergeant standing on the shoulder. The sergeant glanced at Joe, turned, and vanished into the glare of the flashing lights. Minutes later he and David returned. David nodded and said something to the young officer as he headed toward Joe.

Joe got out of his car as the grim-faced detective approached.

"I'm sorry about Tony, Joe. Would you come with me? We'd like you to take a look at this."

Joe followed him into a small open area tightly bordered by

pine trees, palmettos, and undergrowth. Though the sky was getting lighter, David's flashlight was necessary to lead them to where Joe's friend lay.

Carly and a couple of patrolmen stood over Tony's body, mesmerized by something their flashlights had uncovered. It became obvious when the retired detective walked up beside her.

Tony's mouth was frozen open, his jaws and neck painted a deep crimson. A similar swath covered the upper part of his long-sleeve shirt. Most ghastly of all was the severed piece of flesh lying on his chest.

"Is that his tongue?" Joe asked.

Carly nodded as she continued to stare.

Joe slipped his hand around her arm and eased her down with him as he knelt. The concentrated LED beam from her flashlight exposed another disturbing fact.

"He's been stabbed," Joe said.

"We figured as much by the amount of blood," Carly said.

"Can you tell if he was killed here?"

"Criminal Analysis thinks so. Daylight will tell us more."

"Who found him?"

"Anonymous call. Someone wanted us to know he was here."

Both of them had a good idea who that someone might be.

"I'd like to be there when you listen to the nine-one-one recording."

Carly leaned close to him. "You know, Shirley Lyon didn't do this. It had to be someone bigger and stronger."

The face of Tom Vernon settled into Joe's mind. Even as he got on in years, a former telephone lineman like Tom would have no problem subduing someone slight of build like Tony.

"Let me give it some thought."

"Don't take too long. Whoever is doing this has to be stopped."

"Have you notified Emma?"

"We only got the call an hour ago." Carly's eyes darted to Joe then quickly away. "We wanted to be certain it was him before we gave her the bad news. In light of what you've told us, though, I have a feeling she already knows."

After a closer look at Tony's body, Joe returned to his car with Carly and David.

The morning sky brought with it substantial light for the Criminal Analysis Unit to intensify their investigation.

Huddled together, Carly, David and Joe experienced the frustration of not only another murder, but the inability to apprehend the person or persons responsible.

"I think it's a good idea if you stay away from Emma and Shirley, Joe," Carly began.

Joe started to speak.

Carly held up her hand. "We know who's calling the shots. We just can't prove that it's Shirley. Tony's murder was a message. A message to whomever else is involved with her...and you. You're a threat, Joe. Further contact with either of them could get you killed."

Joe recalled the episode of fear he'd experienced the previous night. "Okay, I'll make sure to steer clear of Shirley. I should offer my condolences to Emma, though. It'll look strange if I don't, at least, drop by and..." He stopped when he noticed the look on the detective's face. "Okay, I understand."

"I would like you to keep the lines of communication open. That is, if you don't mind," she said.

"Whatever I can do." He paused and stared at her a second. "What's got you on edge, Carly?"

"I feel like I'm telling the best hitter on my softball team to take a seat on the bench."

The sky was light enough that Joe didn't need to use his headlights when he left. The two-way road meandered through the park, eventually returning to the entrance at Gulf Boulevard. Feeling the weight of guilt over the loss of his friend, he carefully guided his Camry and paid little attention to the enormous parking lot edging the beach and the Gulf of Mexico. Heading in a southeasterly direction, he gazed across Clearwater Harbor into the red-orange rising sun. For no particular reason he glanced to his right. That's when he saw it.

Beside a white, sandy foot trail lay a brown object. Was it a shoe? Joe couldn't tell from his car. If so, it was an old and battered shoe. Joe steered onto the shoulder and got out. Eying the object carefully, he realized that he'd seen a resident at his condo wearing a similar pair. Moccasins were not very popular anymore—not in Florida, anyway. Still, some folks found them comfortable.

Pulling a handkerchief from his right rear pocket, Joe collected the footwear and returned to his car. An easy U-turn pointed him back in the direction of the crime scene.

Carly and David were standing by an unmarked sedan when he arrived, surprised when he approached them with the moccasin dangling from his right hand.

"What have you got there, Joe?" David asked.

"Maybe something, maybe nothing. Do you have an evidence bag handy?"

"Not that big. I'll go get one from Criminal Analysis."

As he watched the detective jog away, Joe turned to Carly. "I found this near the entrance to the park. I didn't see it earlier because it was too dark and on the other side of the road. "

Carly eyed the moccasin. "You believe this has something to do with our case?"

"It might belong to the killer."

"No offense, Joe, but it could belong to anyone. I have to tell you, though, I haven't seen a moccasin in years."

"You may be right." Joe raised the shoe so they could see it better. "Years ago, I read a book on how to cover your tracks after committing a murder. The author was anonymous and supposedly a killer for hire. According to what I read, a smart killer purchases new shoes before a hit so wear marks on the soles aren't evident if his footprints are discovered. After completing the job, getting rid of his clothes and shoes is imperative. The shoes can be disposed of one by one at various points along the escape route, and well away from where the kill took place. After all, who pays attention to one shoe lying on the side of the road?"

Carly grinned and nodded. "Very true."

Joe pointed to the moccasin. "This one has a double soft sole and the wear marks are quite obvious. It isn't new, and it's close to the crime scene."

The detective wasn't moved. "Joe, I appreciate what you're saying, but—"

"If it does belong to the killer, then he isn't very smart."

"Why are you so interested in this particular type of moccasin?"

"Mac, our building manager, wears double soft-soled moccasins. This one is about his size."

Chapter 14

A wave of emptiness filled Joe's insides as he crossed the Sand Key Bridge into Clearwater Beach. The fondness he'd once felt for his small group of friends was now as fleeting as the remaining years of his life. How could they sit by and allow a self-righteous demagogue to play God? Intimidated or not, they should have banded together and taken action.

What does Shirley have on them? Maybe nothing. Maybe witnessing Mac's brutality is enough to convince them to remain silent—if, indeed, Mac is the enforcer.

Joe shook his head. He found it difficult to believe that the divorced, former high school physical education teacher was a killer. Sure, he was irritable at times. Many older people are. His low tolerance for obnoxious residents and loud parties wasn't a unique character trait. Joe held onto the thought for a moment. Maybe discipline *was* the defining point of the man. Follow the rules, behave in an appropriate manner, and he was your friend for life. Buck authority or create a scene, and punishment was swift in coming.

"I hope you have both of your shoes, Mac," he mumbled as he navigated the roundabout to Memorial Causeway.

The salt-tinged air pouring in through the windows felt heavier this morning. Increased humidity meant the chance for rain was good. The parking lot was full as always and looked no different from the day he'd moved into the Crimson Conch. Though he'd parked in the spot bearing his unit number, the walk to the front entrance wore on him—seemed longer for some reason. Maybe the burden of knowing the secret hidden inside the walls of the condominium had purged what little strength he still possessed—his will to continue, the challenge to survive.

"Joyce, if ever I needed you, it's now," he whispered, greeted by the "swoosh" of the automatic doors as he passed through.

Once again, the lobby and hallway were empty. His heartbeat quickened with each tentative step. The elevator carried him to the fourth floor with the usual metallic whine, and, upon exiting the lift, he breathed easier when he met a couple and exchanged pleasantries. Having seen them at other times in the hallway lessened the tension. The release was short-lived when he noticed a folded slip of paper taped to his door. Joe glanced up and down the hall before removing it.

The simple message printed inside leapt out at him: Call me—Tom.

Joe stared at the note, part of him wondering what Tom wanted, and part of him already knowing.

I should call Carly. I may not get the chance later. He took a deep breath and released the air little by little. *If they're not going to kill me then what do they want*?

He shoved his hand into his pants pocket and pulled out his cell phone.

"I was surprised to find you weren't home this morning, Joe," Tom said. "Doris and I were going to have you over for breakfast."

Then why didn't you call? Joe thought. "I was restless and couldn't sleep, so I took a little drive."

"I thought maybe you and Shirley might have..." Tom laughed. "...worked out your differences."

"No, I'm afraid not. What's on your mind, Tom?"

"I need to discuss something with you, but not over the phone."

"Must be *very* important."

"Oh, it is. Can you stop by? Doris can whip us up some bacon and eggs."

Joe hesitated. *He either doesn't know about Tony or doesn't want to tip his hand.* "Sure, I'll be right there."

The minute Doris opened the door and Joe walked into the Vernon's condo he knew he'd been set up. Shirley and Emma sat on a teal sofa. Emma's eyes were red and swollen. Tom stood behind a hunter green felt recliner. The surprise came when Doris closed the door that had been concealing Mac McDougal.

"Joe, I would ask you to sit down, but what I have to say won't take that long," Shirley said.

Joe stood silent.

"To put it simply, you're a nuisance. Your snooping and meddling into other people's lives has become an annoyance that can no longer be tolerated. We know you're working with the police. If you don't stop...well..."

Emma began to sob and covered her face with her hands.

"Who gave you the right to decide who stays and who goes, Shirley?" Joe countered.

"Those who came before me. Who came before all of us, actually. They decided that decency and civil obedience must be upheld. Those of us who followed subscribe to that policy."

"By killing the ones who don't fit in? What kind of monsters are you?"

"Second and, sometimes, third chances are given. If a resident refuses to comply with our requests, then he or she is asked to leave. If they refuse to leave, then steps are taken to remedy the problem."

Joe was chilled by Shirley's cold and insensitive explanation. "Listen to yourself! You sound like a tyrant!"

"We're offering you a second chance, Joe. You would be wise to accept it. You must stop your interfering at once."

Joe searched the eyes of each friend. Everyone but Emma

exhibited a narrowed expression of obedient compliance. Terror dwelled in Emma's eyes.

"Okay, I'll do as you ask."

"Good. We expect Emma will be receiving a visit from the police at any time now. I'm guessing they called you earlier, and that's why you weren't at home."

Joe said nothing.

"You're welcome to stay if you like."

"No, I'll…" Joe shifted his gaze to Emma. "I'll stop by later." He turned and started for the door.

Mac stepped in front of him. "You made the right decision, Joe."

"I hope so," Joe replied and lowered his eyes.

Covering Mac's enormous feet was a brand-new pair of moccasins.

Chapter 15

Wasting no time after walking into his condo, Joe retrieved his cell phone. Angry at himself for allowing fear to control him the previous night, he refused to be threatened by Shirley's ultimatum. He punched in the number and waited.

"Joe, we were just getting ready to call on Emma Dunham."

"They know, Carly. They know I've been helping you. They killed Tony because he told me how they operate."

"Who are *they*?"

"The Committee! Give me a minute and I'll explain." Joe inhaled deeply. He proceeded to inform Carly of the self-appointed group holding sway over the Crimson Conch, and how he was lured into meeting with them. "Shirley Lyon chairs the group. The others bow to her wishes like frightened little children."

"They're hardly frightened little children if they agree to have someone murdered."

"Tony told me that in the beginning they didn't know that murder was going to be the solution. She has to have something on all of them."

"You think she's that powerful?"

"Maybe one or two support her. I don't know."

"And Mac McDougal. What about him?

"I firmly believe that he killed Tony. He was wearing brand new moccasins, double soft-soled, just like his old ones and the one I found in the park."

"You know the problem, Joe. They'll deny everything, and we won't be able to prove they're lying."

The retired detective thought a second. "I told Emma I'd visit her later today. Maybe I can persuade her to give you all the details in exchange for protection."

"You can try, but after what happened to her husband I doubt if she'll agree to it. I don't like the idea, anyway."

"Carly, we have to do something."

"Joe, did you stop to think about how the others found out that Tony talked to you?"

"Not really."

"The only ones who knew were you, David, and me, and the Dunhams."

"You're right. Emma must have told them."

"Had to be her. She's not going to drop a dime on the rest."

"In any case, I'm still going to try."

"You're a stubborn old fossil, you know that?"

Joe chuckled. "You sound like my wife."

"Did you listen to her?"

"Sometimes."

"Well, you'd better listen now! They will kill you!"

The inflection of concern in the young detective's voice found Joe, but he was still determined.

"I don't have to tell you to play it straight when you go see Emma. They're all going to be there."

"Dammit, Joe, don't do it!"

"I'll talk to you later."

He ended the call and sat down at his mahogany dining table. He thought about Carly and her dedication to the job. Dedicated like he had been at that age. He grinned when he thought of her overly-protective outburst that reminded him of Joyce. Then he thought about Shirley. He pinched up his face in disgust at how he'd been taken in by her act. Finally, he gave in to another, more unusual thought. *Strange how the mind works. I'm hungry.*

***

Not long after sunset, Joe stood calmly at the door to the Dunhams's condo. Fear of dying no longer plagued his mind. Calling upon the knowledge and experience gained over years of police work, he'd formulated a plan to persuade Emma to tell all about The Committee. If the plan failed, he most certainly would be killed. Failure didn't enter into his thinking.

The door opened slowly and Emma materialized from the darkness.

"Joe! I didn't think you would..."

"How are you doing, Emma?"

"I'm coping. Or, at least, trying to."

He looked beyond her. "Why don't you turn on some lights?"

"I can't. Not right now," she said and sniffed.

"May I come in?"

"I don't feel like company, Joe. Maybe tomorrow."

"You shouldn't be alone now, Emma. Believe me, I know.

"Please, Joe, I'm not up to it."

"Just for a few minutes, then I'll leave. I promise."

Emma lowered her head and opened the door wider.

Joe stepped inside, heard the door close behind him, and waited for his eyes to adjust.

Without making a sound, Emma moved through the darkness and turned on a table lamp beside the sofa. She dropped down on one end. Joe took a seat on the other end.

"I am so sorry, Emma. If there's anything I can do just..." He stopped when he saw her head slowly turn toward him.

"Haven't you done enough?"

"Emma, I never thought anything like this would happen."

"This is all your fault. If you hadn't been such a snoop then Tony..." Her eyes welled up, and one tear after another escaped down her cheek.

"Tony came to me. He wanted to free the two of you from

Shirley."

"And he was a fool to think he could! No one leaves The Committee!"

"Is Shirley blackmailing you?"

Emma reached out and pulled a tissue from the box on the coffee table. She dabbed each eye and cleared her throat. "Background checks are done on everyone who applies for residency. Everything about a person is revealed."

"How does The Committee gain access to this information? It's supposed to remain confidential."

"Mac can get a hold of it. I don't know how."

"Why the need for a committee then? The bad eggs should be filtered out beforehand."

"No system is perfect, Joe. Some people are bound to slip through the cracks."

"How do these background checks keep a stranglehold on the committee members?"

"Shirley and Mac know everything about everyone. Computers have guaranteed that no one is safe. Tom and Doris wanted to leave a year ago. They have three children. Shirley suggested that one of their grandchildren might have an accident if they left."

"And you and Tony?"

"We...I love our granddaughters very much."

"How long has this been going on?"

"The Crimson Conch was built in 1989. The first mishap occurred in 1992."

"Are you telling me that in all those years no one ever suspected foul play?"

"Joe, we're a bunch of old people nearing the end of our lives. Who questions accidents or death by natural causes?"

"I don't guess the numbers are great enough to attract attention."

"Pretty much the norm, so Shirley told us."

"What about Gary Burgess? He's not an old person, and he was stabbed."

Emma sniffed and dabbed her eyes again. "Have your friends at the Clearwater Police Department figured out who killed him?"

Joe shook his head.

"And they never will. Believe me."

"Emma, you have to tell the police. You have to tell them everything."

"No! I don't want to die!"

"The police will protect you."

"Do I look like a fool to you, Joe? No one can protect me!"

A pounding on Emma's door interrupted their exchange.

Emma's green eyes grew large. "Did you tell anyone you were coming here?"

"No."

Emma slowly got up from the sofa and walked to the door. Peering through the peephole, she moaned and lowered her head. Reaching down, she twisted the doorknob, and pulled the door open.

Shirley and Mac walked into the room. Both of them glared at Joe.

"You just couldn't leave well enough alone, could you?" Shirley said.

Joe felt the prickly spurs of fear ripple up his spine. "What do you mean? I told Emma I was going to stop by. You were here. You heard me."

"When the police came to give Emma the bad news about Tony, they asked a lot of questions."

"It's their job."

"They wanted to know about Millie Barclay and others who met an unfortunate end while living here. Did Tony tell you about them?"

"Three murders, days apart, arouses curiosity, Shirley. Good detectives do extensive research."

"And having a source on the inside certainly helps, doesn't it, Joe?"

Joe could do nothing but return her gaze.

"Mac," she said.

"Come on, Joe. We're going for a ride."

Chapter 16

Outside Emma's condo, Joe's mind geared up. He wasn't going down without a fight, so an infallible plan had to be devised—and fast. Overpowering Mac was out of the question—the man was huge. Maybe he could outrun him. Joe had never been fast or quick on his feet, but if he could get to the door of the fire escape he might be able to get away. Because of his size and age, Mac had trouble negotiating stairs.

As they waited in front of the elevator, Joe glanced at him out of the corner of his eye. The second the building manager turned to look up the hall, he broke for the door. Joe scrambled as best he could, and was surprised by the silence, expecting to hear Mac puffing and blowing in pursuit. His heartbeat doubled when he reached the exit and grabbed the doorknob. A second later his heart sank. The knob came off in his hand. That's when he heard Mac chuckle.

"I gotta remember to get that fixed one day."

Before Joe could turn around, he felt Mac's hefty hand clamp onto the back of his neck.

"Don't do that again, Joe. You're liable to get your skull cracked open."

Joe's misfortune continued as Mac steered him down the hall.

Any other time this place would be crawling with people, he thought. *Where is everybody? It's not that late.*

Of course the elevator was empty when it finally reached

them. Why should he catch a break?

A spike of adrenaline lifted him when they exited the hallway and met a couple at the condo's entrance.

Witnesses! At least someone will remember seeing me with Mac!

Mac relaxed his grip on Joe's neck and let his hand fall. "Pete, Nina. Lovely night, isn't it?"

The old couple smiled and nodded. Neither acknowledged Joe.

"They're as senile as the day is long," Mac said out of the corner of his mouth. He clamped onto Joe's neck again.

The night was clear and warm and the well-lighted parking lot near capacity. No one was around to see them approaching the brown Ford F-250.

Damn! Joe thought. *Where the hell is everybody?*

After opening the passenger-side door, Mac reached inside the glove box and removed a pair of handcuffs. His vise-like grip on Joe's neck tightened.

"Don't try anything stupid."

He released the former detective and snatched his arms behind his back.

The metallic clicking of the handcuffs tightening around his wrists angered Joe. He hadn't been cuffed since the academy. He didn't like it then and he didn't like it now.

"Did you use these on Tony?"

Mac chuckled.

"I would think a big ignoramus like you wouldn't need them to control an old man."

"Shut up, Joe!"

Mac latched onto Joe's arms and threw him into the cab. Slamming the door, he walked around the front of the Ford and got inside. Grabbing Joe again, he grappled him onto the passenger seat. He started the truck then reached down to the controls embedded in the armrest and pressed the master lock switch. As he turned to Joe, he punched the button for the air conditioning, sending a blast of cold air into the cab.

"This can be an easy ride or a hard ride. It all depends on you, Joe."

"Tony didn't put up a fight, did he?"

Mac grinned. "He bawled like a baby."

"Is that what it takes for you to get it up? Bullying people?"

Slamming the truck into reverse, Mac roared out of the parking space.

"That's why your wife left you, isn't it? She got tired of you slapping her around."

Mac hit the gas pedal and the pickup sped off down the rows of cars. When they reached the access road, he stomped on the brakes. Joe flew forward, smashing his face against the windshield. Mac grabbed his left arm and snatched him back into the seat.

"Like I said, Joe, easy or hard. It's up to you."

The onset of pain above Joe's right eye was excruciating. A trickle of blood slipped out of his nose.

Leaving the parking lot, their short drive on Island Way ended with a left turn at Memorial Causeway.

"Where are we going?" Joe asked.

"Somewhere you've never been, I'll bet."

No place in Clearwater to dump me, Joe thought. *Too populated. He can't drown me in Tampa Bay. Courtney Campbell Causeway is too wide open. That means north to Dunedin, possibly Palm Harbor, or south to Largo.*

Silence rode with them until a left turn onto North Fort Harrison.

"How did you get involved in this mess, Mac?"

"Who says it's a mess?"

"What does Shirley have on you?"

"Joe, I don't know what you've been told and, quite frankly, I don't care. Things were just fine until you started poking around. Why couldn't you just let it be?"

"Killing people doesn't bother you?"

"Not people, Joe, vermin. The dregs of society. I provide a

service like any other exterminator."

"Even rats have a right to live."

"I agree, but not at the Crimson Conch. I'm not alone in that thinking."

"The Committee?"

"Others, too. The number would surprise you."

Good Lord! Joe thought. *I'm living in a community of fascists*! "No one has ever complained to the police before now?"

"Not to my knowledge. Why would they? All the bad goings-on in the world don't exist inside our condo. Who in their right mind would want to change that?"

The Yacht Harbor Inn came into view and Mac turned right. A block later he stopped for the traffic light at Broadway Street.

Joe scanned every inch of the crowded intersection in Dunedin. People alone and in groups milled about, oblivious to his dilemma. The windows being up would prevent them from hearing him yell. If he could fall onto his right side and kick Mac in the head fast enough, he might buy the time he needed to unlock the door and bail out. As he swiveled his head toward his captor, a massive fist cracked Joe in the face, sending him hard into the door.

"Don't even think about it," Mac said. He slowly accelerated and made an easy turn.

Joe barely heard him over the ringing assaulting his ears.

They continued north on Broadway until it became Bayshore Drive. Further north, and with the ringing subsiding somewhat, Joe sat up just as Mac steered them onto a side road. Joe didn't catch the name. The pain in his head was so intense that even speaking was difficult.

"Are you going to cut out my tongue?"

Mac chuckled. "Shirley was right. You *did* go to Sand Key Park this morning." He chuckled again. "Tony was a squealer. He deserved it."

"And me ? What do I deserve?"

"I don't know, Joe. I'll have to think about it."

Their ride through the residential area in north Pinellas

County was as quiet as the neighborhood itself. Traffic was light, most of the houses were lit, and no one dwelling in the serene surroundings had any idea that a former detective from Philadelphia was about to die.

Joe was caught off-guard when they came to San Mateo Drive and Mac made yet another turn. An uneasy feeling that their journey was nearing an end consumed him. The F-250's headlights stretched far up the two-lane road until a black wall materialized.

Mac backed off the gas pedal, the wall became a stand of oak and pine trees, and a pair of narrow asphalt roads branched off to the north and east. Mac followed the eastern road past a church sitting on the right. At the sight of a small building and parking lot, he eased the pickup to a halt and shut off the motor.

"Welcome to Hammock Park, Joe. The end of the line."

Chapter 17

Had Joe not been so focused on finding an escape route he would have appreciated the sizeable piece of nature in the middle of suburbia.

Still handcuffed, he offered no resistance as Mac pulled him from the parking lot to the head of the main trail. He didn't know the exact number of trails that snaked through the park, and surrendered to the fact that an inordinate amount of time would pass before his body would be found—*if* his body was found. Hearing the guttural growl of an alligator spiked his already heightened level of anxiety.

Working their way along the dirt path, Mac showed no interest in a second foot trail breaking off to the south. The same was true of a paved trail stretching to the north. Mounting a small bridge over a narrow creek brought Joe's captor to end their trek and inhale deeply.

"Isn't this park beautiful, Joe? I love the smell of the pine trees...especially at night."

Pine, Live Oak, even a sprinkling of palm trees blanketed the world before them.

Mac inhaled again. "I'm going to miss coming here, and it's your fault, you know?"

Joe didn't answer, believing the creek to be his final resting place.

Mac sighed and tugged on his arm. Their journey wasn't over.

A few yards from the bridge, another trail emerged, a smaller, primitive corridor cutting through walls of vegetation. Mac remained silent as he dragged Joe toward it. The former detective sensed that only a few more steps remained in his life. Mac wouldn't take him much farther. He was too fat and too lazy to venture so deep into the wilderness. As the trail began to bend to the west, Joe's worst fear was realized. Mac stopped and faced him, removing a five-inch lockback knife from the pocket of his khaki cargo shorts.

"Like I said before, Joe, this can be an easy ride or a hard ride. Either way, you're not walking outta here alive."

"Just make it quick, you son of a bitch!" Joe growled.

"Oh, it's not going to be quick. Shirley wants you to suffer. You should have listened to her, Joe. You know how some women are when they're pissed off." He paused, and took a breath. "I've decided not to cut your tongue out." He slowly unfolded the knife, "But I am going to cut your throat. Then I'm going to give you a Columbian Necktie. Know what that is, Joe?"

Joe said nothing.

"I didn't think so. Well, it works this way. After you're done choking, I pull your tongue through the opening in your neck and let it hang...like a necktie. Get it?"

Joe cringed at his tormentor's tortuous laughter.

Before Mac could move, the LED beam from a flashlight lit up his face.

"Drop the knife!" a woman shouted.

Surprised, Mac threw up his hands to shield his eyes as he gasped.

Without hesitation, Joe kicked him between the legs.

Mac let loose an ear-splitting howl as he dropped to his knees and fell over on his right side.

"How'd you like *that*, you fat slob?" Joe yelled.

Carly shoved past him with her flashlight focused on the knife and snatched it off the ground.

Joe drew his foot back to kick Mac again. A pair of brawny arms wrapped around him.

"Hold on, Joe!" David shouted. "He's not going anywhere."

"Get these cuffs off me! I'm gonna kill him!"

Carly wheeled her flashlight into Joe's eyes. "Take it easy! You got him!" She froze. "Jesus! Did he do that to you?"

David released Joe and proceeded to unlock the handcuffs. "Are you all right?"

"No, I'm not all right! My head aches, my face hurts, and I think I broke my foot!"

More LED beams danced in the darkness as three Pinellas County deputies ran up from the opposite direction.

"Get him outta here!" Carly barked. "And call an ambulance!"

Two of the deputies cuffed Mac's hands behind his back and strained to lift him to his feet. Joe glared at the hefty building manager as they took him away.

"Now let's see about getting you to the hospital," Carly said.

"Just take me home."

"Joe, you may have a concussion."

Joe ignored her and turned to leave. He didn't make a step before a sharp pain shot up his leg. He grimaced and struggled to remain standing.

"Give me a hand, will you?"

Carly and David went to his side. Joe wrapped his arms around their shoulders and they helped him hobble back to the main trail. The going was slow and gave him time to think of how lucky he was.

"Thank you. Thank you both."

"You're welcome," Carly said. "I'm just glad we got here in time."

Joe yelped when he stepped wrong, and labored to take a breath. "How did you know where to find us?"

"A bit of help and a bit of luck. We got a call from Emma."

"She knew where Mac was taking me?"

"No, but she remembered Mac telling Tony how much he

enjoyed coming to Hammock Park. We took a chance and called the sheriff's office. A deputy patrolling a side street saw Mac's truck on San Mateo Drive and radioed in."

"What if he hadn't brought me here? What if he'd taken me somewhere else?"

"We put out a countywide alert, Joe."

Joe released a groan when he stepped wrong again.

"You want to rest a minute?" David asked.

"Guess I'd better." Joe took two more deep breaths. "Has Shirley been arrested?"

"Tom and Doris Vernon, too. And Emma. She agreed to help us, though."

"I feel sorry for them. They were intimidated into following Shirley and Mac." A short distance away he could see the creek and the small bridge. "Well, let's get moving. By the way, you need to look into all the accidents that have occurred since the Crimson Conch was built. Mac told me The Committee has been intact for years."

They stopped one more time within sight of the park's entrance.

An ambulance with red lights flashing sped into the parking lot. The EMT's hopped out and started toward them with a stretcher.

"I want to thank you, Joe," Carly said.

"Thank me for what?"

"For being a nosey old goat. We never would have known what was going on at your condo if you hadn't brought it to our attention."

Joe chuckled. "You should expect no less from The Gray Detective."

Chapter 18

Being confined in the hospital for two days added more misery to the aggravation of Joe's condition. Diagnosed with a mild concussion and three broken toes, he reluctantly gave in to the doctor's recommendation that he remain for observation. His age, he was informed, being a primary concern. He understood, but was happy to finally be released.

The purple-black bruise adorning his face gradually faded to a sickening yellow after a week, summoning an outpouring of sympathy from many of the other residents. He was a sad sight, indeed, hobbling around the Crimson Conch on his cane.

This day found Joe deeply engrossed in the contract for a pest control company appearing on the computer screen in the building manager's office. He'd assumed the position of building manager as a means to shield him from the temptation of police work. A rapping on the door broke his concentration.

Carly and David entered before he could lift himself out of his chair.

"Well, look at this, David, Joe has a job. And an easy job at that."

David arched his eyebrows. "Building manager, Joe? Are you sure you'll be able to stay awake?"

"There was an unexpected opening," Joe said, "and, anyway, I need to stay active. Besides, it beats being a punching bag."

Both detectives grinned.

Carly looked around the room. "Nice office. How are you feeling, Joe?"

"No headaches or nausea, and my face finally stopped hurting. Still need the cane to get around, though. Other than that I feel pretty good. What's the latest word?"

"Mac McDougal has been very cooperative. Fear of death by lethal injection has that effect sometimes."

"He admitted to all of the killings?"

"He admitted to Beth Randolph, Tony Dunham, Millie Barclay, even Gary Burgess. There may be more."

"What was his reason for killing Gary?"

"He said Shirley Lyon knew that Randolph wanted to become part of Burgess' harem. When she found out that Burgess had snubbed Randolph, she was afraid there might be trouble and ordered her killed. Thinking that Burgess might become suspicious, she ordered him killed, too."

"But why wait to kill Gary? You took him into custody. He could have told you everything then."

"According to McDougal, that's where the plan went wrong. He was supposed to kill Burgess the same night as Randolph, but Burgess left before McDougal realized he was gone."

"Seems awfully risky to kill two people the same night in the same place."

"Maybe McDougal planned to take Burgess on a road trip like you and Tony Dunham."

Joe reflected a second. "I guess Shirley really did have all of them under her thumb."

"The others swore that she called the shots, and because they feared McDougal, went along with whatever she wanted."

"I can't help feeling bad for Emma, Tom, and Doris. They were nothing more than pawns."

"All three have been extremely helpful, but the fact is they were part of the conspiracy. We talked to the prosecutor and recommended leniency."

"It's sad when good people wind up on the wrong side. But

what's done is done."

Carly was staring hard at him.

"Is something bothering you?"

"I keep wondering what would have happened if you'd had a pistol. Why *did* Joyce ask you to get rid of it?"

"She never liked guns. She knew they were a part of the job, and never complained once. When I finally retired she asked that I never carry a gun again."

"You loved her very much, didn't you?"

"I still do." Joe paused, thinking. "You know, with all the excitement, I never got the chance to ask how *you're* doing."

"I'm fine."

"Everything okay at home?"

Carly snapped her head around. "David!"

David threw his hands up, palms forward. "Now don't get mad at me. I was worried about you."

"He's right," Joe said. "Both of us were worried."

A grin turned up the corners of Carly's mouth. "Tim and I had a long talk. We're going to try to make it work."

"Good for you."

Their attention was drawn to a soft knocking at the office door. The door opened, and a thin, silver-haired woman with electric blue eyes stepped inside. Age had been kind to her. A luminous smile complemented her graceful features.

"Excuse me. My name is Victoria Combes, and I'm looking for the building manager."

Joe straightened in his chair, offering his fullest attention. "Yes, ma'am, how can I help you?"

"I understand you have a vacancy."

"Why, yes, we do."

The woman glanced at Carly and David. "I can wait until after you're finished."

"We were just leaving," Carly said.

Joe struggled to his feet and picked up his cane.

"My goodness," the woman said, "what happened to you?"

“It’s a long story.”

Outside the office door, David took hold of Carly’s arm.

“How come you didn’t ask Joe if he’d like to be a consultant like we discussed?”

“David, somehow I get the feeling that he’s tired of police work.”

“But, Carly, he’s one of the best detectives I’ve ever seen. Maybe the best ever.”

“I know. We’ll just have to wait and see.”

DARK ARRIVAL

Chapter 1

Joe Hampton sighed and lifted a glass of Evan Williams whiskey to his lips. Cooled by three ice cubes, the brown liquor easily rolled over his tongue before he swallowed.

Dark clouds from an approaching front were gradually blanketing the brilliance of the sunset. Sitting atop the Gulf of Mexico, the sun fought back with a golden wall of resistance across the face of the invader, but to no avail. Such was the pattern of summer storms in Florida.

The woman lying next to him on the matching chaise lounge eased her head around. "You're not bored, are you, Joseph?"

Joe took another drink. "Sunsets are beautiful in this part of the country. I was hoping this one would be special."

"Any particular reason why you wanted it to be special?"

"I wanted to impress someone."

"Anyone I know?"

Joe smiled and swirled the whiskey in his glass.

The pair turned their attention to the gloomy western sky. The clouds pressed on, burning as enormous red-orange embers, relentlessly attempting to vanquish the stubborn, sinking sun. Joe sighed and rolled his head over.

"Care for another drink, Victoria?"

"I could use one, yes."

Joe reached for his cane.

"Hold on, old-timer, stay where you are. I'll get it."

"I'm *not* helpless, and who are you calling *old-timer*?"

"How long have you been leaning on that cane?"

"Three weeks."

"That long? Hmm."

"What does that mean?"

"Oh, nothing." Victoria picked up his glass as she stood over him.

"My foot's still sore."

"You said that last week."

"It was sore last week."

She grunted again and disappeared from the balcony. Joe tilted his head back, eyeing the ever-widening storm moving in their direction. Inhaling deeply, he could smell the rain.

"Won't be long now," he whispered.

His lovely acquaintance breezed back onto the balcony and set his drink on the folding TV table between the two chairs. Easing into the empty chaise lounge, she glanced at him out of the corner of her eye.

"You really must have kicked that man hard."

"I broke three toes, and considering that he was built like a rhino..."

Victoria took a healthy pull of her whiskey. "Still, it has been three weeks. I would have thought you'd tossed that third leg by now. Oh, well."

Joe shook his head. "How long have you been living here?"

"About as long as that thing has been holding you up. Why do you ask?"

"Seems like I've been listening to your nagging a lot longer than that. Oh, well."

"Why, Joseph Hampton, I oughta slap you!"

A bolt of lightning cleaved the charcoal sky. Glass-rattling thunder immediately followed. Both of them jumped.

"That was close!" Joe said. "We'd better get inside before we get soaked."

Victoria was already on her feet. "Let me help you."

Joe felt the strength in her hands as she took hold of his arm, yet there was gentleness in the way she helped him up from the chair. When they got inside, she carefully steered him to the sofa. She quickly returned to the balcony to retrieve their drinks. Joe leaned back and let the cool breath of the air conditioning pour over him.

Victoria scooted through the opening, closing the sliding glass door ahead of another round of crashing thunder. She set Joe's drink on the coffee table in front of him.

"Is the lightning always this intense?"

"Yes, during the summer."

"We don't have anything like it in Indiana."

"Welcome to Florida." Joe allowed his eyes to linger.

Victoria Combes had come to inquire about a vacancy at the Crimson Conch Condominiums shortly after Joe had assumed the position of building manager. Though he'd sensed her interest in him right away, he had been reluctant to enter into a new relationship, his brush with death at the hands of Shirley Lyon, a former resident, being the obvious reason. But the main reason was his everlasting love for his deceased wife, Joyce.

Victoria hadn't been aggressive in her desire to get closer to him, but her gentle persistence and willingness to accept his need to drag his feet had persuaded him to take a chance. To this point, he was glad that he had. He was hoping that their relationship would continue to move forward and that she felt the same.

Taking a seat in the living room chair near the sofa, she stuck her forefinger into her glass and twirled the ice cubes.

"How *is* your foot, Joseph? No joking, I genuinely want to know."

"It's okay. At times it reminds me that it isn't completely healed."

"I really shouldn't tease you."

"I don't mind."

"Are you certain? I can be unmerciful."

"Can you take it as well as you dish it out?"

"I've been told that I have a good sense of humor."

Joe chuckled. Her playfulness, relaxed manner, and quiet confidence reminded him of Joyce. In other ways she was unique—a mystery hungering to be solved. And what detective could resist the challenge of solving a good mystery? The opportunity to discover more about this beautiful stranger excited him. It was a feeling he thought he would never experience again after the passing of his wife. Now, a renewed appreciation for life had ambushed him whenever he gazed into her alluring blue eyes.

"You're planning something, aren't you, Joseph?"

Her voice chased his thoughts away.

"Why do you say that?"

"Don't be coy with me. I can tell by that whimsical expression on your face. You're planning something to test my sense of humor."

"Maybe I am and maybe I'm not," he said, and bobbed his eyebrows up and down.

"You'll have to wait and see."

"I knew it! I knew you were a rascal! The first time I saw you in the office I had a feeling."

"No you didn't."

"I did!"

"You're teasing me again."

"It's true! I have a sense about those things."

"Couldn't let it go, though, could you? You just *had* to find out for yourself."

Regardless of whether what she'd said was true, Joe enjoyed the banter. Above all else, he hoped the sentiment was mutual. No one could ever replace Joyce—a fact never to be denied. Still, he wanted to believe that Victoria knew as much, and wouldn't try.

A wall of thunder rattled the windows again. Neither of them noticed or cared, locked in an embrace of the eyes and seduction of the senses. A rising compulsion implored Joe to ignore his impairment and move from the sofa to kiss her. Victoria's eyes exhibited a willingness to meet him halfway. They both teetered on the brink of relenting.

Victoria suddenly blinked several times. "I should do the dishes," she said.

"The dishes can wait. I'll do them in the morning."

"Now, Joseph, you were kind enough to fix supper, so it's only right that I should do the dishes...even though the veggies in your beef stew *were* overcooked."

"Overcooked?"

"Next time we'll try my recipe."

Joe picked up a throw pillow and tossed it at her.

Laughing, Victoria juked out of the way as it flew by, bounced along the carpet, and came to rest against the turquoise wall.

"You'll never make the starting team with that arm, old-timer." Victoria crinkled her nose and left him for the kitchen.

Joe leaned back and took a long sip of whiskey.

He knew that at seventy-one she was three years his senior. He had done a thorough background check on her when she applied for residency. No signs of trouble with the law were uncovered, though her record in the arena of marriage was a point of interest.

She'd been married and widowed three times, the last two husbands being successful financiers. To put it simply, she was well-off. She had a master's degree in psychology, yet no employment record was listed. Joe figured she'd resigned herself to being a traditional housewife, even to her first husband, a floor manager in a plastics factory.

"Got any plans for tomorrow?" he asked.

"I have to do some shopping I've been putting off." Victoria's voice carried easily into the living room. "Why? What do you have in mind?"

"Do you like art?"

"Depends. I don't consider a watercolor tin can on a canvas to be art. And I don't care for the glorified graffiti that's being passed off as genius. I do like the works of the Renaissance period and the Impressionists, though. Some of the modern works I don't understand. Oh, and I like Marc Chagall and P.J. Bach."

I've opened a can of worms, Joe thought. *And who is P. J. Bach*? "How about Salvador Dali?"

The ensuing silence led him to believe she cared little for the Spanish surrealist.

"I've never taken the time to closely study his paintings...other than the occasional glance here and there, I mean."

"Would you like to go to the Dali Museum in St. Petersburg?"

"I think that would be—"

The rest of her answer was drowned out by knocking on the door. With the aid of his cane, Joe got to his feet to see who the caller might be. The answer came as he glanced through the peephole. He quickly opened the door.

"Detectives! What a surprise!"

"Hey, Joe," Carly said. Her smile was forced, and her voice without feeling.

David held no expression. "How's the foot doing?"

"Getting stronger by the day."

Joe studied David a second then looked at Carly. Their grim faces told him this wasn't a social call.

"Won't you come in?"

The detectives entered and stopped a couple of steps inside the door.

"Joe, D-M-V records indicate that a man by the name of Steven Echavarría is a resident here," Carly said. "Do you know him?"

"Not by name. Maybe by sight."

"Then you wouldn't know anything about him?"

"Probably not. I could pull up his residency file for you. But you don't need me to check on... I take it he's dead."

"Did I hear you say that someone is dead, Joseph?"

Victoria was drying her hands with a faded blue hand towel as she emerged from the kitchen. Three pairs of eyes settled on her. She stopped, finished drying her hands, and countered with a smile.

"Sorry, Joe, we didn't know you had company," Carly said.

"Victoria Combes, these are detectives Carly Truffant and David Sizemore."

"Pleased to meet you," Victoria said before exhibiting a look of curiosity. "You look familiar. Have we met before?"

"We were in the office the day you came to ask about a vacancy," Carly said.

"Oh, that's right."

Silence carried the next few seconds.

"I should be going, Joseph. Thank you so much for a wonderful supper."

"There's no need for you to leave. We can finish our discussion in the hall."

"I have to get up early and..." Victoria handed him the towel. "I'll talk to you tomorrow."

"Ms. Combes?" David said. "By any chance do *you* know Steven Echavarría?"

"It's *Mrs.* Combes, and I don't believe I do, Detective."

David nodded and stepped aside to allow her to pass.

Once she was gone, Carly resumed the conversation.

"Steven Echavarría was murdered in the Sunrise Motel on Gulf to Bay Boulevard. A maid found his body this morning."

"How was he killed?" Joe asked.

"He was stabbed five times."

An act of passion, Joe thought. *Or not.* "Was it a robbery?"

"Doesn't appear to be."

"Any leads?"

"We talked to the desk clerk who works nights," David said. "He told us there was a woman with him, but she stayed in the car while he checked in. He didn't get a good look at her."

"Was he able to give you any kind of a description?"

"Silver hair was all he could see."

That's more than half the population of the county. "Did

you find a murder weapon?"

"Our luck hasn't been that good lately," Carly said.

"Is Echavarría married?"

"He was a widower."

"Then why take the woman to a motel? Why not invite her to his condo?"

"Maybe they didn't want to run the risk of her husband finding out."

"Maybe he didn't want her to know where he lived," David said.

"Or maybe their meeting wasn't about sex?" Carly added.

Joe arched his eyebrows.

"These days you never know. Would you mind taking a look at the body, Joe? He doesn't have any family in the area."

"Sure, but I don't know if it will do any good."

"Criminal Analysis will need to get into Echavarría's place."

"Of course, but we'll have to go to the office so I can get the master key."

"Thanks for helping out...*Joseph.*"

Chapter 2

Joe secured his condo and followed the detectives to the elevator, making sure to bring his umbrella. By the time the trio reached the first floor and walked to the entrance of the building, torrents of rain were pouring from the menacing gray sky. A Criminal Analysis Unit team waited in the lobby a few feet from the automatic glass doors.

"I'll only be a second," Joe said as he opened the building manager's office. He returned with the key and started to hand it to Carly.

"David, I'll get with you as soon as Joe and I get back from the Coroner's Office."

"Stay dry," David said, took the key from Joe, and motioned for the analysis team to join him.

Carly and Joe left the building and paused beneath the concrete roof over the short walkway in front.

"What do you think?" Carly asked.

"I think we're going to get wet," Joe replied.

"You wait here while I get the car."

"I can make it. I'm not completely incapacitated."

"You'll look like a drowned rat by the time you get there." Carly glanced at his cane.

"Especially if you're still using that thing. Do you really need it?"

"My foot bothers me on occasion."

"Are you getting plenty of rest like the doctor told you?"

"As much as I can. It's not easy when you live alone. I have other responsibilities that need tending to."

"Your lady friend doesn't pamper you?"

"No, she gives me a hard time like someone else I know."

Carly chuckled. "Here goes." She clutched the collar of her dark blue trench coat and sprinted into the deluge, splashing through the countless puddles sprinkled throughout the parking lot.

Joe was impressed by her athletic moves. *Joyce, if we'd had a daughter, I would have hoped she'd be like Carly.*

A moment later Carly pulled up to the curb in a gray, unmarked Dodge sedan. Joe opened the door and struggled to get inside. Once he'd fastened his seat belt, they slowly motored through the saturated parking lot and pounding rain to Island Way. A short ride followed by a left turn onto Memorial Causeway had them headed in the direction of downtown Clearwater.

"So how are you doing?" Joe asked. "Everything okay at home?"

The young detective didn't answer right away. "About the same. Tim and I are trying to work things out. He can't seem to understand all that my job entails. I try to leave my work at the office to make it easier for him. And he does everything he possibly can to show that he loves me." She sighed. "It's not working, though."

"Being a cop is tough—on *and* off the job."

"How did you and Joyce make it work?"

Joe grinned as the image of his wife clad in the flowing white wedding dress she wore on the day they were married slipped into his mind.

"For me it was pure luck, and a great deal of love. Joyce tolerated a lot in those early years. I was fortunate to realize what a special person I'd found before she told me where to get off, and packed her bags to...well, that's when I knew that I truly loved her."

The trip to the Forensics Science Laboratory on Ulmerton Road would take some time. Joe seized the opportunity to learn more about the case.

"Carly, if robbery wasn't the motive, why do you think Steven Echavarría was murdered?"

"I think somebody wanted him dead. At present, there's no other viable motive. The motel room wasn't vandalized, we found no visible evidence of drugs or alcohol being a factor, and no one we interviewed heard them fighting."

"Anyone see the woman leave?"

"The people on either side of the room didn't even hear them come in, which is odd."

Odd, yes, but not unheard of, Joe thought. "Did you check the taxi services and...oh, what's the name of it? Uber. Did you check with Uber and those other people carriers?"

"David called every one of them. No one was picked up at the Sunrise Motel."

"I suppose she could have walked a block or two in either direction before she called."

"We thought of that. No one within a five-block radius of the motel needed a ride."

"How about foreign DNA? Did you find any inside or outside the room?"

"Criminal Analysis found some fluid on a pillowcase. We're waiting to hear the results."

"I'm wondering if this might have been a professional hit."

"At this point anything is possible. We're going to dig deeper into Echavarría's background when we get back to the office."

Carly eased off the gas pedal as Memorial Causeway veered to the right and became Chestnut Street.

Joe leaned back and attempted to recall whether any of the cases he'd worked during his days in Homicide were similar. Some of the killings had occurred indoors, and some out of doors in an area affording the shooter a clean, fast getaway. He couldn't remember a case involving the lure of sex as bait—none that he'd worked, anyway. And he'd never encountered a hired killer that was a woman. But this was a different time. Women claimed empowerment, or so they kept reminding him. Failing to consider a woman as the suspect would be a grievous error by today's standards.

"Joe, there was one thing that David thought was unusual."

"What was that?"

"All of his clothes were gone."

"Everything?"

"Even his shoes, not to mention his keys, money, and identification. He was completely nude when the maid found him."

"How did you identify him?"

"We ran his license plate. His car was still in the parking lot."

"Seems strange that his clothes were taken, but not his car. It could have been dumped anywhere later and would explain how the killer got away."

"I agree."

"Any word on the fingerprints?"

"We're still waiting. Criminal Analysis found quite a few."

Joe pinched up his face. "Hard to believe that his clothes weren't tossed in a dumpster or stashed someplace else."

"If they were, we couldn't find them. And get this, Joe, it appears the killer showered, and took the towel."

"That's pretty brazen." Joe paused as another question entered his mind. "Carly, how does someone traveling on foot and carrying an armload of laundry go unnoticed?"

Carly grinned. "Sounds like a job for The Gray Detective."

"Oh, no. Not me. I'm retired."

A right turn at Missouri Avenue pointed them south, and closer to their destination.

Joe glanced out of the window at the side streets shiny with rain. He had come to accept the season of "liquid sunshine." Florida natives didn't give it a second thought. In a sub-tropical climate, the rainy months were expected like the winter snows burying the north and the tornados ravaging Tornado Alley.

Acclimation was the key to living in the Sunshine State.

But the rigors of relocation weren't important to Joe. His focus was on the faceless Steven Echavarría. Not even a hint of the man's features stirred a memory. Names without faces were not uncommon in a condominium the size of the Crimson Conch. Some folks simply chose to forgo the many weekly gatherings such as bingo and bridge nights. Even the monthly barbeques, courtesy of the condominium association, failed to draw half of the residents. Still, Joe figured that at some point he would have crossed paths with the man.

The right turn onto Ulmerton Road drew him from his thoughts and directed his attention to the busy intersection. The next left would deliver them to the Coroner's Office, and yet another victim of a violent crime. And he'd seen too many victims in his time.

Chapter 3

The room containing the wall of vaults was as cold as expected—chilling, in fact.

Cold as death, Joe remembered someone saying. A baseless idiom meant to propagate fear more than conjure up an image. To one-time visitors the expression was spot-on. To morgue personnel and veterans of law enforcement like he and Carly, it was simply another day at the office.

Along with the pathologist, they looked down at the naked body of Steven Echavarría. The opening in the man's throat was as ugly as the path of five stab wounds running from his chest to his groin. At first glance, a criminal psychologist might label the attack a crime of passion as Joe had. A blatant act of revenge tendered toward a cheating spouse. But a number of motives could apply, and uncovering the right one would take some time.

"I don't know him, Carly, but I believe you're right," Joe said. "Someone wanted him dead. The obvious question is why?" He noticed the pensive expression on her face. "Is there something I'm missing?"

"He was tied to the bed, and there was a pillow over his face."

Joe leaned closer and studied the ugly discoloration on Echavarría's wrists and ankles. "These bruises are severe."

"We think the killer used a rope or cord. Criminal Analysis found some fibers."

"Was he smothered before he was stabbed?"

"Unfortunately not," the pathologist said. "He was very much alive."

"We think the pillow was used to muffle his screams," Carly said.

The pathologist nodded.

"And no one admitted to hearing anything?" Joe asked.

Silence was the answer he received.

Joe pictured Echavarría bound and spread-eagled as the woman riding him held a pillow over his face with one hand while stabbing and slicing him with the knife she clutched in the other.

"She must have been very strong. The bruising tells me that Echavarría was fighting for his life the whole time."

"Unless she was sitting on his face," Carly said.

Joe and the pathologist leveled stares.

"There was some fluid found on the pillowcase. If it's vaginal fluid then she could have been sitting on the pillow, smothering him at the same time she was using the knife."

"What about it, Doc?" Joe asked.

The pathologist shrugged. "It's possible, I suppose. And you're right about it being vaginal fluid. We're running it through the national DNA database. And before you ask, the killer was right-handed."

"Would your conclusion still be true if she was sitting on the pillow?"

"No question."

"Anything unusual about the stab wounds?"

"Nothing, really. They all were deep. Any one of a dozen different knives could have been used."

"Maybe the killer wasn't an older woman," Carly said.

Once again she was the center of attention.

"All the desk clerk said he saw in the car was silver hair. No one else we interviewed remembered seeing a woman. Maybe it was a younger woman with a dye job or wearing a wig...or even a cross-dresser."

The next few moments were as cold as the surroundings and equally still.

Carly released a heavy sigh. "Let's hope the DNA results tell us something."

The rain had stopped and the air was sticky when Carly and Joe began their journey back to the Crimson Conch Condominiums. Joe sat quietly sorting out how the confrontation between Echavarría and his killer might have unfolded. Seduction was the primary factor to getting him alone, and thrill sex the lure for his being tied up. Joe shook his head. Two old people rocking a motel room might seem disgusting to some, especially the younger crowd envisioning grandma and grandpa bouncing up and down under the covers. But the victim belonged to the Woodstock Generation. "Live for today" was their mantra. The era of bell-bottom jeans may have gone the way of the peace sign, but the memory of free love lived on. If two consenting adults agreed to a friendly session of bondage to reignite the spark, so be it. As long as the result was successful, why *not* indulge in some naughty play-acting.

Except this wasn't done for fun, Joe thought. *It was a prelude to murder*.

Carly shifting in her seat broke his concentration.

"Joe, did you ever get a case like this one?" she asked.

"I was called to a B-D-S-M event once. A woman had a seizure while being suffocated."

"That must have been weird."

"Besides her dying, the saddest part of it all was that none of the witnesses seemed to care. They figured she would be all right even as they watched her convulse."

"Did you charge anyone?"

"We charged the organizers of the gathering with second degree murder. Two days later we got an anonymous tip. When we interviewed the woman whose name we were given, she broke down and admitted to playing the role of dominatrix. She said she was scared, and didn't want it to become known publically that she engaged in such activities."

Carly grimaced. "A woman torturing another woman. What kind of person does that?"

"Nothing surprises me anymore."

The retired detective decided against telling her of the other two murders. Snuff films were a totally different indulgence. One of the victims, a sixteen-year-old blond, was the subject of several nightmares that continued to disrupt Joe's sleep. An uneasy feeling brought him to fold his arms and stare at the road ahead.

"Something on your mind, Joe?"

"I was wondering why the killer left the pillowcase. Echavarría's clothes and personal belongings were taken along with the bath towel, but the most damning piece of evidence was overlooked."

"The thought crossed my mind, too. Maybe she got scared like the woman you mentioned, and forgot it."

"Maybe."

Joe's focus was broken by the numerous buildings rising up in downtown Clearwater. Although he had come to appreciate one of the three major cities making up the Tampa Bay area, and the sunsets burning above the Gulf of Mexico every evening, he found himself slipping back into a mode of behavior that he longed to forget. He was totally immersed in a pool of unanswered questions. The old itch from his days in Homicide was back and stronger than ever.

He refused the urge to offer assistance, and decided to wait until Carly asked for his help—*if* she asked for his help. No sense in being meddlesome, he reasoned.

Memorial Causeway gleamed like an incandescent serpent from the headlights of the many vehicles coming from and going to Clearwater Beach. Carly slowed for the right turn onto Island Way, bringing into view more points of light from the condominiums, townhouses, and excess of homes defining Island Estates.

Joe took little interest in the parking lot of the building where he lived. He could navigate the plot of asphalt in his sleep. It wasn't until they rolled up behind a silver Lincoln Continental at the main entrance that a possible answer to one of the important questions surrounding the latest murder case became apparent.

A man exited the car and strolled around to the passenger side to act the gentleman for the woman riding with him. As the man opened the door, Joe slowly turned to Carly.

"I think I know how the killer escaped, and it's so obvious that I can't believe it didn't come to me sooner."

A blank stare appeared on Carly's face. "What is it?"

"The killer had an accomplice."

Chapter 4

Since his near-death experience at the hands of Michael "Mac" McDougal, the former building manager, Joe had been able to benefit from several nights of peaceful, uninterrupted sleep. Some nights, though, were burdened with the faces of those falling victim to horrible deaths in the murder cases he'd worked. Struggling to escape one such nightmare, he was jolted awake, bolting upright and gasping for air in the suffocating walls of darkness within his bedroom.

God! Why can't I let go of them? he thought.

Morning had yet to drive away the night, so Joe got up and hobbled to the bathroom, a ritual of old age and one of many he hated—especially with an injured foot.

A trail of slow, sleepy steps to the kitchen and the coffee maker came next. The machine sat idle, the hour too early to trip the timer. Joe pushed the button, bringing it to life, and then limped to a chair at his mahogany dining table. Serenaded by the sounds of sputtering and burping, and enticed by the alluring aroma of the liquid escaping through the coffee grounds, he sat idly by between thoughts.

I don't know how much longer I can do this, Joyce. One day blends into another. They all seem so meaningless. I wish you were here.

Stop it, Joe, he heard her say. *Stop being so melodramatic.*

I can't help it. I'm close to losing all hope.

You know I'm here with you. I'll always be with you.

I know, but I...

Now stop feeling sorry for yourself, and go get your coffee.

Joe remembered how she used to brush his nose with her forefinger before she kissed him. He smiled as he got up from the table.

After a breakfast of waffles with three crisp planks of bacon, Joe enjoyed a long, hot shower before leaving his condo for the building manager's office on the first floor.

He encountered a number of couples during his ride on the elevator and the labored trip down the hall, knowing some of them, but speaking to all. As he rounded the corner, he noticed a folded piece of paper taped to the office door.

Now what is this? he thought.

Seeing his name neatly printed on the note, he carefully removed it and began to read. A smile slowly turned up the corners of his mouth. The message was from Victoria, inviting him to lunch. He unlocked the door, went to the desk, and picked up the receiver to the light brown phone before sitting down.

"I was beginning to think that you weren't going to call," Victoria said.

"I got a late start this morning. I couldn't seem to get going."

"Are you all right? You're not feeling ill, are you?"

"I'm fine. I didn't sleep very well."

"Is something on your mind?"

"Nothing in particular."

"Oh well, we'll just chalk it up to old age."

Joe cringed.

"I thought if you were up for it, we might do lunch somewhere on the beach today."

"Sounds good."

"Okay. Is eleven-thirty a good time for you?"

"Better make it twelve-thirty. I've got some orders to place and some errands to run."

The ensuing silence left Joe wondering if his suggesting a later time had made her unhappy.

"I don't see a problem," Victoria finally said. "Someone recommended a place called Frenchy's. Are you familiar with it?"

"I am."

"Is that all right with you?"

"Fine by me."

"Joseph, are you sure you're all right?"

"Certainly. Why do you ask?"

"You don't sound the same."

"I'm just tired."

"Are you sure it isn't something else?" Playfulness tinged her voice.

"Nothing a good night's sleep won't cure."

"Oh. Okay. Then I guess *I* should drive since your foot is still bothering you."

"Whatever you decide, but I'm quite capable."

"Can the macho act, Joseph. If you drive we'll most assuredly wind up having an accident."

"You don't quit, do you?"

"I told you that I can be merciless."

"I believe you."

"Okay. I guess I'll see you at twelve-thirty then."

Joe leaned back in his chair. Victoria was most perceptive. Something *was* on his mind—someone, actually. Steven Echavarría. He wanted to look over the background check done on the man when he had first applied for residency. If Mac McDougal had bothered to do a background check. And he hadn't been lying when he'd said he had orders to place and errands to run.

"Now's as good a time as any to get started," he muttered.

He didn't get the chance.

"Good morning, stranger."

Joe looked to his left and saw Russell Goodfellow standing in the doorway. "Good morning, Rusty."

Russell, or Rusty, as he preferred to be called, and his wife Nancy had come to the Crimson Conch a year ago. They were a stocky and perfectly matched gregarious couple from Michigan. In truth, she was gregarious. He was loud and obnoxious.

Rusty walked to the front of the desk and helped himself to a chair. "Haven't seen you out and about lately."

"My foot's been bothering me. I'm resting it as much as possible. Doctor's orders."

"And I'll bet the R and R involves Vickie Combes, doesn't it?"

Rusty didn't pretend to hide his joking, bobbing his eyebrows up and down.

"Now that's not true and you know it," Joe said.

Rusty laughed and threw up his hands, palms forward. "Hey, it's none of my business. Nancy was wondering where you've been hiding, that's all."

"I haven't been hiding."

Rusty hooted again. "Now, Joe, just some friendly ribbing between friends. Actually, I came here to invite you to lunch. Nancy and I were thinking of going to the Sloppy Seagull for some beers, burgers, and a few laughs."

"Sorry, I already have plans for lunch."

"Oh." Disappointment appeared on Rusty's face. Then revelation. "Ohhhh! I get it! You and Vickie. Well, she can tag along, too. The more the merrier. Whaddaya think?"

"I don't know. She invited me."

"So what?"

"She has another place in mind."

"Great! Nancy and I are flexible."

"I'll have to call her and get back to you."

"Call her now."

"Rusty, I have some business I need to tend to, and it has to be done today."

"Fine. Is noon okay with you?"

"I'll let you know."

Rusty got up to leave.

"Say, Rusty, I realize that you and Nancy haven't lived here very long, but do you know Steven Echavarría?"

The man from Michigan brought his right hand up and pulled on his chin. "Steven Echavarría, Steven Echavarría. Yeah! Nice little guy. Cuban, I think. Real quiet. Keeps to himself. I haven't seen him around lately. Why?"

"Someone was asking about him."

"Oh." Rusty started to leave, stopped abruptly, and spun around. "Wait a minute! He's dead! I saw it on the news this morning! Is that why the cops came here last night?"

"Who told you the cops were here?"

"I saw them. The same two that came here before when you got smacked around."

"They were asking for some personal information on him."

Rusty's eyes grew large. "Did you go with them to the Sunrise Motel? Did you see his body?"

"Rusty, I'll get back to you about lunch."

"Oh! Right! Nancy and I will be waiting for your call. She'll love gabbing with Vickie. Girl talk, ya know."

Rusty slammed the door behind him when he left.

Joe sighed deeply and picked up the phone. He needed to call the yard maintenance company about some additional landscaping before he contacted the others on his list. Next, he would figure out an efficient route to run his errands so he could get back in time to meet with Victoria.

An hour later, right before he was getting ready to leave, the phone rang. He recognized Victoria's voice immediately.

"Joseph, I just ran into Nancy Goodfellow. Did you tell Russell and her that we were going to have lunch with them?"

Joe rolled his eyes. "Victoria, let me explain."

Chapter 5

Uncomfortable couldn't begin to describe how Joe felt as he, Victoria, Rusty, and Nancy sat down at a table in Frenchy's Rockaway Grill. He and Victoria preferred a peaceful meal in a relaxed atmosphere and subtle conversation. They were soon to be subjected to an unwanted dose of Rusty's flamboyant personality.

"Nice place," Rusty said, his head swiveling in all directions. "Glad you suggested we come here, Vicki."

Victoria strained a smile. "I'm told the entrées are delicious. And Russell, my name is Victoria."

"Well, excuse me! I didn't know we were being so formal." Rusty let loose his loud, staccato laughter that boomed off of every red, yellow, and blue wall in the eatery.

Victoria glanced at Joe with disapproving eyes.

Nancy seemed unfazed. "How's your leg coming along, Joe? I see you're still using a cane."

"Actually, it's my foot, and it still bothers me on occasion. I try to rest it as much as I—"

"He's gotta good nurse, honey," Rusty interrupted. "Victoria's keepin' a close eye on him."

"—as much as I can," Joe continued. "I broke three toes. They take time to heal."

"Especially with someone as old as you!" Rusty roared once more, louder.

"Now tell me again how you hurt yourself?" Nancy asked.

"I told you, honey, he kicked the crap outta Mac McDougal, the fat guy who used to be the building manager."

"Oh, that's right." Nancy laughed, a higher-pitched staccato than her husband's, but equally annoying.

A couple at a nearby table made known their discontent by frowning at the unruliness.

To the relief of Joe and Victoria, a blond-haired server worked her way to their table.

"What can I get you folks to drink?" she asked.

Rusty didn't hesitate. "Beers all around, guys? Whaddaya think?"

"I'll have iced tea," Victoria said.

"Make it two," Joe added.

A look of surprise shaped Rusty's face. "Don't you wanna brew, Joe? A cold beer always tastes good on a hot day."

"I still have some work to do."

Rusty looked at the server and shrugged. "Two drafts for me and the wife."

"I'll be right back."

"Hold on, Sweetie, we'll order now!" Rusty bellowed and offered a wide smile.

The server looked over her shoulder toward the kitchen then back to him. "Okay."

"I'll have a dozen oysters on the half shell, the eight-ounce big boy grouper sandwich, cole slaw *and* potato salad, and a basket of fries."

Rusty showed little interest in Nancy and Victoria ordering salads, and peered through the window at the outdoor deck and the growing number of people claiming small areas along the shore. When he heard Joe order a mahi mahi sandwich, he snapped his head around.

"Don't you want some oysters, Joe?" He glanced at Victoria. "You know what they say about oysters." He made no attempt to hide his bouncing eyebrows.

"The sandwich will be fine," Joe said.

The server collected the menus and scurried away.

Rusty again set his sights on the Gulf of Mexico. "We shoulda sat outside. There's a better view of the beach. I like lookin' at the water."

"What he *really* likes is looking at the girls in their skimpy bathing suits," Nancy said to Victoria.

Nodding, Victoria offered the hint of a smile. "Nancy, why did you and Russell decide to move to—?"

"Say, Joe, heard any more about the dead Cuban guy?" Rusty interrupted.

Victoria frowned.

The couple at the table nearby was staring at them again.

"No, Rusty, I haven't, and I don't think this is the proper place or time for that discussion."

The hefty Michigander arched his eyebrows. "Oops! Sorry, Joe."

The server returned with their drinks, and the topic was lost to Rusty's incessant babbling. A short time later their food was served. The kitchen staff lived up to their reputation, and everyone commented favorably about their delicious meals, with Rusty going overboard as expected.

At the end of a long and boring two hours, Joe and Victoria said goodbye to Rusty and Nancy.

The trip along Mandalay Avenue was quiet—too quiet for Joe. Although their relationship was in the beginning stages, he knew that Victoria was unhappy. Silence was easy to interpret, and often more painful than yelling.

Better get this over with, he thought. "I hope you're not too upset with me about lunch."

Victoria steered her blue Mercedes Benz SUV into the roundabout leading to Memorial Causeway.

"I'm not upset."

Not much. "But you *are* disappointed."

"Very!"

"I'm sorry. I promise I won't let it happen again."

"Joseph, I hope you realize how much I enjoy your company. I wanted today to be reserved for the two of us. I would like to get to know you better."

Joe grinned. "I'd like to get to know you better, too. We'll do something special next time."

The red light at the intersection to Island Way presented Victoria with an opportunity, so she casually turned to Joe.

"Another reason I wanted to go to lunch was to tell you that my daughter is coming to vacation with me."

"How wonderful. I'll bet you're excited."

"She arrives next Tuesday, and I thought you might come to dinner some evening to meet her."

"I'd like that."

The turn signal appeared, and Victoria eased the SUV onto Island Way.

"She's a beautiful young woman and as smart as they come."

"You must be very proud. What does she do for a living?"

"She marries rich old men like her mother." A second later Victoria laughed at the befuddled expression Joe was wearing. "I'm joking. She's a doctor, and a very good one. Mothers always say that, I suppose."

Joe's puzzled expression vanished. *Glad she's in an upbeat mood again.* "I'll look forward to it. What's her name?"

"Cicely. She works in Worcester, Massachusetts, where she lives."

Victoria brought the SUV to a halt in the space designated for her in the condominium parking lot. Exiting the Mercedes, she went to the passenger side and helped Joe get out. As they slowly made their way to the main entrance, Victoria tugged on Joe's arm.

"And the next time Russell and Nancy want us to join them for lunch, I'm going to be sick."

Chapter 6

The next morning was Friday, and Joe was in the office at the usual time: eight o'clock. The week's paperwork was close to being finished. The contractors' schedules for the coming month had been charted. He was looking forward to a short work day. A pair of visitors broke his concentration.

"We figured we'd find you hiding in here," David said.

Joe looked up from the papers scattered over his desk. "Well, if it isn't my two favorite detectives."

Carly and David casually walked to where he was seated. She looked solemn. He looked indifferent.

Joe eyed them warily. "Don't tell me you found another body."

"Nope, the truth is we didn't find anything," Carly said.

"Other than the stain on the pillowcase *is* vaginal fluid," David added.

"No luck in identifying her?"

"Not one match in the database," Carly said. "We went back to the Sunrise Motel yesterday afternoon and questioned the staff again. One of the maids remembered seeing a woman sitting in a car in the parking lot."

"A woman with silver hair?"

"The maid didn't recall her hair being silver. She said she just sort of glanced at the woman."

"What time was this?"

"Late afternoon...about five-thirty."

"The same day Echavarría was killed."

"The same day."

"Five-thirty? But that's hours before the estimated time of death, isn't it?"

"Maybe she was checking out which motel would be best for the set-up," David said.

"Or maybe she didn't have anything to do with the murder at all," Carly said.

The trio fell silent for a moment.

"Could the maid tell you *anything* about this woman?" Joe asked.

"Only that she *might* have had brown hair. Or auburn hair."

"And no one else noticed her in the parking lot?"

"No one we interviewed."

David's cell phone rang and distracted them right before Nancy Goodfellow walked into the office with a look of deep concern. "Oh, excuse me. I didn't realize you were busy, Joe."

David held the phone to his ear, glanced at Carly, and walked out the door.

"We're done," Carly said. She smiled at Nancy, noting the woman's uneasiness.

"I'll be in touch, Joe." She left them to join her partner in the lobby.

"What can I do for you, Nancy?"

"Have you seen Rusty this morning?"

"No, is something wrong?"

"He went to the Circle Food Mart last night to get some junk food. He gets these cravings and, well, he hasn't come back."

"What?"

"I don't know where he could be."

"What time did he leave?"

"Around a quarter after ten."

"Did you try calling him?"

"Five times. He didn't answer. I called the police at midnight and they said they'd look into it. I haven't heard back from them."

"Did you call the Circle Food Mart?"

"Yes, a little before midnight, but no one answered. I guess they were closed. I'm scared, Joe."

"The man and woman who just left here are detectives. Stick your head out the door and see if they're still in the lobby."

Nancy stepped to the door before disappearing.

Joe struggled to his feet and felt a sharp pain shoot through his injured foot. Taking a moment to recover, he wondered if Rusty's absence was the result of an argument between him and Nancy. As he started to reach for his cane, Nancy, Carly, and David came back into the office.

"Nancy, these are detectives Truffant and Sizemore. Tell them what you told me."

Nancy recounted her story, adding that she had attempted to reach Rusty shortly before she came to see Joe. Again she received no answer.

David glanced at Joe with troubled eyes.

"I realize that missing persons is not your department," Joe said, "but I thought you might—"

"Detective Sizemore, would you take Mrs. Goodfellow into the lobby and get a description of her husband, please," Carly said. "I need to speak with Mr. Hampton."

Carly's formal tone filled Joe with trepidation. He sensed something terrible was about to unfold.

When Nancy and David were gone, Carly turned to him.

"There's been another murder. A man was found in the scrub brush at the end of the beach access off El Dorado Avenue and Juniper Way.

"Do you know who he is?"

"No identification on him. He was naked."

"Any idea of how he was killed?"

"Stabbed multiple times and his throat cut according to the first officer on the scene." Carly paused. "I've got a bad feeling that this victim's wounds are going to be similar to those found on Echavarría."

"Carly, is there something you're not telling me?"

"It's just a feeling."

Joe understood what she was experiencing. The feeling, or "go with your gut" philosophy employed by all good cops, had helped him many times in chasing down murderers.

"What can you tell me about Russell Goodfellow, Joe?"

"Not much, I'm afraid. He and Nancy have been living here for about a year. They came from Michigan. They're amiable and socially interactive. He's about six feet tall and close to three hundred pounds, I'd say, ruddy complexion, bushy brown hair, and brown eyes."

"Other residents ever have a problem with them? Any complaints?"

"Not that I'm aware. No official complaints, anyway."

"What does that mean?"

"Rusty can be loud and obnoxious at times, very irritating. I've seen people offended by his rudeness." The face of Shirley Lyon appeared in Joe's mind. *I know what she would have done*, he thought.

"Joe, I don't have to tell you that Goodfellow and his wife may have argued, and he could have disappeared just to piss her off."

"Thought the same thing myself except, and I don't know them that well, she has a worried look in her eyes and she told me she was scared."

"I noticed that look, too. It still doesn't mean that his disappearing act isn't on purpose."

"Well, let's hope he comes home soon and we can forget the whole thing."

"I'm all for it." After a few seconds she said, "Guess I'd better go check out the latest victim."

When he was alone, Joe allowed an unpleasant thought to strengthen. He hoped the latest victim Carly alluded to was not Rusty Goodfellow. His gut feeling had him believing otherwise.

Chapter 7

Sliding the desk drawer closed, Joe took a moment to unwind and allow the throbbing in his foot to lessen. His responsibilities as building manager had been met for another week, more work than he realized when he took the job, and he was looking forward to a peaceful weekend—starting immediately.

Carefully lifting himself out of the chair, he picked up his cane and took a quick look around. Everything appeared to be in order, especially the top of his desk, so he hobbled to the office door and locked it behind him. Once he was in the lobby, the next trick would be getting to the elevator without having to stop numerous times. A couple who'd resided at the Crimson Conch long before he'd arrived greeted him in the hall. He smiled and nodded politely the way well-mannered people do—those people he knew, anyway.

The elevator was kind to him this day, and took next to no time to reach the first floor. More grateful than usual, he couldn't wait to rest his foot on the coffee table for an hour or two—or three or four.

Maybe I'll stretch out on the sofa and take a nap, he thought. *R and R is what the doctor ordered.*

The elevator door closed, the car began its ascent, and Joe welcomed the gratifying feeling of being lifted homeward. He leaned against the back wall and closed his eyes. As often times happened, the beautiful face of his wife materialized.

Hello, handsome. How are you?

Hello, gorgeous. I'm tired.

Her loving smile was one of the many things he had adored about her. *You're always tired.*

True, but not like this, and I'm having trouble facing the day.

Her smile vanished. *Don't do this to yourself, Joe.*

I've always told you the truth, Joyce.

I know, but don't do this.

Joe felt the elevator slow to a halt. He opened his eyes and gazed at the line of numbers above the door. The numeral three was glowing, one landing shy of his floor. The door opened, and he was ambushed by the smothering fragrance from two women—two beautiful women. One was Victoria. The other was her mirror image, only younger, with darker hair and the same speculative expression. Their resemblance took him by surprise, and he was unable to speak.

"Joseph!" Victoria said. "What a coincidence. We were on our way up to see you."

Joe chuckled, glancing at the other woman. "I'm glad you pointed out that there are two of you. I thought I was experiencing double vision."

The woman unknown to him smiled, her perfect teeth white and gleaming.

"Do you have some time to visit?"

"Certainly."

Joe hobbled out of the elevator as the door was starting to close.

"Joseph Hampton, this is my daughter, Cecily Dearmin."

"A pleasure, Cecily, or would you prefer I call you doctor?"

"If you do I'll never speak to you again."

Joe noticed the brilliance of her auburn hair as she lowered her eyes to his cane.

"I broke three toes."

"And he's been playing the *woe is me* card for weeks," Victoria chimed in.

With a tight smile, Joe shook his head.

"Joseph, are you getting enough rest?" Cecily asked.

"As much as I can. When your mother isn't pestering me, that is."

Cecily laughed—a pleasant melody.

Victoria was grinning as she took hold of his arm. "That's quite enough, Joseph. Allow me to assist you." She looked at her daughter. "He's helpless without me."

The trio started down the hall at a slow and deliberate pace.

When they reached Victoria's condo, Cecily unlocked the door, and waited to follow them inside. Victoria helped Joe settle onto her lavender sofa. Cecily chose a matching chair positioned nearby.

"Have you had lunch, Joseph?" Victoria asked.

"No, I just finished working in the office."

"I'll fix us something to eat while you two get acquainted."

Joe winked at Cecily. "Something other than your boring salads, okay?"

Victoria placed both hands on her hips and glared at him. "If my daughter wasn't here I'd slap you."

Joe brought up his cane. "Bring it on, Sassy!"

The music that was Cecily's laughter filled the room. "All right, you two, am I going to have to call the police?"

Victoria was already on her way to the kitchen. "No need, my dear. He sits before you."

"Is that true, Joseph?"

"I'm retired from Philadelphia P.D. And please call me Joe."

"But you said you worked in an office."

"I'm currently the building manager by proxy."

"He thinks he can run the place!" Victoria shouted. Her laughter followed.

Joe chuckled and shook his head again.

"By any chance were you a detective?" Cecily continued.

"Eighteen years in Homicide."

"Did mother tell you that I'm a pathologist?"

"Really? I would never have guessed."

"Why, because I'm a woman?"

"I didn't mean it that way. I simply meant that I would have guessed you to be a surgeon or pediatrician."

"I'm teasing you, Joe. Most people are surprised when I tell them."

"What made you decide on pathology?"

Cecily tilted her head. "Curiosity, I guess. And I wanted to do something different...different and challenging. I found pathology to be exactly what I was looking for."

"Your mother said that you live in Worcester, Massachusetts."

Cecily rolled her eyes. "I don't know why she keeps telling people that. I *work* in Worcester. I *live* in Shrewsbury. I used to live in Worcester before my husband died."

"Oh, I'm sorry."

"He left us four years ago."

"Us?"

"I have a twenty-five-year-old daughter—Vicki—named after you-know-who." Cecily leaned forward, and whispered, "If we had named her after my husband's mother, I would never have heard the end of it."

Liking her more and more, Joe said, "I'll take a wild guess and say your daughter's in medical school."

"Good guess. She's following in her mother's footsteps."

"Too bad she didn't come with you. I'm sure your mother would have loved to see her."

"She thought about it. But she has a full schedule this semester. As a matter of fact, I had to shuffle *my* schedule to get away Wednesday."

Wednesday? Joe thought. *Victoria said she was arriving next Tuesday. She must have gotten the days mixed up.*

"Lunch is ready!" Victoria sang out from the dining room.

Cecily rose and helped Joe to his feet.

"Thank you. I really hate being in this condition." He winced after a couple of steps, but kept moving. "I'm not a big fan of getting old, either."

Victoria had a chair pulled out for him when he and Cecily reached the table.

"Nothing special, just some cold cuts, and tomato, lettuce, and onion." As he sat down, she added, "The baloney's for you, Joseph, because you're full of it."

"Mother!" Cecily gasped.

"You may find this hard to believe, Cecily, but your mother really likes me," Joe said.

"She just has a funny way of showing it."

Once all were seated, they began to eat.

By three-thirty that afternoon, Joe was stretched out on the sofa in his own condo. The "Dagwood" sandwich Victoria had created for him had definitely satisfied his hunger. Now he could close his eyes and drift undisturbed for a few hours.

Subdued knocking ruined his plan.

Joe let loose a mild groan, rolled over on his right side, and sat up. Slowly rising, he limped to the door and peered through the peephole.

Uh-oh, he thought, and reached for the doorknob.

"Hi, Joe," David said. "Sorry to bother you. Can I come in?"

"Sure." Joe pulled the door open wider.

David stepped inside and faced him.

"Carly figured you'd want to know that our latest victim *is* Russell Goodfellow. We found his car on Juniper Way and ran the plate."

"I was afraid of that. Where *is* Carly?"

"Delivering the bad news to Mrs. Goodfellow."

"How was Rusty killed?"

"Almost exactly like Steven Echavarría."

"Almost?"

"Goodfellow had a large bruise on his left temple. Criminal Analysis believes a metal pipe or rod was used to bring him down.

Then he was stabbed multiple times and had his throat cut."

"Same pattern of wounds?"

"Almost identical."

"Find any clues?"

David shook his head. "We couldn't come up with any footprints in the sand because the rain obliterated them. And we didn't find either weapon."

"Rusty was a big man. His killer must have surprised him...if the killer was a woman."

"We came to the same conclusion—surprised him, I mean. There were no signs of a struggle."

"No witnesses, I suppose."

"We should be so lucky." David took on a defeated look. "I'd better go see how Carly's doing with Mrs. Goodfellow."

Joe saw him out, locked the door, and limped back to the sofa. The face of the boisterous Michigander appeared in his mind as he lay down.

"You may have been obnoxious, Rusty, but you didn't deserve to go out like that."

Chapter 8

Joyce was standing at the sink doing the dishes. Joe lingered at the dining table after enjoying another fine meal prepared by his beautiful young wife. A wicked thought seeped into his mind, so he got to his feet and walked to the kitchen, pausing in the doorway as his eyes pored over every inch of her curvaceous body.

As lovely as the day I married her, he thought.

Moving across the black-and-white-checkered linoleum floor, his indigo socks muffling each step, he stopped an arm's length behind her. He wanted to hold her, to kiss her, to make love to her. The desire was nearing eruption, and the urge to move closer growing stronger.

"Did you actually think you could sneak up on me?" she said, placing a clean plate in the dish rack to dry.

Joe chuckled, the urge close to uncontrollable, and slipped his arms around her waist. "You know me too well, my dear," he whispered. He began to kiss the nape of her neck, her familiar scent and the fragrance of her favorite soap fueling his passion.

As he pressed his body against hers, she felt the stoutness of his manhood. A soapy glass slid from her wet hands into a white mountain of suds.

"What are you doing?" she moaned softly.

He continued to kiss her neck, raising his right hand, unbuttoning her blouse, and gently fondling her breast. When he heard her moan a second time, he removed his hand and eased her around. Bringing his lips to hers, he kissed her forcefully while pulling her slowly to the floor.

As his fingers danced down to unzip her slacks, the dream exploded and darkness prevailed, startling him awake. Unsure of where he was, Joe sat up straight, jerking his head in every direction.

The rays from a late afternoon sun stealing through open mini-blinds lined the carpet in his living room. Coming to realize that he was alone, sadness dampened his dreamy desires. An unexpected knocking directed his eyes to the door.

"Wish you could have given me a few more minutes," he mumbled. He forced himself to stand, the pain in his foot unbearable. *Must have bumped it when I was playing with Joyce*, he thought and forced a grin. His pace toward discovering the identity of his visitor was slow. He winced a moment later as he reached the door and gazed through the peephole.

Carly was waiting patiently in the hall.

Joe opened the door and immediately sensed the detective was in a gloomy and troubled mood. A mood made stronger by her pitch-black pantsuit.

"You look like you could use a drink," he said.

"I do, but I'm still on duty. Mind if I come in?"

Joe stepped back and winced again.

Carly noticed as she passed by. "Your foot's not getting any better, is it?"

"It's fine. I bumped it earlier today."

"Uh-huh."

"Now don't *you* start."

She helped him to one end of the sofa and took a seat on the other.

"You look concerned," Joe said through his pain. "Is it the job...or something else?"

"I just came from the Medical Examiner's Office. I spent an hour going over the bodies of Echavarría and Goodfellow."

"David told me the wounds were similar. Is that what's

bothering you?"

"Joe, the stab wounds on their torsos are not identical, but they're close enough. What's bothering me is the path of their wounds."

"Identical?"

"Professional...according to the pathologist."

Joe was reluctant to suggest that she may have described the work of a serial killer. No need, really. The idea of a psychopath being on the loose was not one he cared to entertain at any time, and though he hadn't known her very long, he was certain the thought had already crossed her mind."Professional, as in done by someone who possesses medical skills?"

"Not a pleasant thought, is it?"

Triggered by a lasting, deepening suspicion, Joe entertained another troubling and unpleasant notion. He thought carefully before he spoke.

"Carly, do you know any women that whittle?"

"I don't believe so. What made you think of that?"

"Deanna Kenny, a resident here, has an online woodcarving business. She creates small busts, statues, totem poles, and the like."

"So she's an artist who's good with her hands."

"And with knives."

"I'm no expert, Joe, but don't wood carving knives have small blades?"

"I would think so."

"And aren't some of them designed primarily for digging and gouging wood?"

"You know more than I do. My point is that she's good with the use of a knife. Maybe a knife of any size. Like a carving knife or a fillet knife."

"Point taken. Are there any other reasons why you thought of her?"

"She prefers the alternative lifestyle."

"Meaning she doesn't like men."

"Up until last year she had a partner living with her."

"That doesn't make her a killer, Joe, and it's a short-sighted motive for suspecting her."

"I couldn't agree more, but if an insufferable loudmouth like Rusty Goodfellow said the wrong thing to her, she might be offended enough to do something about it."

"What about Echavarría? We don't know the first thing about his personality."

"Rusty told me he was quiet and kept to himself."

"Not anything like Goodfellow?"

"Doesn't sound like it."

"That doesn't reinforce your theory."

"True, but like you said, you don't know that much about him."

"When did Goodfellow tell you this?"

"A day or so ago."

"Can you tell me anything else about this Deanna Kenny?"

"She's about five foot six, stocky, and has sandy blond hair and brown eyes. Every time I've run into her she's wearing a red baseball cap."

Carly stared at him.

"I know, you're looking for a woman with gray hair and a woman with brown or auburn hair, but like you said, she could have worn a wig." Joe sighed. "I don't know, maybe I'm all wrong about Deanna."

"I'll have a talk with her anyway, just to be on the safe side."

Joe hadn't noticed that she was sitting slumped over. "Carly, is there something else you want to talk about?"

Carly quickly straightened. "No! I mean, no. Why would you think there was something wrong?"

"I didn't ask you if anything was wrong. Is there?"

"Tim... Tim left me this morning. He said he couldn't do it anymore. We tried, Joe. Honestly. I don't know why we couldn't save our marriage. I guess it wasn't meant to be."

"Did you see it coming?"

"I had an idea. We stopped talking a week ago. Pretty easy to figure out what was going to happen next."

"Does David know?"

"I think so. He hasn't said anything, though."

"Why don't you take some time off? I'm sure your superiors will understand."

"Take some time off and do what? Sit around and feel sorry for myself? I've cried enough, Joe. Besides, we need to find the killer."

"Carly, *you* need to get away from the job and figure out what you're going to do."

"I know what I'm going to do. I'm getting a divorce."

"Then take a vacation. Do something to relieve the stress."

"I'll have plenty of time for a vacation *after* we find the killer."

"Is that a promise?"

A scowl was etched into the detective's face as she got to her feet. "So what are you now—my father?"

Joe looked away and sharply exhaled disgust. He slowly stood up and started for the door.

As Carly reached over to take his arm, Joe jerked his arm away.

"I don't need your help!" he barked.

"Joe, I was only trying to—"

"Go on! Get out of here! Go find your killer!"

Carly stood stunned. "What is wrong with you?"

"Nothing! I don't need your help or anyone's help! Now go on! Get out of here!"

Carly left without saying another word.

After she closed the door, Joe limped back to the sofa and collapsed.

"God, my foot hurts."

He placed both hands under his calf and raised his leg, bringing his foot to rest on the coffee table. Easing back, he closed his eyes.

You shouldn't have shouted at her, he heard Joyce say.

She insulted me, Joyce. No one insults me. You know that.

She's young and she's hurting. Young people say things they don't mean when they're hurting.

I know, but she didn't have to be a smart-ass. I was only trying to help.

You should be more patient with her.

Don't start, Joyce. My foot is killing me.

You need to apologize.

When it snows in Clearwater!

You know, she reminds me of someone.

Don't even go there!

A sound Joe had come to despise found his ears.

"And, of course, the damned phone is on the dining table!" he bellowed.

Gingerly setting his foot on the floor, he hoisted himself up and struggled to get to the table.

"Joe, this is David. By any chance is Carly there?"

"She just left."

"I've been trying to reach her, but I keep getting her voicemail. I've uncovered some important information."

"What is it?"

"I was researching Russell Goodfellow and getting nowhere. I decided to talk to the cashier at the Circle Food Mart again. The woman who works the night shift."

"What did she tell you?"

"After thinking it over, she remembered seeing Goodfellow talking to a woman outside the store."

"Did she describe the woman?"

"Not really. The woman was medium height and had dark hair."

"Let me guess. The cashier was too far away."

"Right."

"What about the video camera?"

"They have two, and we looked at them this morning. Unfortunately, they only show the inside of the store. We saw

Goodfellow and some others come in and leave, but no woman who fit the description."

"I'll go downstairs and see if Carly is still in the parking lot."

"Thanks, Joe. I'll keep calling her."

Joe slid his phone into the pocket of his khakis, seized his unwanted cane, and limped out of his condo. Every step he took was more painful than the one before. He shifted his weight to the other foot during the elevator ride, did his best to act cordial when greeted by residents, and finally hobbled through the doors of the main entrance, gritting his teeth when he stopped.

Disappointment tugged at his insides when he scanned the parking lot and didn't see her. His spirits rose when he eventually caught sight of a gray Dodge sedan. The going was slow, and the drizzling rain relentless, but as he neared the car, he recognized her short raven hair. She was holding her head down, so he gently tapped on the windshield.

Carly looked up, her eyes red and swollen, embarrassed as she lowered the window.

"I'm sorry, Joe. I didn't mean to—"

"No, Carly, I'm the one who needs to apologize. I shouldn't have shouted at you."

"I'm not thinking straight. You were trying to help me, and I…" She sniffed, and a fresh cluster of tears joined the others on her cheeks.

"David called. He has something important to tell you."

Carly raised her hands and wiped her face. "Did he say what it was?"

"I'll let him tell you. I need to get out of the rain."

Picking up her iPhone from the passenger seat, Carly brought it to life. "My god! He's called five times." She sniffed again. "Thanks, Joe. I'm really sorry."

Joe motioned with his head. "Go do your job, Detective."

As he slowly shuffled back to the entrance, he was smiling.

You're right, Joyce, she is a lot like me.

Chapter 9

After a ham and cheese sandwich for supper, Joe was relaxing on his sofa with his bare foot cradled in a throw pillow atop the coffee table. The pain had subsided, but still left him feeling uncomfortable.

His television was tuned to a comedy he and Joyce had enjoyed early in their marriage. He'd seen nearly every episode about the U.S. Army surgical team stationed in Korea, some more than once. Even now the antics of the doctors and medical staff made him laugh—and he needed to laugh.

During a commercial break, he closed his eyes and tried not to think about his foot, difficult since every sharp and stabbing pain reminded him of Mac McDougal, and how close he had come to being murdered by him. A moment of introspection resulted in an interesting observation. He had been consumed by fear when it appeared The Committee's enforcer was about to end his life, and yet, during his bleakest moments, when he entertained thoughts of being with Joyce again, the fear was completely gone.

Odd that death would be welcome, he thought.

A soft knocking on the door garnered his attention. He winced when lowering his foot, wondering if it would ever heal, and braced himself against the discomfort he knew he must endure.

"I'm going to take a vacation deep in the woods where no one can find me," he muttered.

Struggling to his feet, he silently cursed as he limped to the door. When he gazed through the peephole, he saw two women he recognized.

This ought to be good.

Taking a deep breath, he swung the door open.

"Joe, we'd, uh, like to talk to you," one of the women said. She looked down at his foot. "Oh, my goodness. Is this a bad time?"

"No, Ruth, please come in."

Ruth Sterling was a quiet, pudgy widow with thin, graying hair eternally wrapped in a bun. Her politeness was the hallmark of her character.

"You're limping, Joe. Is your foot still bothering you?"

"I bumped it earlier." He directed Ruth and her friend, Betty Hough, to the sofa and eased into the dark blue chair nearby. "Now, ladies, what can I do for you?"

Ruth and Betty looked at each other before turning to him. Ruth spoke first.

"We heard about Rusty Goodfellow on the news today."

"Very sad," Betty said. "Very sad."

"Ladies, I don't mean to sound terse, but is there a problem I can help you with?"

Betty set her serious, dark brown eyes on him. "Joe, I...what I mean to say is that we've seen Rusty with other women."

"Younger women," Ruth added. "And on more than one occasion."

"To be honest, Joe," Betty continued, "we didn't see him *with* these women in the sense that he was...what I mean is, he was just talking to them."

"I'm not sure where you're going with this, "Joe said.

"We saw Rusty at the Circle Food Mart on Thursday night. We were coming in as he was leaving."

They must be some of the people that Carly and David saw on the video, Joe thought, and leaned forward. "Was he with anyone at the time?"

"Not right then," Ruth said, "but when we came out, he was talking to a woman."

"A *young* woman," Betty said.

"How young?" Joe asked.

The pair looked at each other again.

"I'd say she was in her late thirties or early forties," Betty said, "but no older."

"What did she look like?"

"They were standing in the corner of the parking lot," Ruth said. "We weren't that close to them, but I'd say she was a couple of inches taller than me, maybe. I'm five-foot-five."

"And she had dark brown hair," Betty said.

"I think it was more auburn than brown."

"No, Ruth, I'm certain it was brown."

"Betty, I think I know the difference between brown and auburn."

"Then you should get your eyes checked, Ruth, because her hair was brown."

"Ladies," Joe interrupted, "is there anything else you can tell me?"

A look of regret shaped Betty's mousy features. "They left before we got to my car."

"Did they leave together?"

"I don't believe so," Ruth said.

"No, they didn't," Betty said.

"What kind of car was the woman driving?"

Ruth and Betty looked at one another a third time.

"A little white car," Ruth said.

"Yes, definitely white," Betty agreed.

"Do you know the make or model of it?"

"I don't know cars, Joe."

Joe looked at Betty.

"I have a Nissan Sentra. That's the only car I know."

"Would you recognize this woman if you saw her again?"

"I think so."

Ruth agreed.

Joe started to reach for his phone. "You need to talk to the police right now."

"Oh, please, no!" Ruth begged.

"We don't want to get involved!" Betty said, her brown eyes growing wide.

"But you're already involved. What you witnessed is important. The police need to know."

"Can't you tell them for us, Joe? They'll believe you," Ruth pleaded.

"It's not the same as eyewitness testimony, Ruth. You were there. *You* saw Rusty and this woman."

Ruth and Betty said no more.

Joe sat back and took a moment to study them. A hint of terror inhabited their eyes.

"Is there a particular reason why you don't want to talk to the police?" he asked.

The women remained silent and hung their heads.

"Okay, Ruth, what is it you're not telling me?"

Ruth looked up, her face drawn into an uneasy expression.

"Neither of you is leaving here until I get some answers."

"We wouldn't want this to become fodder for the gossip mill, Joe," Ruth began slowly, "but Betty and I were, uh...we were canoodling with Rusty."

"Canoodling?"

"You know, having an affair."

"Both of you?"

They nodded.

"Please don't tell anyone," Betty said. "We don't want to hurt Nancy."

"How long has this *canoodling* been going on?"

"A couple of months. He kept on joking about it and I was...we were...don't you ever get lonely, Joe?"

The face of Gary Burgess flashed into Joe's mind. The former maintenance man murdered by Mac McDougal had admitted to servicing some of the female residents in the condo.

Does this kind of thing go on all the time around here? he wondered.

Pausing to consider all he knew and what he had heard, Joe leaned forward and picked up his phone from the coffee table.

Chapter 10

The next morning, Saturday, Joe sat quietly at the dining table after a breakfast of toast and coffee. No appointments or meetings were scheduled on his calendar, the necessary chores around his home had been completed, and his foot no longer ached, a miracle in itself. He sat back and considered a number of things he could do.

I wonder if Victoria and Cecily have anything planned today, he thought. *Maybe they'd like to go to the Dali Museum.*

He held off moving forward with the idea when he heard the steady pattering of rain against the windows.

The storm had awakened him well before sunrise, a momentary interruption before he drifted off back to sleep. When he got up later for his morning ritual in the bathroom, he'd again heard the drizzling rain. He figured a front had stalled over the Tampa Bay area and the shower might last all day. Unfortunate in one sense, not so in another. While the precipitation put a damper on some outdoor activities, its persistence lowered the temperature and the humidity. For the time of year, cooler days were always a welcome change.

The memory of his sitting in on Carly's interview of Ruth and Betty ended Joe's short episode of daydreaming. Reluctant at first, his neighbors had recounted their story to the detective, unable to hide the shame glowing red on their faces. Carly promised to do her best to keep word of their "canoodling" under wraps. She and Joe knew the truth would surface sooner or later.

Joe looked down at his empty plate as another uninvited memory came to light. The ages of the murder victims played an important part in determining the identification of the killer. However, the sighting of a younger woman in the vicinity of the crime scenes again triggered his curiosity. He stuck by his belief that two women were working in tandem. The younger of the two, now appearing to be the bait, left herself open to being seen—a bold move for a murderer. Even an accomplice.

Late thirties to early forties with dark brown or auburn hair, he thought. *And around five-feet-seven inches tall—maybe.* He listened to the rain a moment. *I'll call Victoria later.*

He got up from his chair and picked up his plate, deciding that a slow and easy gait to the kitchen sink was the wisest way to go. He wasn't about to give in to overconfidence and risk hurting his foot again. Pain was the reward for stupidity.

Deciding he needed to take a look at where Rusty Goodfellow had been murdered, he was in no hurry to get to the bedroom to dress for the drive. His choice of a forest green polo shirt, khaki trousers, and favorite black running shoes defined a modest uniform comfortable enough for a miserable day. A dark blue rain jacket would aid him in weathering the storm.

The trek from his condo to the main entrance of the building was uneventful. As always, the maroon carpet and pink carnation walls in the hallway disgusted him. And, as always, the residents he encountered offered polite greetings and wishes for a speedy recovery.

He did his best to avoid the numerous puddles collected in the parking lot. Having forgotten his umbrella, limping through the downpour was punishment enough for absentmindedness.

Behind the wheel of his car, he took a moment to glance in the rearview mirror. He heard Joyce laugh when he discovered his thick gray hair plastered down.

"I know, I know," he muttered. "I look like a drowned rat."

He started the car, turned on the headlights, and carefully backed out of his parking space.

The traffic on Island Way was light as he left the parking lot. Not so on Memorial Causeway. An ever-increasing caravan of cars and trucks was moving in both directions as he attempted to merge onto the causeway and instead came to a halt in the right turn lane. Patience made the time he was forced to wait insignificant before he eased his way into the flow. Relief from the morning stampede came as soon as he exited the roundabout onto Mandalay Avenue. He took a deep breath and tried to relax. His next point of interest was Juniper Way.

The homes and condominiums on either side of the street became a blur as thoughts of the involvement of a younger woman in Rusty's murder intensified. With the right amount of flirting and suggestive offerings, she could have easily enticed an older man into a trap.

"Even me," he mumbled.

Though a clear-cut description of the woman was unavailable, what little that *was* known about her was starting to irritate him.

"Why do I feel like the answer is right in front of me?"

A couple of things jumped out at him as he motored onto Juniper Way. The two-lane road was narrow, and "No Parking" signs stood in plain sight along the right shoulder.

"Why didn't someone report Rusty's car?" he wondered aloud, then recanted, "Maybe they did."

A familiar gray Dodge sedan came into view as he neared the intersection of El Dorado Avenue. Joe parked his car and got out. The downpour at the beginning of his ride had become a drizzle, the variation typical in a sub-tropical climate. He cursed the fact that he'd forgotten his umbrella.

The beginning of the beach access was an extension of the sidewalk off of El Dorado Avenue, less than a half-block long and quick to vanish into the sand.

Hours of rain had compacted the sand, providing a smooth surface investigators would have gladly welcomed when working this crime scene—impressions were easily identifiable in saturated sand. Unfortunately, an ongoing shower would obliterate them.

Looking toward the Gulf of Mexico, Joe spied a lone figure standing where the access flowed into the beach. As he drew nearer, the man turned around.

"Never figured you for one who liked to walk in the rain," David said.

"I got bored sitting at home. What brings you out here?"

"I don't know." David stared at the cordoned-off area of sopping scrub brush and sodden sand dunes. "How does a guy wandering through the darkness with someone he just met allow himself to be bashed in the head?"

"Do I really need to tell you if that someone is a woman? Especially an attractive woman?"

"I guess not. A quickie in the dunes would be first and foremost on his mind."

Joe felt several beads of rain run down the back of his neck, and pulled up the collar of his rain jacket.

"Have any luck finding witnesses in the neighborhood?"

"No one saw or heard anything. I even talked to some residents I met walking their dogs this morning. They were oblivious until they heard about it on the news."

"Did Carly tell you that I thought there might be two women involved in the Steven Echavarría killing?"

"She did. And it makes sense to me."

"Even though the kill methods are similar in both cases, only one woman was seen talking to Rusty Goodfellow at the Circle Food Mart. That puts a wrinkle in my theory."

"Not if the other woman was already here. It's not that difficult to hide in the dunes when it's dark."

"Carly and I discussed the possibility that the woman seen with Steven Echavarría might have been wearing a wig."

"Right, she told me. So what are you saying? Now you think there's only *one* woman?"

"My money's still on two. If there *is* only one, then she's a very smart woman. Every move she makes is calculated and decisive. I believe she has knowledge of the area, too. She might even be homegrown."

David stood silent, thinking.

"By the way, where *is* Carly?" Joe asked.

"She took the day off. She, uh, said she needed to take care of some personal business. I don't think things are going well at home."

Joe nodded, knowing the truth.

"Well, Joe, there's nothing here to help us. I guess I was hoping we might catch a break." David stared at the cordoned-off area again. "I don't know about you, but I'm tired of getting wet."

"Agreed. Let's go."

The pair trudged through the wet sand to the sidewalk. As they reached El Dorado Avenue, a short, stout man wearing a yellow raincoat and a dark blue Boston Red Sox baseball cap approached them.

"Hey! You two blind or somethin'? Can't ya see the no parkin' signs?"

David brought out his badge. "I'm Detective Sizemore, and this is Joseph Hampton, a police consultant."

"Oh! Sorry. Since the other night people have been flockin' here ta see where the guy was killed. Damned nosey busybodies. They need ta get a life."

"And who are you, sir?" David asked.

"Harvey Dortmunder. I live right there." He pointed to a quaint little white house.

"I don't remember interviewing you."

"Ya didn't. I talked to the lady cop. Her name was Truffle or something like that."

"You mean Detective Truffant?"

"Yeah, that's it. Couldn't help her, though. Me and Melinda, she's my wife, we didn't hear nothin'. Not unusual, though. It's usually pretty quiet out here."

"I don't suppose you noticed any illegally parked cars," Joe said.

"Nah. Melinda said she passed a little white car when she was comin' home from shoppin'. That's about it."

"A little white car?"

"Yeah, some foreign job, she thought." Dortmunder looked at David. "She told the lady cop."

"Is your wife home now?" David asked.

"Nah, she went ta breakfast with her girlfriends."

"Do you know where they went?"

"Nah. It's always some place different."

David pulled out his wallet, removed a business card, and handed it to the man. "Ask her to give me a call when she gets home."

"Sure thing. Well, I'll be seein' you guys."

Joe waited until he and David were alone. "That's the second time someone has mentioned seeing a little white car."

"Really? Well, it's news to me. Did Carly tell you?"

"No, two women who live in my condo saw Rusty Goodfellow at the Circle Food Mart the night he was killed. Carly interviewed them at my place last night."

David looked puzzled. "I left work early yesterday. Carly called me sometime later and said she was leaving to do an interview. I didn't hear anymore after that."

Joe hesitated as the rain pelted his jacket. "David, I didn't tell you this, but you were right about her. Things aren't going well at home."

Chapter 11

Sitting in his car, Joe was watching the rain cascade down the windshield. David and Harvey Dortmunder were gone, and the "old itch" that drove him to view the crime scene had been satisfied. He felt no need to hurry home. Nothing but washing his breakfast dishes and silverware needed to be addressed. Victoria was entertaining her daughter. He was free to do as he pleased—fortunate to his way of thinking. Sort of. Another irritant was plaguing him now—the little white car.

"Like trying to find the ripest watermelon in a watermelon patch," he whispered.

Light-colored cars were plentiful in Florida—especially silver and white cars. Dark colors drew the heat during the summer months, putting a strain on the air conditioning to keep the interior cool. That was the belief, anyway. A belief to which he certainly subscribed soon after he arrived in his adopted state. And what shade of white was the car? A cool white offered on the inexpensive base models, or a stark white common among the fleets belonging to rental companies and corporations? Was there really a difference? The advertising gurus who thought up the names believed so.

A woman in a little white car, he thought. *What better way to hide in plain sight.*

Joe brought the engine to life, turned on the windshield wipers and headlights, and pulled away slowly. The dwellings on either side of El Dorado Avenue were of no interest to him. His focus lay solely on finding a murderer.

Even without the assistance of a meteorologist, Joe felt his personal forecast of an all-day rain to be accurate. The drizzle accompanied him back to his condominium, giving no indication of ending any time soon. When he found the parking space reserved for him, he shut down his car and struggled to see through the rain sheeting the windshield. Working up the gumption to get out and figure out a way around the larger puddles in the parking lot, his attention locked on a small white car making its way to the main entrance. The driver quickly exited and scurried around the back to the passenger side. Although wearing slacks and sneakers and a parka with the hood pulled up, the driver's body language told Joe he was looking at a woman. The lavender parka was another clue.

The driver pulled several plastic shopping bags full of groceries out of the back seat and disappeared through the automatic doors.

I need to get a look at that license plate, he thought.

As he grabbed the door handle, he saw the driver reappear, get back into the car, and drive away.

Damn!

Joe left his car and limped as fast as he could to the entrance. Once inside, he noticed the bags sitting on the floor.

That's odd. Why would she leave them here? Must be a friend or relative parking the car. Or maybe a resident.

He hobbled to the building manager's office, pausing to insert his key into the lock. He glanced toward the entrance to see if anyone was approaching.

Standing under the concrete roof over the walkway, the driver of the white car slid back the hood of her parka.

Joe couldn't make out who it was and shifted his eyes back to the door, pretending to fidget with the key. When he heard the automatic doors slide open, he casually turned his head.

"Cecily, what are you doing out on a day like this?"

"Joseph! I didn't see you standing there." She picked up the shopping bags and walked over to him. "I went to the grocery store for Mother." She grinned, a mirror image of Victoria. "I see that you're all wet, too."

"I realized I had forgotten to run an errand yesterday. My memory isn't what it used to be."

"I wish I had known. I could have driven you."

In your little white car? He eyed the shopping bags. "Let me give you a hand with your groceries."

"Absolutely not!" Cecily protested and stepped back. "You can barely walk!"

"My foot doesn't hurt today."

"Good. No need to aggravate it then."

"Planning something special for supper tonight?"

"Uh, well, yes. It's, uh, something special for a special occasion...for someone special I'm told." A look of mild disgust settled on Cecily's face. "Oh, I was never good at hiding things. Mother is planning to invite you to join us. She wanted it to be a surprise."

"How nice."

"I guess she hasn't called you yet."

"She may have. I don't have my cell phone."

Cecily chuckled. "You'd better go check."

"And prepare for the hard time she's going to give me," Joe added.

An ensuing silence quieted them.

"Joseph, I guess you know my mother is quite fond of you."

"She's an interesting woman."

"And I get the feeling that you're attracted to her as well."

"It's true, Cecily, I won't lie to you."

"I love my mother very much, Joseph, and I wouldn't want to see her, uh...I'm not saying you would intentionally do anything to, uh...now I don't mean to offend you, but I..."

"Cecily, I appreciate your concern, and your reasons are certainly justified. In the short amount of time I've known your mother I've learned that she's not shy about speaking her mind. I appreciate her candor. We've been open and honest with each other from the beginning, but we're taking our time." He noticed her relaxing.

"Thank you, Joseph, and thank you for understanding."

"You're a good daughter, Cecily."

"Well, I'd better get going." She rolled her eyes. "You know my mother."

Joe watched her all the way to the elevator and offered a brief wave as she entered the car.

"Yes, Cecily, I know your mother. But I don't know you."

He waited a couple of minutes then went outside. Though he hated to slosh around in the rain again, he needed to confirm a detail he found most troubling. And that meant locating the car Cecily had been driving and running a check on the license plate.

Chapter 12

The cold air filling the hallway and circulating throughout his condo gave Joe chills. Though he needed to dry off, he decided to wait until after he had made an important phone call. Inadvertently, he may have discovered the identity of the woman driving the white car. Thinking Cecily might be a killer left him with a hollow feeling as he picked up his cell phone from the coffee table where he'd left it.

"What can I do for you, Joe?" David asked.

"Something has come my way that may be of interest to you. Are you in the office?"

"I'm in my car. Give me a minute to pull over."

Joe shivered as a frosty wave danced without pity down his spine. He took off his rain jacket, dropped it on the floor, and sat down on the sofa.

"Okay, Joe, what's up?"

"Write this down." Joe passed along the tag number."

"Got it. You want me to run this plate, right? Is it a Florida tag?"

"Yes, it belongs to a Chevy Sonic—a *white* Chevy Sonic."

"Are you telling me that you think this car is the one driven by our mystery woman?"

"I'm not telling you anything of the sort. Run the tag and see what you find. I believe it's a rental."

"Oh, I see."

"Is there a problem?"

"Not really. Even if there is, I think I can get around it. Any chance you might have a name connected to the car?"

"No positive identification, but it might be Cecily Dearmin."

"I don't suppose you know her home address."

"Only that she lives in Shrewsbury, Massachusetts."

"Why the sudden interest in this woman, Joe?"

"She's visiting a relative who lives here. Some inconsistencies and interesting coincidences have arisen."

"Care to share any of them?"

"I was led to believe that she was arriving next Tuesday. She told me that she got here three days ago. I know that doesn't sound like much."

"She's staying at your condo?"

"With her mother."

"By any chance is her mother Victoria Combes?"

"Yes, and I hope I'm wrong about her."

"Is it really worth going to all this trouble just because she arrived earlier than you expected? Maybe she decided to take a few extra days. Maybe you were misinformed."

"Steven Echavarría was murdered Tuesday night. A dark-haired woman in a white car was seen in the motel parking lot earlier the same day."

"Joe, you just said that she told you she came here on Wednesday."

"And maybe she was lying."

"Hmm."

"Rusty Goodfellow was murdered Thursday night. The same night witnesses saw him talking to a dark-haired woman who drove a small white car."

"You don't like coincidences, do you, Joe?"

"There's no such thing."

"I don't like them, either. I'll see what I can do. I have an acquaintance who works for—"

"Names aren't necessary, David. I trust your judgment."

“So, Joe, what else can you tell me about this Cecily Dearmin?”

“She’s a pathologist.”

“Which means she’s efficient with surgical equipment.”

“Right.”

“And I suppose she has dark hair?”

“Auburn hair.”

Joe ended the call and took a moment to wipe his brow with the back of his hand. Questions surrounding Cecily Dearmin ran one after another through his mind. A belief that she couldn’t be involved in such heinous undertakings battled hard to dissuade him from condemning her. Yet, the sighting and description of a woman at or near both crime scenes was too significant to ignore.

“And her job requires the use of a scalpel,” he mumbled.

A single bead of moisture left the hair on the back of his head and trailed down his neck. He shivered. Having noticed that he’d missed three calls, all from the same number, he punched the button that would dial and connect him with the caller. He sat back and prepared for the onslaught.

“Well, it’s about time you called,” Victoria grumbled.

“Miss me, did you?”

“Like a pimple on my tookus. You know, some of us don’t have the time or the inclination to sit around waiting all day.”

Joe chuckled. “You do miss me.”

“I was going to invite you to join Cecily and me for supper tonight, but now I’m not so sure. I’m not very fond of such inconsiderate behavior.”

“Depends on what you’re having.”

“Depends on what I’m having?” Victoria bellowed.

Joe could hear Cecily laughing in the background.

“Cecily and I are having pot roast! For you, I think I’ll scrape off what the sea gulls left on the balcony and fry it up!”

Joe burst into laughter. “Pot roast sounds terrific. I’d be honored to break bread with you two.” He paused. “What kind of vegetable are you having?”

"You are *really* pushing your luck, mister!"

Joe laughed again. "What time does this feast begin?"

"I'm thinking five-thirty, unless that's too early for your majesty. We can have a cocktail and eat around six."

"I'll see you then."

"Don't be late."

"What did you say?"

"I said don't be late."

"Victoria?"

"You'd better be on time, Joseph!"

"Victoria, are you there?"

Joe heard her growl and was still laughing when he set his phone on the coffee table.

I should get out of these damp clothes and take a hot shower. He hesitated as a vision of his wife appeared. *You don't mind, do you, Joyce?*

Mind what, Joe?

Me being with Victoria.

She seems like a nice lady.

She makes me laugh the way you used to.

But she isn't me.

I know.

Take your time with her.

I will.

A hot shower made Joe feel like a new man—a new man with a sore foot. Cecily had warned him about aggravating it. He now wished he hadn't tried to hurry through the parking lot.

He was thinking about lunch when his phone's familiar tune drifted into the bedroom. Not bothering to put on socks, he ignored his injury and ambled to the living room, snatched the phone off the coffee table, and dropped down onto the sofa. There was no name showing on the caller I.D.

"Joe, we've got a problem."

"David! That was quick. Do I want to know what the problem is?"

"The car belongs to Rent-Way Car Rentals in Tampa. It was leased to a Lawrence Lombard of Fall River, Massachusetts, at Tampa International Airport."

"Lawrence Lombard? Are you sure?"

"As sure as I'm talking to you."

"No chance there might be a mistake?"

"That's only the half of it. Lawrence Lombard was found dead Tuesday morning in rural Pasco County near Wesley Chapel."

"When did he pick up the car?"

"Monday afternoon."

Joe went silent and attempted to work out a timeline for the three murders—and the supposed arrival of Cecily Dearmin.

"Joe?"

"I'm here. I'm just trying to piece things together."

"It gets better. The rental agent at Rent-Way reported seeing a woman with Lombard. She couldn't give me a good description because—"

"I know, the woman was standing too far away."

"And the terminal was crowded."

"Did her description match the other reports?"

"Dark hair, maybe five-five or taller. Pasco County Sheriff's Office has been looking for the woman and the car."

"I'd be interested to hear what Cecily has to say."

"That's our problem. My problem, really. If I tip Pasco S.O. as to the whereabouts of the car, they'll want to know how I found out about Lombard leasing it. My friend, uh, a certain person who was very helpful, might get into a lot of trouble. I don't want to see her lose her job."

"How could your friend get into trouble for assisting the police?"

"I don't know about company policy. I'd feel bad if she—"

"David, they put out an alert for the car and the woman, right?"

"I haven't confirmed it, but I'm sure they did."

"Then if you're asked, tell them you noticed the car and decided to check it out."

"But I haven't seen the car."

"By the way, have you heard from Carly recently?"

"What?"

"I'm concerned about her."

"Joe, I told you that she's at home. She's taking care of some personal—"

"Why don't you stop by and see me. As soon as you can."

"But, Joe, there's nothing we can do to...oh! Right! I'm concerned about her, too. I'll go over right away."

Joe set his phone on the coffee table and took a deep breath.

Supper should be very interesting, he thought.

Chapter 13

Waiting for David to arrive, Joe rested his bare foot on the coffee table. The discoloration painting his injured toes was barely noticeable. Soreness, however, was another story.

I should rest it more, he thought. He closed his eyes.

The sound of the drizzling rain filled his ears with a soothing rhythm, pleasant, not distracting.

A video of Cecily played vividly in his mind. She was chatting with a man he didn't know, Lawrence Lombard he supposed. They met on the plane. Maybe sat next to each other. Friendly conversation carried them to their destination along with some harmless flirting or consent to a brief affair before going their separate ways.

But Lombard's name is on the car.

Had he agreed to pay for the rental in exchange for sex?

Stupid on his part if he did. Cecily doesn't strike me as a flirtatious woman, though. But I've been wrong before. Joe released a long, slow sigh. *So she takes the car to her mother's condo in Clearwater Beach, and for whatever reason he winds up dead in Wesley Chapel. Is that the way it happened? Is Cecily completely ignorant of and blameless in Lombard's death? Or did she kill him? No, Cecily's not that dumb. If she killed him she would have dumped the car and rented another.*

The Echavarría killing was an entirely different matter.

The time between landing in Tampa, doing away with

Lombard, and driving to Clearwater Beach was a possibility, but when did she meet Echavarría? And how could she lure him to a motel in an unfamiliar city so quickly? Had she visited the area before? Or was she that competent a seductress?

It has to be someone else.

A more plausible scenario was her possible involvement in the Rusty Goodfellow murder. Victoria may have complained to her about Rusty's rude and obnoxious behavior. A chance meeting at the Circle Food Mart presented her with an opportunity. With Rusty's penchant for ogling younger women, she could easily have baited him into a rendezvous—assuming, of course, that she knew who he was.

Joe sighed again. The argument for Cecily being a serial killer was as strong as it was weak. Too many counterpoints supported her innocence. Why would she keep the car? How did she meet Echavarría? And why risk killing Rusty Goodfellow in a community unknown to her—unless she was the quintessential psychopath.

The video of Cecily and the rhythm of the rain vanished with a knocking on the door.

I'm starting to hate that sound, as well as my cell phone.

He lifted himself from the sofa, considered moving to another condo, and fully expected his visitor to be David.

"Carly!"

"I should have called first, Joe. Can I come in?"

"Certainly."

With her head bowed, Carly stepped into his living room, her demeanor tentative, and her hair damp and disheveled. She, in no way, appeared the strong, confident woman he remembered from the first time he'd met her. Defeated best described the person standing before him.

Joe gestured to the sofa. "Have a seat. Would you like something to drink?"

"No, thanks. If you want something, I'll get it for you." She looked down at his bare foot. "Are you still hurting?"

"I need to get more rest."

Together, they took seats on the sofa.

"I've just come from seeing Deanna Kenny. We can forget about her as a suspect. She's been out of town for the last two weeks at some wood carver's convention and visiting friends. She has the airline tickets to prove it."

"Guess I had her all wrong. She didn't give you a hard time, did she?"

"On the contrary, she was most accommodating. She had no idea what had happened."

"So what are you going to do now?"

Carly stared straight ahead.

"Carly?"

"I need someone to talk to. Do you mind?"

"Not at all."

"I've been doing a lot of thinking. Probably too much thinking. I'm going ahead with the divorce. I'm all out of options. And I have to tell you that the idea is pretty scary." She offered a tight smile. "About as scary as getting married."

"I can understand," Joe said.

"What I'm really worried about is..."

As distressed as she seemed, Joe resisted the urge to hold her.

"I'm worried about living alone," she finished.

"How long have you and Tim been married?"

"Almost nine years. Seems a lot longer...a *lot* longer. I was still living with my parents when we started dating. We lived together for two years before we decided to do it. There's always been someone else in the house, you know? But now...I'm not sure I can handle it."

Joe saw the advancing fear in her eyes. "What about your parents? Could they help you?"

"My parents died in an auto accident five years ago."

"Oh, I'm sorry. What about your friends? Don't you know someone who might want to rent a room?"

"All my close friends are married. And I don't want a stranger in my house...if I stay in the house...especially when I'm not there."

"Carly, I'm not one to give advice when I'm not asked. Never having been in your situation, I'm reluctant to do so. But as your friend, I think you need take this a step at a time." He paused, feeling like the father he never was, talking to the daughter he never had. "Start the divorce proceedings. It's what you want. Then get some professional counseling. There's no shame in asking for help. I'm sure your superiors will support you. As far as your living arrangements, I honestly don't know what to tell you. I believe a counselor will provide you with a much better perspective."

Carly nodded and lowered her head. The sound of the rain serenaded them for a moment. Joe sensed she was thinking over his suggestions and hoped she would agree. She finally raised her head.

"Joe, I believe you're right. But I was wondering if I could...could I stay with you for a while? Just for a few days. I promise not to be a pest."

The only thing Joe found more startling than her request was another round of knocking on his door.

"I'll get it," Carly said, and hopped up before he could move.

When she swung the door open, both she and the person standing in the hall were surprised.

"Carly!"

"David!"

"What are you doing here?" they said together.

They looked at Joe.

"Hey, I'm just the intermediary. I think you'd both better sit down."

An explanation—short and to the point—was delivered to the detectives with specific details omitted. Joe reasoned the pair could fill in the blanks themselves.

"David, why didn't you call me?" Carly demanded.

"Because you needed the time off to, uh, you know."

"Everyone knows. You should have called. This could be the break we've been looking for."

"I understand, and it's being handled the best way possible." David glanced at Joe. "And legally."

"Now what does that mean?"

"It means that I can swear under oath that I acted accordingly and followed procedure."

Carly studied him. "Joe, did you have anything to do with this?"

"We discussed the situation. Like you and I have done in the past."

"And when you got here, David, you saw a white car, remembered that Pasco County S.O. had put out an alert, and followed up on it."

"Right. The car is the one they're looking for, so I notified them. The lead detective is on his way over."

"So why did you *happen* to come up here? You talked to Joe earlier at the crime scene."

"I saw your car in the parking lot. I thought maybe something was wrong. I came to see if you or Joe needed help."

Carly eyed one man and then the other. "You know, whenever my husband was hiding something from me I used to get this weird feeling. I have that same feeling now."

The soothing sound of falling rain was all she heard for several seconds.

"David, don't you think you should be keeping an eye on the car?"

David's eyes widened. "You're absolutely right! I'd better get down there!"

Before he could get to his feet, someone knocked on the door.

"That can't be the detective," Carly said. "Not coming all the way from Pasco County."

"He's supposed to call me," David said. "I'm supposed to meet him in the parking lot."

"I'd better throw together some hors d'oeuvres if we're going to have a party," Joe said, and got up from the sofa, gingerly testing his foot on the way to meet his latest visitor.

Glancing through the peephole, he stepped back when he recognized the person. He turned to Carly and David and arched his eyebrows before opening the door.

"Joseph, I was wondering if I might—oh! I didn't know you had company."

"It's okay, Victoria, won't you come in?"

Chapter 14

Victoria was unable to disguise the look of surprise on her face. She tentatively walked into Joe's condo, glancing at the detectives before speaking to him.

"I wanted to talk to you about tonight," she said.

"Excuse us, ma'am, but we have to run," David said. "I'll call you later, Joe."

"Never a dull moment," Carly said, and smiled at Victoria.

"Please don't leave on my account. I invited Joseph to supper. We can talk when it's convenient."

"We just got a call," David said.

Victoria stepped aside and the detectives disappeared into the hallway.

"Now what is so important that you came all the way up here and chased off my friends?" Joe asked. He tried not to grin.

"Joseph, I am *so* embarrassed. I didn't mean to interrupt you. I hope it wasn't police business." Her blue eyes brimmed with sincerity. "I haven't seen you in a couple of days—alone, I mean. And I..." She reached forward, pulled him into an embrace, and kissed him.

Not expecting the passionate overture, Joe wavered between astonishment and appreciation. His body was starting to warm when she eased him back.

"But if you'd answered your damn phone then I wouldn't have made a fool of myself."

She must have called while I was in the shower, he thought. "I do have a bad habit of—"

His explanation was cut short as Victoria pulled him close and kissed him again—hard. The warming trend intensified.

"Now I want you to be on your best behavior tonight," she whispered, "and in a few days when Cecily goes home, I'll show you how appreciative I am."

Joe felt his living room getting warmer. "Victoria, you don't have to—"

She kissed him again. "Don't talk, Joseph. Imagine."

Caressing his cheek, she eased him away, and left him stranded in fantasy.

Joe took a deep breath and released a long, slow sigh. *I haven't felt this good since Foster and I solved that double homicide in '99. I should call ole Bill and see how he's doing.*

He walked to his sofa, sat down, and propped up both feet on the coffee table. Wiggling his injured toes, he noticed they were no longer sore. *Magic*, he thought. *Amazing what a little TLC can do*. He laid back and closed his eyes, feeling Victoria's tender hand on his face. A lingering trace of her perfume filled his nostrils. *I may have to open the windows and let some cool air in.*

He chuckled when he realized the windows were already open. The moment of ecstasy was shattered by his cell phone.

"I knew it was too good to last," he mumbled.

"Joe, it's Carly. Is Victoria still there?"

"She left a couple of minutes ago. Why?"

"The white car is gone. David told me that you saw Cecily driving it."

"Maybe she forgot something and went back to the grocery store."

"Would you call Victoria and find out?"

A frosty shard of anxiety ripped Joe's insides. "I'll need a minute to come up with a good excuse. I don't want her to think I'm—"

"Right! I got it! I'm sorry to drop this on you, but if I call her then she'll *know* that we're looking for her daughter."

"She may come to the same conclusion if I ask her."

"David showed me the Pasco County S.O. alert. He swears they're looking for the same car."

"You'd better put out an alert, too, in case she's taken off. Don't waste any more time."

Joe laid his phone down on the sofa cushion. Whether or to what extent Cecily was involved was the prime concern at the moment. Apologies could be dealt with later. His empathy for her was fading. He hoped that a computer glitch or human error had drawn her into this tangled web. At the same time, he knew the worst was a possibility.

Glad it isn't me that's after her. He picked up his phone.

Pushing all emotions aside, Joe punched in Victoria's number and waited.

"What's the matter, Joseph," Victoria cooed, "all steamed up with nowhere to blow?"

Joe let loose his best chuckle. "Actually, I wanted to speak with Cecily. Is she available?"

"I don't know where she is. She was gone when I got back. Why do you want to talk to her?"

"As crazy as this might sound—"

"I would expect no less from you."

"You never let up, do you?"

"I gave you fair warning."

"After you left, I started thinking about an old case. Don't ask me why. It just popped into my head. Anyway, being that Cecily is a pathologist I thought she might be open to letting me pick her brain."

"This couldn't wait until tonight?"

"Victoria, I just thought if she was—"

"What do you really want?"

Joe felt a spike of apprehension. "To talk to her, that's all."

"Why, Joseph Hampton, you should be ashamed of yourself!

I get you all worked up, and now you want a ménage-a-tròis! With my daughter? Why, you unscrupulous degenerate!"

"What! No! How could you even think that I..." He stopped in the middle of his fumbling when he heard her laughing. He exhaled sharply. "Victoria Combes, you are incorrigible."

She continued to laugh. "I'm sorry, Joseph."

"No you're not."

"You're right, I'm not." She laughed louder and harder. "I'll have Cecily call you when she gets back."

Joe wasn't laughing when he called Carly. He still wanted to believe his friend's daughter was innocent, but found no humor in the possibility that she might be a psychopath.

"Victoria doesn't know where Cecily went, Carly."

"We put out an alert. We'll find her."

"I hope this is nothing more than a paperwork snafu."

"I don't know what that means, but I've got a feeling that she's the one we want."

"Yeah, me, too."

"Oh, Jesus!"

"What is it, Carly?"

"The Pasco sheriff's detective just pulled up. Now we'll look like a couple of idiots without the car being here."

"I'd better let you go."

Joe dropped his phone onto the sofa and leaned back. More and more he sensed that the personable woman who was the mirror image of her mother was the perpetrator of several heinous crimes. Driving a car rented by one of the victims put her in an extremely bad light. And vague as they were, the descriptions given by witnesses at two of the crime scenes placed her squarely in the person-of-interest category. Yet, with all that going against her, part of him didn't want to believe it.

"I hope it's not you, Cecily," he whispered, "but I've been wrong before."

Chapter 15

Endless bands of showers rolled in from the Gulf of Mexico throughout the afternoon. Gray skies appeared as an omen to more gloomy and dismal expectations. The troublesome thoughts whirling about in Joe's mind warned of an equally dark arrival.

Preparing for his evening with Victoria and Cecily, he stood uncomfortably in front of a floor-length rectangular mirror, his chosen wardrobe a royal blue polo shirt and navy-blue Dockers. He was geared up for the criticism he knew was coming, joking or not, and armed with a pocketful of witty comebacks. He'd had plenty of time to work on his ruse.

Not having heard from Victoria, he wondered if she was still unaware of her daughter's plight. Surely Cecily had been located by the Clearwater Police if she'd simply gone to the grocery store. If she was running—he thought of giving Carly a call to find out for sure.

"She's not running, she's hiding," Joe whispered. "But who tipped her off? She doesn't know that I saw her in the white car." *Or does she*? he thought. "I guess I'll find out soon enough."

He glanced in the mirror once last time, made certain his keys and cell phone were in his pants pocket, and slowly walked to the door.

This may turn out to be the most unusual invitation to supper I've ever received.

A quick look around the room preceded his leaving.

He quietly strode down the hallway, noting a profound silence that normally was reserved only for the late evening hours.

Where is everyone? They must be staying indoors because of the weather.

After a brief pause, he was on his way to the third floor, alone in the elevator, alone with his thoughts.

How could Cecily kill two men hours apart, miles apart, and hide out somewhere for a day before coming to see her mother?

The elevator door opened and he stepped into the hall, finishing his thought. *The fact is, she couldn't. Not without prior arrangements and the perfect setup. No one is that good or that lucky.* As he stood in front of the door to Victoria's condo and rapped lightly, he remembered something he'd mentioned to Carly: An accomplice aided in the escape of Steven Echavarría's killer. He believed it then, and he believed it now.

Victoria opened the door, dashing his thoughts. Her silver hair glistened, complementing the sparkle in her eyes. She wore a short-sleeve plum blouse, opened slightly and alluringly revealing, atop cream-colored slacks that clung to her body. The scent of her perfume reminded him of the elevator ambush and left him fumbling for a friendly greeting.

"Well, don't just stand there like an idiot," she said, "come in."

Joe entered the living room, still enamored by her presence and unable to find the right words.

"I must say you look awfully handsome tonight, Joseph. Quite frankly I'm surprised."

"I have my days," he finally said.

"Would you like a cocktail, or should we get right to the sex?"

Joe's mouth dropped open.

Victoria burst into laughter. "I'm sorry, Joseph. I am in such a good mood."

"Really? I hadn't noticed."

She laughed again then looked him over. "You don't have

your cane."

"I don't need it anymore."

"Good for you." She motioned to a living room chair. "Have a seat. You like Evan Williams on the rocks, right?"

"If you have it on hand." He watched her walk to a table full of liquor bottles and glasses against the far wall.

"Do you think this rain will ever stop?"

"Hard to say. Looks like the front has stalled on top of us. It might be a day or so before it decides to move on."

Victoria turned around with his drink in her hand and started toward him. "You sound like a meteorologist. Anything you'd care to add to your forecast?"

"Tonight will be dark, continuing until morning."

"Now you're being silly."

She held out his drink and he took it from her.

Victoria sat down on the sofa and leaned back. "I hope you like potatoes au gratin and asparagus."

"Two of my favorites."

Joe sipped his whiskey and wondered if he should ask about Cecily. Her obvious absence led him to believe she was still away.

"Joseph, I hope my being so forward earlier didn't upset you."

"You surprised me more than anything."

"I guess you've figured out that I've grown quite fond of you in the short time I've been living here. Do you hold any feelings for me?"

Take your time, he heard Joyce say.

He sipped more whiskey. "I do, and I'm hoping we can see more of each other."

Victoria beamed. "You get a gold star. Can I freshen your drink?"

"I'm fine."

"Let me go check on our supper."

As he watched her enter the kitchen, he breathed in the aromas hanging on the air. If the taste was as good as the smell, then this meal would be one of the finest he'd had in a while. He tilted his glass and poured down more whiskey.

Victoria emerged from the kitchen, plucked the glass from his hand, and headed to the liquor table.

"You must introduce me to your friends sometime...formally, I mean."

"Which friends are you talking about?"

"The policewoman and her partner. They seem like a couple of nice young people."

Joe cringed inside. "Yes, they are."

"How did you meet them?"

"We...had some trouble here a while back. They were sent to investigate. We struck up an acquaintance after they discovered I had been in law enforcement."

"Do they come to visit you often?"

"Not really. They stay pretty busy."

Victoria handed him a fresh drink.

"There's been talk around our condominium that two of the men who live here were murdered recently. Is that why they came to see you?"

"Part of the investigative process is doing a records check. It makes me feel sad, though."

Joe took a healthy pull of whiskey.

Victoria looked puzzled. "Why, Joseph?"

"Homicides don't make you feel sad?"

"Well, of course. What I meant was, after all those years around such atrocities, didn't you become somewhat immune?"

Joe stared at her. "No one should ever become immune to the killing of a human being. If they do, then they're no longer human."

"I'm sorry, Joseph, I didn't mean to sound insensitive." She rose from the chair and glided into the kitchen.

The next belt of whiskey rolled easily over Joe's tongue. He thought no more of their exchange and considered how he would shift the conversation to the whereabouts of Cecily. Victoria hadn't mentioned her once since he'd arrived—unusual, since the purpose of this soiree was for him to get to know her better. He enjoyed another sip.

A sudden tingling crawled up his neck before dissolving into a numbing sensation that blanketed the back of his head. Joe fell back in the chair and fought to retain focus. The numbness slowly spread throughout his body until he found he couldn't move. The glass of whiskey slipped from his hand and spilled onto the carpet.

A satisfied smile brightened Victoria's face as she came out of the kitchen. She walked to where Joe was sitting and leaned over him.

"How do you feel, Joseph? Like you've never felt before, I bet."

Her voice echoed deeply. She knelt down to pick up the glass and ice cubes.

Joe's vision kept drifting in and out of focus. He was helpless to resist.

"You shouldn't have gotten involved, Joseph. No one would have been the wiser if you hadn't been so damned nosey. Are you wondering what gave you away? Cecily knew that you saw her in the rental car. She's very observant. She told me the minute she got back from grocery shopping. I told her that she should get rid of it."

Victoria straightened up, her satisfied smile more apparent than before.

Joe heard a door close.

Seconds later, Cecily walked up beside her mother.

"Hello, Joseph."

Chapter 16

Anxiety more than surprise flooded Joe's mind. The sight of Victoria and Cecily standing side-by-side, mother and daughter conspirators, positively confirmed his doubts and fears. They worked in tandem to overpower their victims, one aiding the other to ensure a successful getaway—and a successful killing.

The satisfaction in Victoria's eternal, glowing smile had given way to a look of ravenous empowerment—a voracious craving too deep-seated to be contained.

"Look at him, Cecily, helpless, stupid, and trapped."

"They're all alike, Mother, easily led, easily deceived."

"Some things never change."

Mother and daughter laughed.

"I'll bet you're wondering how Cecily outsmarted your friends." Victoria paused, viciousness mounting. "She drove the car to another condo up the street and left it. Then she walked back here and sneaked in through the rear exit. While your friends were chasing their tails, she came up the fire escape stairs."

"Hide in plain sight," Cecily taunted. "I'm surprised that *you* didn't think of it first. Is old age slowing you down? I guess we gave him too much credit, Mother."

"Obviously. Just look at him. Taken in by beauty and charm like all the rest."

Mother and daughter laughed again.

Although debilitated, Joe's mind was still functional. He

wondered what plan they'd conceived to escape. Did they actually believe their intelligence and feminine wiles could spirit them away to some safe haven? Clearwater Police would be watching the building and searching the streets. Carly and David were smart enough to extend the alert to the Pinellas County Sheriff's Office as well as the agencies in the neighboring communities. The county was a peninsula with limited incoming and outgoing roadways. Even if they chose to use Victoria's SUV, there was no rock-solid guarantee of alluding capture. From Joe's standpoint, their only options were surrender or commit suicide. He couldn't imagine either of them surrendering, and their egos wouldn't permit a terminal solution.

Cecily bent over him. The look on her face reflected the same inhuman desire inhabiting her mother's. "Joseph, you may not believe this, but I do like you. You remind me of my grandfather."

"Oh, brother!" Victoria scoffed, and left for the kitchen.

"Unlike the others, I'm going to make certain that you're dead before I start carving on you." Her eyes suddenly widened. "I just thought of something. I've never seen my grandfather naked."

Her ear-piercing laughter, no longer melodious and pleasing, reverberated throughout the living room as she left him to join her mother.

Not since he'd stood face to face with Mac MacDougal in Hammock Park or watched Joyce's casket being lowered into the ground had Joe entertained the thought of dying. His life ending at the hands of a psycho pathologist certainly hadn't found its way onto his finality list. His mind reeled as picture after picture of himself materialized—grisly scenes similar to those of Steven Echavarría and Rusty Goodfellow. At the height of the gruesome parade of visuals, a notion far removed turned aside the imagery. *What are they going to do with my body? They can't leave me here.* Horror hit him hard, stealing the breath from his lungs. *They're going to chop me into pieces!*

Keep my body parts in a freezer and dispose of me little by little! Sudden reckoning pushed horror aside. *That will take too long. Carly and David will be all over this place before I've disappeared completely.*

An unexpected noise ended his journey through the macabre.

Cecily came running into the living room. She stared hard at Joe before hearing the noise again, lowering her eyes to his pants.

"Mother, it's his cell phone!" Grabbing Joe's shoulder, she pushed him over onto his left side, and dug her hand into his right front pocket. Once she'd retrieved the phone she let him fall back, staring at the caller I.D.

Victoria rushed out of the kitchen. "Who is it?"

"There's no name or number."

The phone rang a third time.

Cecily thrust the phone at her mother. "You answer it. Tell them he's in the bathroom or something."

"What if it's the police?" Victoria said. "They'll want to talk to him. Let it go to voicemail."

"But they'll know something's wrong when he doesn't call back."

After the fourth ring, there was silence.

"Turn it off, and let's get him into the bathroom!" Victoria ordered.

She and Cecily grabbed Joe's arms and hauled him out of the chair. Together, they dragged him into the undersized hallway before turning into the bathroom.

Joe was surprised at the strength exhibited by both women, and the effortless manner in which they hoisted him into the bathtub. A shower curtain covering the bottom of the tub and draped over the open side answered the question of how they would avoid the spilling of his blood. Helplessly he watched them leave. A hushed conversation ensued.

"We've got to figure out what we're going to tell his cop friends if they come looking for him," Cecily said.

"I'll tell them he hasn't come by yet, and I don't know where he is. I'll tell them I called him, but got no answer," Victoria said.

"What if they want to come inside and look around?"

Joe heard nothing as the seconds passed.

"I'll tell them that I called Joseph, and he said that he was on his way. Then I'll suggest we go check on him. While I distract them, you take his keys and go downstairs. When you're able, go to the parking lot and take his car. It's a silver-blue Camry. He has a reserved parking space. Drive it somewhere and leave it. I'll call you when it's safe."

"Good idea. Let's hope we can stick to the original plan."

"There's no reason we can't if we're careful, but getting rid of his body will be more difficult now. Dumping him on the beach may be out of the question. We'll have to wait and see."

The conversation ended, and Joe attempted to focus, struggling to come up with an idea on how to get the help he so desperately needed. Whatever drug they used to disable him was powerful and lasting. Though his thought processes were not affected, he was only successful in the moving and blinking of his eyes.

Clattering sounds in the kitchen was all he heard for the next couple of minutes. Each sound brought with it a new kind of terror. When Cecily appeared in the bathroom doorway clutching an eight-inch carving knife, Joe figured he was about to be killed. Setting his eyes on her, he refused to show fear.

It's almost over, Joyce. I'll be with you soon, my love.

Don't give up, Joe! he heard her shout.

What can I do?

Fight back!

How?

Cecily stepped into the bathroom. Victoria was right behind her. Hovering over him like a pair of vipers sizing up their prey, they seemed in no hurry to finish him.

"Get his keys," Victoria said.

Cecily handed her the knife, knelt down, and stuffed her hand into his pants pocket. After removing his keys, she laid them on the floor.

Victoria set the knife on top of a marble vanity. "Now let's strip him."

Cecily let loose chilling, maniacal laughter as she began to loosen Joe's belt and unfasten his Dockers. Victoria bent over and untied his shoes. Yanking off his socks, she watched her daughter slide her thumbs inside the waistband of his pants and start to pull them and his undershorts down.

Both women froze when they heard a loud pounding on the door. Cecily's eyes were riveted onto her mother.

"Don't make a sound," Victoria said. "I'll take care of whoever it is."

Out of the corner of his eye, Joe watched her stand up and step quickly from the bathroom, careful to ease the door shut behind her. He knew that now was the time to act. Problem was, the drug hadn't worn off.

Chapter 17

Joe concentrated as best he could while Cecily rose and crept to the bathroom door. She stood with her head lowered and eyes closed. After several seconds, she cracked the door open.

The voices were low but discernible. Victoria's voice was most recognizable as she fabricated a lie about his being late for their supper date. The other voice, high-pitched like hers, was muffled and more difficult to distinguish.

I sure hope it's Carly, he thought.

A strange sensation, warm pins and needles, began in his toes, crept into his feet, and slowly up through his ankles. Elation flooded his mind as he came to realize he was regaining feeling. The drug was wearing off. He strained to get another look at Cecily. Standing motionless, she was focused on the others in the living room, so he took a chance and attempted to wiggle his toes. His triumph intensified when he was able to move them.

A little more time. All I need is a little more time.

Sensation was gaining momentum as its prickly tentacles gradually climbed to his knee. In a minute or two he might be able to stand. A few more minutes and he might be able to defend himself. The eagerness to overcome his captor vanished once he heard the condo door close.

Cecily wore a satisfied grin as she straightened up and opened her eyes.

"The best laid plans," she said. Her voice was barely above

a whisper.

She moved to the vanity, wrapped her slender fingers around the handle of the carving knife, and leveled a feasting gaze.

"Try not to worry, Joseph. Death comes quickly by my hand."

With all life vacant from her eyes, she took two steps, dropped to her knees, and raised the instrument high above her head.

Joe's right foot slammed into the side of her face with amazing speed and strength. What didn't surprise him was the pain that followed. A reminder of the booting he'd given Mac McDougal.

"Ahh!" Cecily screamed as she crashed into the wall, the knife sailing from her grasp and rattling along the floor.

Joe fought to reposition himself, but feeling had yet to reach his waist.

Dammit!

Cecily released a groan before pulling herself upright. Wearing a look of uncertainty, she seemed unsure as to what had happened. A trickle of blood trailed down her forehead.

"Why you old son of a bitch, for that I'm going to slit your throat and watch you choke while I cut your balls off!"

She rolled over onto her hands and knees, scooped up the knife, and rising up, came at him again.

Before she made good her threat, the bathroom door flew open. Two loud gunshots sent a pair of bullets deep into her back. Frozen at the height of her attack, she then crumpled into the bathtub and Joe.

Carly lowered her automatic a bit and stared hard, watching for any signs of movement. With her eyes still trained on Cecily, she eased her head to the right.

"He's okay, David, but we're going to need an ambulance!"

Raising her weapon, she inched her way inside.

Joe still couldn't move, and feebly attempted to relay that fact with his eyes.

When Carly reached them she kept her automatic leveled as she leaned down and snatched the knife from the dead woman's hand. She holstered her weapon and pulled Cecily off of him.

"Can you stand, Joe?"

His silence was a message she understood.

"Did they drug you?"

Joe blinked several times.

Setting one foot into the tub, she slid her arms under his shoulders, and locked her hands behind his back.

"Try to use your legs if you can."

Joe used all the strength he had to help his struggling friend lift him to his feet. Much to his embarrassment his pants fell down to his knees.

Carly propped him up against the wall and made certain to steady him.

"We can't have you leaving here looking like this." She hoisted his Dockers, fastening and zipping them before cinching his belt. "Now try to walk."

Carly held onto both of his arms, and Joe labored to lift his left leg over the side of the tub. With equal difficulty and a great deal of pain, he managed to lift his right. Wrapping her left arm around his waist, she helped him stumble out of the bathroom.

When they emerged from the hall, Joe saw Victoria sitting hunched over on the sofa with her head bowed. David was standing beside her with his weapon drawn.

"Are you all right, Joe?" David asked.

"They drugged him," Carly said. "He can't talk yet."

Joe's eyes were blazing and locked onto Victoria.

She slowly raised her head. Her expression mirrored his.

"Damn you, Joseph Hampton! Damn you to hell!"

"Shut up!" David growled, stuffing his automatic into its holster. He grabbed Victoria's arm, jerked her to her feet, and wrested her hands behind her back to put on the handcuffs. "Let's go!" he barked.

"Call the Medical Examiner's Office, will you, David? I'm going to wait for the ambulance with Joe."

David nodded and hauled Victoria to the door.

Joe never took his eyes off the silver-haired woman until they were gone.

Carly eased him down onto the sofa, and took a seat beside him.

"Getting more feeling back?"

Joe blinked.

"Someone must be looking out for you."

And I know who that someone is, Joe thought.

"We caught a break on this one. A uniform was patrolling the north end of Island Estates when we put out the alert for Cecily's white car. He began a search of the houses and condos, and eventually found it in a parking lot two blocks from here. I remembered that Victoria had invited you to supper. I took a chance on Cecily coming back. I guess they'd worked out some kind of plan for Cecily's escape."

More and more feeling crept back into Joe's body.

"David and I decided to talk to Victoria. When she met us at the door, she told us you hadn't arrived. She suggested we go check your condo. I knew something was wrong because we'd already beat on your door, and you didn't answer when I called. David grabbed Victoria when she stepped into the hall while I came inside to look for you. That's when I heard Cecily scream, and, well, you know the rest."

Joe forced his left arm from his side and reached out to her. Carly took his hand. He tried to speak, but couldn't.

"That's okay. I understand. You'll be all right in a few minutes."

Bustling and murmuring in the hall drew their attention to the open door.

As Carly started to get to her feet, a pair of EMTs guided a stretcher into the room while a half-dozen or more residents crowded together outside the doorway.

"He's been drugged," she told them, "but he's got most of his feeling back. Be careful with him, all right?"

The EMTs helped Joe onto the stretcher and started to wheel

him away. Joe caught hold of Carly's arm.

"Thank you," he croaked.

Carly squeezed his hand. "I'll see you at the hospital."

Chapter 18

Sporting a white cotton sock on his badly bruised right foot and a black running shoe on his left, Joe took a moment to appreciate a warm, mid-morning sun coupled with a mild breeze blowing in from the Gulf. This was the Florida weather he'd come to know, and the first sunny day he'd seen in quite some time. Lifting his coffee mug to his lips, he heard the young brunette in the matching chaise lounge beside him release a heavy sigh.

"You're not bored, are you, Carly?"

She sighed again. "For the first time in weeks, I'm relaxed, Joe. Really relaxed. I'd almost forgotten what it feels like."

Joe grinned and sipped more coffee. "I'm glad you stopped by so I could properly thank you for saving my life...again."

"Just doing my job, sir."

"I'll call and thank David later."

"I'm sure he'll appreciate it." She chuckled. "I don't envy him filling out all those reports, though."

"But he pushed for you taking time off, didn't he?"

"I think I was driving him crazy. Anyway, I can use the time to follow through with my divorce."

"I'm sorry it didn't work out for you and Tim."

"Me, too. But it's best that we go our separate ways."

Joe allowed the thought to linger a moment. "I don't suppose we'll ever know for sure whether Victoria and Cecily were behind the killings of Steven Echavarría and Rusty Goodfellow."

"Hard to say. David is going back to the Sunrise Motel and the Circle Food Mart with their pictures. Maybe someone will recognize them."

"Talk to Ruth Sterling and Betty Hough as well. They may point to Cecily as being the woman they saw talking to Rusty."

"David is way ahead of you, Joe. It's on his to-do list."

"I should have known."

They paused to take in the daily goings-on of others down below and across the channel.

"Joe, ever since this ordeal ended I've been thinking about Cecily. The possibility exists that she might have been a serial killer. I mean, in the short time she was here, three men died...and almost a fourth."

"Three men?"

"The Pasco County Sheriff's Office is pinning the murder of Lawrence Lombard on her. He was the man who rented the car at the airport."

"Oh, that's right. I forgot about him."

"I don't believe that Lombard was stupid enough to lend Cecily the car. And I still can't believe that Victoria didn't know about her daughter."

"She knew. I can attest to that, and I'll swear to it in court. In fact, Victoria may have gotten her started. She's been married and widowed three times. And remember, you told me that a silver-haired woman was seen with Steven Echavarría at the Sunrise Motel. Add to that the young woman seen earlier in the parking lot. I think Victoria set him up and Cecily killed him."

"Sounds about right, Joe. The timeline of the car rental supports your theory."

"If that's the case, then I believe Cecily left the motel after she killed Echavarria and rendezvoused with her mother at another location a short time later. Since Victoria was somewhat familiar with Clearwater, they made a nice, clean getaway."

"And when they tag-teamed Russell Goodfellow, they simply traded places. Cecily was the bait, and Victoria bashed him in the head at the beach before her daughter put the knife to him. We determined the stab wounds were similar to those on Echavarría." Carly shook her head. "Mother and daughter serial killers. I don't think I've ever heard of such a thing."

"I know I haven't."

"Something bad must have happened to both of them for their minds to become so twisted."

"I agree. All in all, a sad situation. Almost makes me feel sorry for them."

"Really?"

"I said *almost.*"

Another breeze whistled through the balcony.

Joe closed his eyes. A second later they opened wide. "I just remembered something."

"What?"

"Cecily told me that she has a daughter, Vicki, in medical school."

"So what are you saying?"

"Alerting the local police to what happened to her mother and grandmother, and recommending they do a background check on her might not be a bad idea."

"You mean like mother, like daughter...a second time?"

"Better to be wrong than not."

"I'll call David right away."

"In the meantime, I need to use the bathroom."

"Do you want some help?"

"No, thank you. My cane is lying right here on the floor. I'm starting to think I'll never get rid of that thing." Joe reached down and picked it up.

"I know your foot is only bruised, but I want you to promise me that you'll use your cane until the doctor says otherwise."

"I appreciate your concern, Carly, but I'll be back to my old self in no time."

"I'm not kidding, Joe."

"All right, I promise."

Carly kept an eye on him as he struggled to his feet. "Are your pants fastened?"

"Yes, Carly, my pants are fastened."

She laughed at his exasperated expression. "Don't worry, what happens between us, stays between us. After all, no one needs to know that I caught The Gray Detective with his pants down."

DEADLY SEPARATION

Chapter 1

The past two months had seemed like two years to Joe: Slowly unwinding, deliberate in passing, and never a clear sign to signal the end. The length of time it took for his foot to heal was definitely frustrating. When the doctor gave him the go-ahead, Joe tossed his trusty cane aside, happy to be self-reliant again and thankful he'd taken Carly's advice.

Carly had been a model tenant during her brief stay. Quiet when she left for work each morning, respectful of his desire for rest when she came in late. Her helping with the cooking and cleaning, and seeing to his needs accelerated his rehabilitation. Though he was certain their living arrangement had raised the eyebrows of quite a few residents in the Crimson Conch Condominiums, he ignored their whispers and stares, happy to be of assistance. Now, with the process of her divorce nearing an end, she had moved into a duplex in north Dunedin to begin a new chapter in her life.

With the worst of his predicament behind him, Joe was beginning again as well. He discovered new-found enjoyment in bingo and bridge nights, and in mingling with the residents in general. Even the dances, held once a month in the Rec Room, lifted his spirits. To remain active and productive, he continued with his position as building manager. Seeing to the placement of new arrivals, and the requests and complaints of the current homeowners gave him a sense of purpose.

A bright, bold, full moon hung above the shadowy waters of the Gulf of Mexico this morning. Waking early, and unable to return to sleep, Joe decided to get some fresh air and bathe in its brilliance.

Strange how the forces of nature can affect you, he thought, *even when you're asleep.*

He'd been dreaming of Joyce, and how they had often delighted in taking moonlit strolls when they were first married—on the beach, through a park, even around the block in their neighborhood. Waking for no reason, he wished the dream had lasted longer, for being with her again made him feel appreciated and loved.

Languid as the moments passed, he drifted with the memory of her beautiful face. Her beauty, her soft and low voice and her engaging smile were some of the many reasons he loved her, but also the reasons he now wandered aimlessly without her. Resisting the impulse to drown himself in self-pity, he slowly got out of his bed. Throwing on a gray flannel shirt and faded blue jeans, he went into the kitchen to brew some coffee.

After filling his coffee cup, he noticed that the moon had painted his balcony floor a lustrous grayish-blue, beckoning him to soak in its glow. As he lay in the moonlight on his chaise lounge, its twin visibly vacant and lonely, he paused to greet the luminous orb by raising his mug in salute. Appreciative of the gesture, the old lunar gentleman smiled back at him. Although sunrise was an hour away, he was in no hurry to see to his responsibilities as overseer of the building.

One of the benefits of managing the condominium complex was no set office hours. It was also one of the drawbacks, but they were few.

You can do as you please as long as your chores get done, he recalled his mother saying. He grinned as he remembered her soothing voice and endearing eyes—like Joyce's.

Joe enjoyed this time of day—the fading of night into a pre-dawn glow, and the invigorating freshness of a new beginning.

He took a drink of coffee and wondered how Carly was doing. A fondness for her had grown in the short time since they had met. His appreciation of her artful approach to being a detective was without question, but he was concerned that her total immersion in the profession might prevent her pursuit of pleasures in the outside world. Since her separation from Tim, she had severed those necessary lifelines, and he worried that she might end up burned-out, jaded, and bitter.

He lifted the mug to his lips, watching the moon slip closer to dipping into the Gulf.

Why don't you call Carly, Joe? Joyce whispered in his ear.

She hadn't spoken to him since her short stay at his condo after death had stared him in the face at the hands of Cecily Dearmin and her mother, Victoria Combes.

I don't want to be a pest.

You won't be a pest. She likes you.

She's a grown woman. She doesn't need me looking over her shoulder every minute. She might miss having someone looking after her—like someone else I know.

That's different. The way I feel about you...

Now don't be stubborn, Joe. Call her.

All right.

Promise?

I promise.

The moon is beautiful, isn't it?

Not as beautiful as you.

The Gulf had swallowed the moon by the time Joe finished his coffee, and dawn's fingers were reaching across the sky, pushing away the night. As he lingered on his balcony, he knew he had to make a decision. What was he going to eat for breakfast?

Maybe I'll go out to eat. If I leave in the next few minutes, I can be well on my way to finishing the meal by the time the world arrives.

Giving it no more thought, he left the chaise lounge. Passing through the kitchen on his way to the bathroom to splash some water on his face, he set his cup in the sink. Even though the weather was cool, he skipped putting on socks and donned his favorite black running shoes. He paused a moment to check the pockets of his jeans.

Keys, change, and wallet. I'm all set. And I think I'll go to Frenchy's.

The popular eatery sat on the sands of Clearwater Beach, and as soon as Joe thought of it, he remembered Rusty Goodfellow and the lunch date he and Victoria had had with the deceased Michigander and his wife Nancy. He hadn't been back to Frenchy's since.

I'll go in your honor, Rusty. It's the least I can do...as soon as I find my cell phone.

After locating his phone, he was about to open the door when an important fact caused him to hesitate.

Frenchy's doesn't open until eleven.

He debated whether he should go at all until the name of another eatery popped into his mind.

The Clear Sky Café. I haven't been there in a while.

Before he could open the door, his cell phone rang. He stared at it a second, puzzled as to why someone would be calling so early. The caller I.D. was of no help, either.

"Joe, this is David Sizemore. I'm, uh, sorry to bother you at this time of the morning."

"David! What's got you up and running at this hour?"

"I need your help...I mean, we need your help."

"You need help with a case?"

"Yeah, a man living in one of the townhouses on Duncan Loop North in Dunedin has been murdered, and he, uh..."

"David, I'm confused. Where is Carly?" As the words left his mouth, Joe was jolted by a revelation. "Wait a minute! Isn't that the area where she used to live?"

He heard David sigh.

"The dead man is Tim Truffant. Carly made the call. She's sitting here in front of me. Her hands are covered in blood."

Chapter 2

Joe struggled to locate the part of Dunedin where David and Carly were waiting, all the while refusing to believe that Carly had killed her soon-to-be ex-husband. He was barely familiar with the town that bordered Clearwater and entertained no desire to return to any place associated with Hammock Park. Nightmarish visions of the preserve where he was almost killed by Mac McDougal remained fresh in his mind. Just thinking of it still made him tremble. Instead of following the road along the coastline, he motored down Gulf to Bay Boulevard until he came to Keene Road. He made a left turn, then traveled nearly three miles before MacAlpine Way came into view, where he turned left again.

A short distance later, MacAlpine Way became Duncan Loop North, the beginning stretch of a pristine and well-tended neighborhood. The sight of many sheriff's office and forensics vehicles led him straight to the MacAfee Townhomes.

Joe steered his silver-blue Toyota Camry into the parking lot adjacent to the building, taking care not to park in a reserved space. Several steps away from his car, he was confronted by a deputy.

"I'm sorry, sir, but I can't let you pass."

"Deputy, my name is Joe Hampton. I was asked to come here by Detective David Sizemore of the Clearwater Police Department."

The trim, young, blond-haired deputy narrowed his blue eyes. "Sir, I have been instructed not to allow anyone to pass."

"I understand your position, but it's imperative that I speak with Detective Sizemore."

The deputy took a step forward. "Sir, please don't be difficult. I'm asking you to leave."

"Just a minute, Deputy," said a woman approaching them from the direction of the townhouse.

Joe looked over the young man's shoulder to see a stocky woman in a gray pantsuit, her short, black hair clinging to her round face and highlighting her chestnut-colored eyes.

The woman walked up beside the deputy. "Sir, are you Joe Hampton?"

"I am."

"I'm Detective Ramsey. It's okay, Brewer, we've been expecting him."

The deputy stepped aside and nodded as Joe passed by.

Joe followed Ramsey across the sunbaked asphalt parking lot in silence, mounting the blanched concrete sidewalk before either of them spoke.

"Have you known Sergeant Truffant very long, Mr. Hampton?"

"A few months," Joe said. "She and Detective Sizemore solved the cases of some people in my condo who were murdered. And she saved my life…twice."

"Really?"

Ramsey opened the door and Joe followed her inside.

A sand-colored sofa and two matching chairs sat on a dark blue wall-to-wall carpet. On one of the four walls hung a fifty-inch high-definition television with a white ash entertainment center beneath. The other walls held paintings of seascapes and fishing villages.

I guess someone likes the seashore, Joe thought.

The room was teeming with forensics technicians and deputies. Each one gave Joe a curious and unsympathetic eye—branding him an outsider with no reason to intrude. Joe was impervious. He'd received worse receptions in his time.

Ramsey led him up a flight of carpeted stairs to the larger of two bedrooms. David and a tall, unknown man in a dark brown suit stood on either side of Carly. Sitting on the foot of a massive king-size bed, she had her head bowed, legs apart, and arms resting on her thighs. Her hands were streaked with blood. She looked up at Joe through red, swollen eyes, staring a second before looking away. David turned to Joe and gestured toward a corner of the room. The other man didn't move. They quietly moved away from him and Carly.

David looked like someone had just told him that his favorite dog had been run over by a car.

"Thanks for coming, Joe. I'm still in shock."

"What happened?"

"The guy standing beside Carly is Ben Kaczmarek, a detective with the sheriff's office. He and his partner, Kathleen Ramsey, were called here a couple of hours ago. Ben and I went to high school together. When he found out it was Carly, he called me."

"They think that Carly killed her husband?"

David sighed. "This is the way he said it went down. When he and Ramsey got here, Carly was standing inside, by the front door. She appeared disoriented, but told them that Tim was upstairs."

"She called nine-one-one?"

David nodded. "The three of them came up here. Tim was over there."

Joe looked to his left, and saw the sheet-covered body lying a few feet from the bed.

"He'd been shot square in the chest," David continued. "Carly told them that Tim had called her earlier. He wanted to talk more about finalizing their divorce. She said she could tell that he'd been drinking. He got belligerent, but she agreed to come over anyway."

"Her apartment isn't that far from here, is it?"

"About a half-mile away. When she got here, she said the front door was slightly open and the lights in the living room were on. She came inside, didn't see Tim, and called out to him. When he didn't answer, she figured he'd passed out, and went upstairs."

"Did he attack her?"

"According to what she told Kaczmarek and Ramsey, when she turned on the bedroom light, he was passed out on the floor, so she decided to try to wake him up and put him to bed. After she shook him a couple of times, he came to and they struggled. She figured he didn't recognize her. Then she, uh...said that someone hit her from behind and knocked her out."

"So someone else may have shot him."

"They found the gun."

"Where?"

David looked to his right, and again Joe looked at the body. Two feet from where Tim Truffant lay sat a plastic evidence marker.

"It's Carly's backup piece, and there was a spent cartridge in the chamber."

"David, are you sure it belongs to her?"

"I know it's hers, believe me."

"Look, there's no way to know if she shot her husband until they test for residue on her hands."

"I know, Joe, and she's got some scratches and a couple of bruises on her arms. That tells me there *was* a struggle. Hopefully when she's examined they'll find a bump on her head to corroborate her story. But right now it doesn't look good."

"Did she say how she got the blood on her hands?"

"When she came to, she saw that Tim had been shot, and instinctively applied pressure. Then she called nine-one-one. She admitted that she wasn't thinking straight."

Joe glanced at Carly, then back at David. "How do Kaczmarek and Ramsey see it?"

"The same way you and I do. They'll follow procedure, study the evidence, and once they're certain, they'll either charge her or they won't. Ben doesn't play favorites, and I'm betting his partner doesn't, either."

"Like two other detectives I know," Joe said.

David lowered his eyes.

Joe walked over to where Carly was sitting and faced Kaczmarek. "I'm Joe Hampton, Carly's friend."

The detective offered a tight smile and held out his right hand. "Ben Kaczmarek."

Joe turned to Carly and gently squeezed her shoulder.

"We'll contact your union representative about a lawyer as soon as we can...and whatever else you might need."

Carly slowly raised her head.

"Joe, I don't know what the hell to do."

Chapter 3

Detective Ramsey escorted Carly from the bedroom, an awkward situation that embarrassed her as well as Joe and David. Both men bowed their heads and averted their eyes as she was being led away. Humiliation was not becoming to a stalwart public servant with an exemplary career. She would be driven to Mease Hospital to be examined, and once samples of her DNA and the dried blood on her hands were taken, she would end up at the sheriff's office for more questioning. She'd been part of the drill many times, but never on the receiving end.

Joe held hope that Ben Kaczmarek would allow him to remain in the townhouse. In no way did he believe that Carly had killed Tim Truffant, and he wanted to assist in the search for evidence to prove her innocence.

David stood shoulder to shoulder with him. "Ben, I'm going to ask a favor. It goes against procedure because I'm too close to this, and if you refuse me, I'll understand."

Kaczmarek's expression suggested that he sensed what was coming.

"I'd like to help with your investigation. I have a couple of hours before I have to report. If Carly and I didn't have two cases pending, I'd take vacation leave to devote more time."

"I don't have a problem, Dave," Kaczmarek said. His voice was deep and commanding, befitting his daunting stature. "Besides, if I said no, you'd investigate on your own, anyway."

"And I'd like Joe to help us. He's retired homicide from Philadelphia P.D. He's worked with Carly and me on some of our cases."

The sheriff's detective trained his slate-gray eyes on Joe and exhibited a thin smile. "Anyone who can put up with you is okay by me. But fellas, I have to say that what we've discovered so far doesn't look good for Carly."

Tim Truffant's body had been removed, and the men stared down at the blood-stained carpeting.

"Now, Carly said that when she came in, she turned on the lights, and saw him lying on the floor over there." Kaczmarek pointed with his right hand. "She assumed that he'd passed out. By the tracks on the carpet, it appears he was dragged to this spot and shot, where we found him."

The raised lines in the carpeting, leading to the dried pool of blood, drew Joe's attention. He scanned the area near the bed, stepping from the foot to the side, focusing on the bedspread.

"Detective Kaczmarek, there's no blood pattern on the floor or on the bed, so it's doubtful he was standing when he was shot."

"I agree, Mr. Hampton, which makes me wonder why she would bother to drag him. And with all due respect to our female counterparts, I don't think she'd be able to drag him."

"I see your point, Ben," David said. "If he was already down, why not shoot him where he lay?"

Joe looked across the room. A small walnut dressing table and dresser sat against the wall, separated by a louvered door. He glanced over his shoulder to the opposite wall, catching sight of another door. It was partly open and revealed the tan floor tiles and small white vanity in the bathroom. As he returned his gaze to the first door, a forensics technician clad in dark green fatigues passed in front of him.

"Excuse me. Do you know where that door leads?"

"To a walk-in closet," she said.

Joe thanked her, and she left to continue with her duties.

"I know what you're thinking, Joe," David said.

"I believe I do, too," Kaczmarek said.

"Then we all agree that if someone was hiding in the room when Carly came in, she would have seen him come out of the closet."

"But not someone hidden in the bathroom," David added.

"And Carly *could* have gotten cracked in the head if she was facing the other direction while she was trying to wake Truffant," Kaczmarek said.

"She would never have seen him," Joe finished.

"Or her. My partner is a constant reminder of the empowerment of women."

"Mine, too," David mumbled.

Kaczmarek excused himself, and left to converse with a forensics technician.

Joe took that moment to further study the bloody carpeting.

"What're you thinking, Joe?"

"I'm thinking that I'm a dinosaur."

"Because you've been out of the game for a while?"

"David, twice in the past few months I've come close to being killed. The first time, a woman gave the order. The second time, two women nearly succeeded, and knowing that, I still presume a man to be the perpetrator when it comes to murder."

"I guess old habits die hard, Joe—pun intended."

Kaczmarek returned from his meeting.

"Okay, forensics says they lifted scads of fingerprints out of the bathroom. Quite a few from the closet, too. I can see this case is going to be a lot of fun, but here's my question: If someone other than Carly was the shooter, how did they manage to get her revolver...presuming that her back-up *is* the murder weapon?"

"Good question," David said. "Not many people think to search for a snub-nose in an ankle holster...especially in the clutch."

"No bullet found in the walls or furniture?" Joe asked.

Kaczmarek shook his head.

"A second gun could have been used."

"Ballistics will tell us soon enough."

The men paused to consider their assessments. Kaczmarek was first to break the silence.

"And then there's the obvious, of course."

David narrowed his steel-blue eyes. "I don't wanna hear that kind of talk, Ben."

"Come on, Dave, you know how easily she could have set this up."

"I said get off it!"

Joe eased between them, the fire in his young friend's eyes apparent.

"I don't want to believe it, either, David, but you know the routine. It's his job. You'd have to consider the possibility of Carly being the shooter if you were handling this case. It stinks, but it's what we do."

David's glare shifted from Joe to Kaczmarek and back to Joe again. "I have to go to work. I'll be in touch."

Neither man attempted to stop him as he stormed out of the bedroom.

"Thanks, Mr. Hampton, I thought Dave was gonna lose it there for a second."

"He believes in his partner...like you believe in Detective Ramsey."

"You're right about that."

"And, please, Detective, call me Joe."

"Well, Joe, I'm going to look around some before I head back to the office. You're welcome to join me."

"I appreciate that...Ben. And I'd like to be there when you interview Carly...as an observer, I mean."

"I don't see a problem."

Joe spent the next hour doing a meticulous search of the townhouse, thinking the whole time what none of them wanted to admit. He'd witnessed Carly's edginess, seen her take action, and knew she possessed the willingness to pull the trigger. Seeing that she and Tim were embroiled in divorce proceedings, the shadow of doubt hanging over her was enormous.

Chapter 4

Joe and Ben Kaczmarek stood outside the interview room waiting on Kathleen Ramsey. Sickened by the thought of a fellow officer being on the other side of the table in a murder investigation, and more so because it was his friend, Joe glanced through the one-way glass at Carly and the union attorney seated beside her. She looked better than she had at the townhouse, but not much. Seeing her with her head bowed and her hands clasped together on top of the table irritated him. It was as if all her confidence and reason for being had been drained from her, and for the moment, he was unable to help her.

Ramsey arrived on silent feet and stood beside them, allowing herself some time to come to terms with the unenviable task she was about to perform.

"Did she say anything on the way here?" Kaczmarek asked.

"Nothing useful. She asked me the time. That was it."

"She never asked if she was under arrest?"

"Nope."

"David told me that she claims to have been knocked unconscious," Joe said. "Did they find anything when she was examined?"

"She's got a good-size lump on the back of her head, but, uh..." Ramsey sighed. "The location could be a point of contention."

"Meaning an argument could be made that the injury was self-inflicted."

"That or she might have been pushed or fallen backward."

"The doctor didn't recommend that she remain for observation?"

"She chose to leave."

"You got a sample of the blood on her hands, right?" Kaczmarek asked.

"By the book."

"See if you can get more out of her, Kathleen."

He and Joe watched the stocky detective enter the room, pull out a chair, and sit down across from Carly.

Carly slowly raised her head.

"Detective," Ramsey began, "I'd like you to tell me again exactly what happened."

Although totally exhausted best described her appearance, Carly stared at Ramsey, resolute. "Am I under arrest?"

"No, we just want to make certain we have the facts straight."

"I've said all I'm going to say."

"You have her statement," the attorney said. "If you're not going to charge her then I believe we're done here."

Joe's eyes were riveted on Carly as he recalled David's explanation of her predicament.

His recounting of the details matched hers word for word, and sounded rehearsed and employed to deceive.

David said that Carly called 9-1-1, and later he was notified by Kaczmarek, Joe thought. *But he also said that she wasn't thinking straight when she came to and discovered that Tim was dead. Could she have called David before she called—*

His thoughts were dashed when he heard Ramsey say, "Okay, then I guess we're done here."

Kaczmarek turned to Joe. "Well, it was worth a try. She's smart enough not to be led into a trap."

"Does that bother you?"

"Not really. She knows the drill...as do you, I'm certain."

Joe looked back into the interview room. Ramsey was getting up from her chair.

"Is something on your mind, Joe?"

"No, it's just that..."

Ramsey closed the door and faced them. "Well, Ben, I guess that's that. I didn't think we'd get anywhere."

"Did she say anything on the way to the hospital?"

"Not a word."

"I'll make sure she gets home safely," Joe said.

"Make sure you do," Kaczmarek added.

Nothing was said between Carly and Joe during their trip back to Dunedin until they pulled into the driveway of the duplex off Patricia Avenue.

"Thank you for bringing me home, Joe."

"My pleasure. Are you all right?"

"No, I'm not. The doctor gave me something for my headache, but I still don't feel right."

"Then you stay put."

Joe got out of the car, went to the passenger side, and opened the door. Taking both her hands, he steadied her as she eased out of the seat.

"Now I know what a concussion feels like," she said.

After several tentative steps to the front door, she stuffed her hands into the pockets of her black slacks, trying to find her keys.

"I don't recall ever seeing you carry a purse," Joe said.

"I sometimes do when I'm off the job. They're too big a hassle."

Joe wore a tight grin as he remembered Joyce's fondness for handbags.

As Carly shoved the key into the deadbolt lock, she hesitated. "I just thought of something, Joe."

"What is it?"

"My car is at the townhouse."

"Don't worry. I'll make arrangements to get it back to you."

"But I need it to get to work."

"You're not going anywhere...not for a couple of days, anyway."

"Is that right? So what're you now, my father?"

"If I were, I'd wash your mouth out with soap for sassing me. Do you need anything?"

"No, I'm, uh, fine." Carly raised a hand to her forehead. "Could you, maybe, stick around for a while?"

"Certainly."

Her studio apartment was bland and cramped. Her unmade bed, kitchenette, discount-store-two-seater sofa, and scuffed wooden chair filled up the room.

Joe helped her to the couch, and took a seat in the chair, keeping close watch on her as she leaned back and closed her eyes. Five minutes passed before she sat up.

"Joe, there's something I didn't tell the detectives."

"Is it a good idea to share it with me? Maybe you should hold off just to be safe."

"You don't even know what I'm going to say."

"I think you should talk to your lawyer first."

"Would you stop worrying. Besides, I trust you."

She must be feeling better. "Whatever you think best."

Carly dug into her pocket and pulled out her smart phone.

"Someone has been sending me videos."

"How did they get your phone number?"

"I don't know. The videos are of Tim and some woman...a *young* woman."

Carly fiddled with the phone, then handed it to Joe. "Tap the arrow to start it."

Joe did as she instructed and waited until he saw two naked figures in a full embrace.

"Doesn't leave much to the imagination, does it?"

Carly didn't answer.

"Do you know who she is?"

"I have no idea."

"You said *videos*. How many did you receive?"

"I've been getting one a week for the past five weeks."

"Are all of them this...explicit?"

Carly nodded, grimacing a second later.

"Do you recognize the bed? Where they are exactly?"

"I haven't a clue."

"Any messages to go with them?"

"No, I hear the tone for notifications, and there they are."

"No traceable number?"

"I haven't tried."

Her answer set Joe to wondering. He refrained from asking her why. The video ended, so he returned the phone.

"Do you think this has anything to do with your divorce?"

"I'm not sure. When Tim and I decided to call it quits, it seemed like the split was going to be smooth and civil. We'd pretty much figured out who was going to get what before we contacted the lawyers."

"But something changed."

"Yeah. Tim. He decided he wanted more."

"Is that why he stayed in the townhouse and you left?"

"The townhouse was his idea to begin with. I never really liked it. I wanted a house with a fenced-in backyard in suburbia. I guess it made him feel more important at work."

"Where *did* he work?"

"At Holden Fidelity Mortgages as a loan officer."

"The townhouse is very nice. He must have been quite successful."

"His loans were always a half-million bucks or more."

Joe had never been introduced to Tim, and wouldn't have guessed that Carly was married to a money man. Maybe the woman in bed with him had aspirations of becoming the next Mrs. Truffant. But who was sending the videos?"

"Joe, I could really use a shower. Can you hang around in case I, you know, pass out or need your help?"

"I said I would."

"Oh. Right."

Carly started to get up. Joe was quicker.

"Let me help you."

She waved him off as she labored to get to her feet. Purposeful steps guided her to the bathroom door.

After he heard the water come on, Joe allowed his mind to slip back to his conversation with David. The facts he was given were identical to what he'd learned from Kaczmarek and Ramsey about Carly's statement. Granted, she had provided the information to both parties, but nothing had been omitted or added. For someone receiving a blow to the head, that seemed unusual to him. Aware that many years in a profession that demanded attention be paid to details, he knew that some detectives possessed the ability to recall with clarity the events surrounding them. But an uneasy sensation had grown inside him—a feeling that she hadn't revealed everything.

I'll ask her to tell me more about the videos. Then, maybe, I can figure out what really happened between her and Tim.

Chapter 5

Carly emerged from the bathroom after a twenty-minute shower. Wrapped in a lime sherbet-colored towel, her brown pixie hair disheveled, she moved on unsteady legs to a small mahogany dresser and opened the top drawer. Removing a pair of yellow and white-striped bikini panties, she closed the drawer then searched the next one down, pulling out a white tee shirt and cut-off, blue-jeans shorts. A shaky path back to the bathroom was obvious before she disappeared behind the door. Not once did she look at Joe.

I know what you're thinking, he heard Joyce say.

No, you don't.

You love her, don't you?

Like the daughter we never had.

The bathroom door opened, and Carly stepped out clad in her casual wardrobe and drying her hair. Her stride was more confident, but she quickly retreated to the sofa. After a final going-over of her hair, she draped the towel around her neck.

"That did the trick."

"Feeling better?" Joe asked.

"A little. My head still hurts."

"Feel like talking?"

Carly stared at him a second. "I didn't kill Tim, Joe."

"No one will convince me that you did. I'm curious about the videos."

"I am, too. I kinda figured that Tim was seeing someone. I didn't think it had gone that far, though."

"What tipped you off?"

"A wife can tell."

"Carly."

She offered the trace of a grin. "Little things. He was always in a hurry when I called. And he objected when I wanted to come by the townhouse to discuss the details of our divorce. He would suggest that we meet somewhere else."

"Did you ever call him out?"

"No...I just wanted it to be over."

"Why do you think you started getting the videos?"

"Someone was trying to make me jealous, I guess."

"No one comes to mind?"

"It makes no sense to me."

"What do you mean?"

"For argument's sake, let's say it's the blond bitch humping Tim who's sending the videos."

Blond bitch? Joe thought. *You're not bitter.*

"What could she hope to gain?" Carly continued. "She's younger, prettier, she's already given him what he wants, and she's probably going to move in with him if she hasn't already. What would be the point of sending me the videos?"

"To rub your face in it."

"Why aggravate the situation? Tim and I had agreed to an even split—until recently. Pissing me off would only make matters worse."

"I remember your saying that he wanted more. What did he want?"

"I did?"

"After we got back from the sheriff's office."

Carly pinched her face into puzzlement. "Oh. Well, we have a joint savings account. We initially agreed to split it fifty-fifty. Tim decided that wasn't fair, since he'd put in more money."

"What did he consider fair?"

"Seventy-thirty."

"That's quite a difference."

"I argued that since he was getting the townhouse *and* the cabin, I should get fifty percent of our savings."

"The cabin?"

"We own a cabin on the Rainbow River near Dunnellon."

This guy must have been very successful. "What else did he want besides the money?"

"Nothing...just the money."

"Did you agree to it?"

"No way! I've earned what I feel I deserve."

Joe didn't bother to ask the amount of money they had in their savings account. He figured the shock would be too much for his system. Carly had presented a sound argument against the mystery woman being the agitator. The same argument could be made for Tim. But what was behind his suddenly feeling that he deserved more? Was it the want of satisfying a new bedmate?

"Is there anyone you can think of who might want to get back at you?"

"There are a few, but how would they know where to find Tim and Blondie?"

"It *would* take a tremendous amount of time and effort, I suppose."

Carly nodded, grimacing again.

"Are you all right?"

"As long as I don't move my head."

"You probably don't want to hear this, but I haven't had anything to eat yet."

Carly laid a hand on her stomach. "You're right. I don't want to hear about it. I'm not sure my head would allow me to keep anything down."

"Is there a place close by where I could grab something to go?"

"Eva's Kitchen on Patricia. Head north a few blocks. Their food never disappointed me."

"I'll only be gone a few minutes, okay?"

Carly gave him a look of disgust. "I'm not a baby, Joe."

You're not yourself yet, either. "I'll be back as quick as I can."

A hollow feeling was building inside Joe as he closed the front door and strode to his Toyota, pausing a moment as he grabbed the door handle. Hunger aside, he couldn't rid himself of the notion that Carly hadn't told him everything that had gone on during the meeting with her soon-to-be ex-husband. Her defense of Tim and his young consort added strength to a possibility he'd pondered earlier. If David had lied to him about how the series of events in the townhouse had gone down—if Carly had called him first, and he had helped her with her alibi before corrupting the crime scene—then, maybe, it was David's idea to send her the videos. A co-conspirator in the plot to dispose of the man caught cheating on his partner and friend.

And maybe their friendship runs deeper than anyone really knows, Joe thought.

Chapter 6

Eva's Kitchen was closer than Joe had figured, and his order of two pancakes, sausage links, and a medium coffee took little time to prepare. The hollow feeling he'd felt earlier was overcome by hunger pangs, but the notion that David might be a confederate in Carly's situation remained entrenched in his thoughts. The unpleasantness rode with him back to her apartment.

Once he'd parked his car and stood at her door, he decided it best to knock instead of barging inside. When she didn't answer, his anxiety intensified and he tested the doorknob. The door was unlocked, so he eased it open. The aroma of freshly brewed coffee filled his nostrils.

Carly was standing next to the sink in the kitchenette staring at the coffeemaker. Expressionless, she turned to him.

"It's okay, Joe, I just didn't feel like walking all the way over there."

Joe closed the door behind him and headed to the straight-back chair. Setting his cup of coffee on the floor, he removed a Styrofoam container and package of utensils from the white plastic bag. When he'd unwrapped the knife, fork, and napkin, he opened the container.

As he placed a pat of butter on top of each pancake and covered them with maple syrup, Carly sat down on the sofa with a mug full of black coffee in her hand. Joe carved out a wedge of pancakes and stuffed them into his mouth.

"Did the doctor say it was okay for you to drink that?" he asked.

Carly glanced at him as she blew across the top of her mug. "She didn't say I couldn't."

"What *did* she tell you?"

"To rest."

"Promise me you will?"

"Yes, Daddy."

Joe leveled his brown eyes. "Don't get smart with me! Chances are you've got a concussion! It's no laughing matter!"

Carly took a drink of coffee.

Joe ate more pancakes.

"Did you find any clues at the townhouse after I left?"

"Nothing that led me to believe anything different than what you told Kaczmarek and Ramsey."

"Who?"

"The detectives. You don't remember talking to them?"

"Oh. Right. I forgot their names. Guess I got bashed in the head harder than I thought."

The next few minutes were cloaked in silence.

Joe finished his breakfast.

Carly sipped her coffee.

Joe placed the empty container back into the plastic bag and grabbed his half-full cup as he stood up.

"Leave that on the chair," Carly said. "I'll throw it in the garbage later."

"Are you going to behave if I go?"

"I'm fine, Joe...really."

"I can stick around."

"You need to take care of the business at your condo."

Carly eased up off the sofa as he laid the bag on the chair.

Together they walked to the door.

"Now if you need anything, I want you to call me. Understand?"

"I'll have to. My car is still at the townhouse."

"You don't need to be driving."

"I know, but you *will* make sure to get it back to me, right?"

"As soon as I can."

Carly reached into the pocket of her slacks and pulled out her keys. As she handed them to Joe, she leaned forward and kissed him on the cheek.

"I can see why Joyce fell in love with you."

A surprise awaited Joe when he passed through the automatic glass doors of the Crimson Conch Condominiums. David was standing next to the building manager's office, talking on his phone. Seeing Joe, he ended the call.

"David, I thought you were working."

"I am. I..." The detective lowered his blue eyes, his apprehension unmistakable. "Care to take a ride? I could use some experienced assistance at a crime scene."

"Another one?"

"A pending case."

"Sure, let me check the office phone for messages first. There shouldn't be a problem."

"How's Carly? I mean, is she still being questioned by the sheriff's office?"

"No, she's home. Still a little shaky."

"I guess she's got a concussion, huh?"

Joe studied him. "She'll be okay as long as she follows the doctor's orders."

A meek grin shaped David's lips. "That should be interesting. Carly's her own woman.

She's never been one to..." His grin widened. "I guess I don't have to tell you."

Joe unlocked the office door and they went inside. Straight away he focused on the desk phone. No one had left a message. He checked the Post-it Notes stuck to the calendar covering the top of the desk. The tasks awaiting completion and correspondence to contractors were not a pressing concern.

"We're good to go."

After Joe locked the office door, he and David ambled to the parking lot and climbed into a dark blue sedan. He waited until David had steered the car onto Island Way.

"So what's the skinny on your case?"

"A twenty-seven-year-old woman was found dead in her apartment night before last," David began. "There was no break-in, and nothing was stolen."

"How was she killed?"

"She was shot once in the chest."

"Were there signs of a struggle?"

"Not a mark on her. And nothing in the apartment looked out of place. We think she might have known the killer."

"Any witnesses?"

"A neighbor heard the gunshot. He thought it was a car backfiring."

"He didn't bother to investigate?"

"Not at first. He was in bed and half-asleep. Then he heard a car start, and decided he'd better check it out. The car was gone by the time he got to the living-room window. When he stuck his head out to have a look around, he noticed that the victim's front door was slightly open."

"Was he the only one who heard anything?"

"The only one."

David turned off of Memorial Causeway at South Fort Harrison and drove three blocks. A left turn onto Druid Road led them to an apartment complex near Glen Oaks Park. Finding a vacant parking space wasn't difficult, but he was in no hurry to leave the car.

Joe shifted his eyes to a white door striped with yellow and black barricade tape, curious as to why David was hesitating.

"Shall we go inside?"

"Joe, I, uh...sure, I need to...sure."

David's odd behavior set Joe to thinking: Was he correct is

suspecting that the detective was part of a cover-up to protect Carly? Even if he were, why would he feel the need to form such an alliance with Carly?

After leaving the car, David unlocked the door and cleared away the barricade tape, allowing Joe to enter. No sooner had the retired detective set foot inside than he was struck by the abnormally clean living room.

This looks like a window display, he thought.

Plush white carpeting lay beneath an overstuffed white futon, twin white leather recliners, a chrome-framed coffee table with a glass top, and gleaming frosted walls. Evenly spaced pictures hung in chrome frames on the walls, along with a strangely out-of-place black fifty-five-inch high-definition television.

Joe stood awe-struck. "Is this the décor of the whole place?"

"Every room. I don't know how she kept it clean."

"I'd go snow-blind if I stayed in here very long. What's the victim's name?"

"Karen Bachmann. She's an investment counselor for Thomas Harper Financial."

"Where's the crime scene?"

"In the guest room." David pointed to a hallway on their right.

Joe started in that direction.

"Uh, there's something I'd like to show you first."

Joe turned around as David removed a latex examination glove from his coat pocket. As he pulled it on, he led Joe to a large chrome shelving unit containing four glass tiers. The shelves held several certificates of achievement and numerous photographs, all in chrome frames. On the top shelf sat a first-place award for a college debate team. On each side of the award sat a blank chrome picture frame.

David motioned to the frame on the right, a troubled expression etched on his face.

"Joe, I, uh...didn't exactly tell you the truth about why I wanted you to come here. This is a digital photo frame. It contains ten pictures that appear on a continuous loop. There's one, in particular, I'd like you to see."

He carefully reached behind the frame to turn it on. A photograph glowed into view. A beautiful young blond-haired woman stood in front of a mountainous villa, smiling at the camera.

Joe took a step forward to better see the image.

Five seconds later, another photo replaced the first—more affluent homes sitting along a coastline of iridescent blue water. A third photo appeared, followed by a fourth. When the fifth photo materialized, David reached behind the frame. The image remained frozen.

"Take a look at this, Joe."

The blond and a handsome man were holding each other, cheek to cheek, obviously mugging for the camera.

Joe leaned in closer and focused on the woman. "So that's Karen Bachmann."

"Right. And the guy with her is Tim Truffant."

Chapter 7

The photograph of the mystery woman in the arms of Tim Truffant left Joe speechless. It was obvious to him that Carly had seen it during the initial investigation two nights ago. Add that to her possession of the videos of Bachmann and Tim romping in the sack, and Carly sure looked guilty. *Hell hath no fury…* But a troubling thought entered Joe's mind: Why would Carly have told him about receiving the weekly videos if she *had* murdered Tim? Erasing all of them would have been the smart thing to do. Hearing David's heavy sigh brought Joe back to the moment.

"Joe, I really hate what I'm about to say, but I *have* to tell Ben and Ramsey about this."

"It wouldn't bother me if you waited a day or two. Tell them it slipped your mind or something."

"Would *you* believe me if I told you that?"

"Nope."

"Exactly. Besides, Ben knows me too well. And what would a day or two matter?"

"I see your point." Joe thought a moment. "Who discovered this photo first?"

"I did."

"And you pointed it out to Carly right away?"

"I had no choice. She made it clear in no uncertain terms how we would operate when I first became her partner."

Joe understood and appreciated the detective's situation. Trusting one's partner to do the right thing was imperative. Withholding anything, especially the truth, undermined the association.

"How did she react?"

"She didn't—initially. I think she was stunned. Then she started swearing."

"Did anyone hear her?"

"Only me."

"Did she threaten to do anything about it?"

"Her rant was directed at Bachmann."

"At Bachmann?"

"She was saying things like, 'I guess the blond bitch got what she deserved,' and 'When we catch the little whore's killer, I'm going to thank him.' She ended her tirade with 'I'll be so happy when Tim is out of my life.'"

"But she didn't say that *she* was going to get him."

"She didn't need to. I saw the look in her eyes."

Joe was now knee-deep in the proverbial quandary. Whether David knew about the videos or not, telling him about the one he'd seen would only aid in the case against Carly. David would be forced to admit to what he knew under oath. Worse, his knowledge of the videos supplied a motive for Carly to kill Karen Bachmann, as well as Tim. Along with David's testimony, she could be charged with two counts of premeditated murder.

"I hate being a rat, Joe, but I don't know what else to do."

Joe wore a stern expression. "You act like the good cop that you are and do what your conscience tells you to do."

David nodded and lowered his eyes.

"Is there anything else you want me to see in here?"

"No, that's it. Oh, there is something we intended to follow up on. When we checked Bachmann's phone, one number appeared more than a dozen times. It belongs to a guy named Rogan Cavanaugh. I'm going to pay him a visit later today."

"David, could I ask a favor of you? I need help in getting

Carly's car back to her apartment."

"No problem."

Neither of them moved right away. Joe eyed the young detective.

"David, do you think that Carly killed Tim?"

"Absolutely not."

Joe and David got Carly's car back to her by mid-afternoon. After returning her keys, Joe rode with him back to the Crimson Conch Condominiums.

David left to interview Rogan Cavanaugh.

Joe went to the office to address some of the responsibilities awaiting him. About to phone the yard maintenance company contracted to groom the grounds, he hesitated when his mind wandered back to his friend's predicament.

Carly, you are in one grand mess. And it's only going to get worse when Kaczmarek and Ramsey find out about the videos.

He leaned back and stared straight ahead. Even if he were investigating the murders of Tim Truffant and Karen Bachmann separately, he could easily formulate a theory of revenge. Carly had the means readily available to uncover the identity and residence of Bachmann. A confrontation led to an argument that led to murder. Bachmann's case being dropped into her lap was a simple twist of fate, or not, and presented the opportunity for a cover-up—if she was careful. Tim Truffant posed an easier problem to solve, and Carly had an explanation ready.

"Except for her back-up revolver being the murder weapon," Joe whispered. "She could have said that he attacked her and she was defending herself. Saying that a phantom knocked her out is pretty far-fetched." *And why kill Karen Bachmann? Why not use the videos to gain more leverage in the divorce?*

If Tim really *was* as materialistic as Carly indicated, then cavorting with Bachmann before the divorce was final was damned foolish. When, and if, they appeared before a judge,

Carly could legally take more than the usual fifty percent set down by Florida law. Tim may not have been able to keep it in his pants, but was he dumb enough to risk provoking his future ex-wife?

Joe sighed. He refused to believe that Carly was a murderer, and nothing else he was privy to made any sense. He lowered his eyes to the Post-it Note as he reached for the receiver to call the yard maintenance company. The phone rang and he jumped, laughing a second later before he answered.

"Maybe you can help me," the unfamiliar female voice said. "I'm trying to get in touch with Joseph Hampton."

Shock rocketed through Joe. Victoria Combes had always called him by his given name. "This is Joe Hampton."

"Joe! My goodness! You sound so different."

"So do you."

"You don't remember me, do you?"

"I'm afraid not."

"It's Martha Berkshire. Lionel and I used to live next door to you and Joyce in Philadelphia."

Joe's mind went blank. A flood of memories soon followed. The outgoing blond and her taciturn husband were occasional visitors to their home.

"Martha! What a surprise. How long has it been?"

"Too long! Lionel and I finally made it down to Florida for a vacation. I told him that we simply *had* to go to Clearwater Beach to see our good friend Joe Hampton."

"I'm happy you did." Joe rolled his eyes. The Berkshires were more Joyce's friends than his. He was indifferent. Holding a conversation with Lionel had been like talking to the stone statues on Easter Island. "How long will you be here?"

"Three weeks. We're renting a place right on the Gulf of Mexico, at the Tropical Sunset Condominiums. Do you know where it is?"

"I'm familiar with it."

"We looked at the Crimson Conch, but you're full up."

"Yes, people do like living here."

"Joe. I was sorry to hear that Joyce passed away. And I'm sorry we couldn't make it to the funeral. Lionel was ailing that day."

"Thank you, Martha. We had a good life together."

"Anyway, we can't wait to see you. Do you have plans for supper tonight?"

"Well, no, I don't, but—"

"Why don't you come by around seven o'clock. We can have a cocktail or five and chat a while. You can decide on the restaurant. I'm sure you know dozens of places."

"Well, okay."

"Good! We'll see you at seven o'clock. We're in unit seven-nineteen. Oh, and Lionel says hello."

Joe hung up the receiver and shook his head. *Wonderful!* he thought. *Supper with strangers. Almost strangers, anyway. I barely remember them.*

Setting to work on making the necessary phone calls, he hoped that Carly would be able to tell him more about what had happened in the next day or two. Planning for his fun-filled evening with the Berkshires would take up the rest of the day.

Chapter 8

Regret accompanied Joe to the Tropical Sunset Condominiums on the north end of the beach off Mandalay Avenue. Like so many others, the gargantuan building was an alluring seductress to those desiring a warmer climate. And with the Gulf of Mexico for a backyard, a different interpretation of a glowing western sky was on display every evening.

Hesitating in front of the tangerine door to unit seven-nineteen, he drew a breath and tried to settle into the right frame of mind.

Go ahead, Joe, he heard Joyce say.

Don't rush me.

They're our friends.

I haven't seen them in years.

They like you.

I should have told them I was sick.

Now, Joe.

All right.

Joe rang the doorbell, drawing another breath while attempting to smile. Hearing the door being unlocked and the deadbolt released, he stiffened.

Martha wasted no time in throwing open the door, then reached out to wrap her flabby arms around him.

"Oh, Joe, it's so wonderful to see you!"

Joe staggered a step backward, trapped in the stocky woman's bear hug. "Good to see you, Martha."

She held onto him as the door slowly closed behind her.

"Uh, how's Lionel doing?"

Martha released him, her blue eyes lacking enthusiasm. "Oh, his usual self. He never says more than ten words a day. Sometimes I have to poke him just to make sure he's alive."

Joe's smile took on life.

Martha's eyes were locked onto his.

"Shall we go inside?" he said.

Martha laughed—more a cackle. "Oh, my, yes!" She spun around and grabbed the doorknob. "Oh pizzlefritz! I forgot the door locks by itself." She punched the doorbell three times. Several seconds passed. "Come *on*, Lionel!" She punched it three more times.

Finally, the door opened.

A tall man, slight of build, stepped into the doorway, his full head of black hair graying at the sides, and brown eyes as dull as his demeanor.

"Evenin', Joe."

"Good evening, Lionel."

"Why don't ya come in and I'll fix ya a cocktail."

He turned around and released the door. Martha latched on to it before it closed.

"After you," Joe said.

Martha led him into a typical Florida-themed living room with powder blue walls, floral-print fabric furniture, and creamy-orange curtains. The sliding glass door to the balcony perfectly framed the blue-green Gulf of Mexico.

"Have a seat," she said, gesturing to a sofa on her left.

Lionel was standing a few feet away in front of a small mahogany table, holding a green liquor bottle. "Scotch-on-the-rocks for you, Joe?" he asked, already tilting the Dewar's.

"That'll be fine."

"So what have you been up to?" Martha inquired. "I'm sure there are plenty of goings-on at your condominium to keep you busy."

"That's true. With bingo and bridge and dancing in the Rec Room, not to mention a cookout once a month, I barely have time to rest."

"Oh, that's wonderful. I was worried you might be sitting around like a bump on a log like someone else I know."

"Here ya go, Joe," Lionel said, handing him a tumbler wrapped in a napkin.

Martha sat down on the other end of the sofa from Joe. Lionel took to a living room chair with his drink.

"We have so much planned for the next three weeks," Martha began. "I never realized there was so much to do in Clearwater, St. Petersburg, and Tampa. Maybe you could act as our tour guide."

Joe forced a tight smile. "I don't know. I'm the building manager at my condo. There's a lot of work to be done."

"Oh, my, you *do* stay busy." She proceeded to lay out their itinerary, step by step.

Joe quickly lost interest, tuning out her babbling, but kept the smile fixed on his face while nodding occasionally. He was concerned about Carly, not only her physical state, but her mental state as well. And as much as he balked at the idea of her being a murderer, a nagging feeling that refused to go away kept whispering that she might be. A trained professional didn't hesitate to pull the trigger. Carly was a true professional.

"So what's your final decision, Joe? Where are we going to eat?"

"Well, I...wasn't sure what type of cuisine you preferred."

"No fish," Lionel said.

"Okay, I know a quaint Italian restaurant in—"

"Nope! Gives me the shits."

"Lionel!" Martha scolded.

"Well, it does."

"Then how about a nice ribeye?"

Lionel didn't answer.

Martha expressed interest.

"They have other entrées besides steak. And it's not too far from here."

"That sounds wonderful. You boys see to your cocktails while I go to the little girls' room."

Lionel nodded as she scurried away.

Joe turned up his glass to finish his drink.

"So, what have you been up to, Lionel?"

"Nothin' much."

"How long have you been retired?"

"A little more'n four years."

This is going to be a long night, Joe thought.

Martha appeared from the hallway with a large brown purse dangling from her arm "I'm all set. Shall we go?"

Lionel poured down the rest of his drink, got up, and approached Joe.

Joe rose and handed him the tumbler.

He and Martha waited for Lionel to put the tumblers in the kitchen sink. Once he returned, they headed out for supper.

Martha maintained her incessant babbling from the condo to the Sand Key Bridge. At one point, Joe contemplated abandoning his car and jumping off.

In sight of the restaurant, she stopped talking as if a switch had been flipped. Lionel never said a word. They parked in the lot of a small strip mall, and joined the line of people waiting to get inside.

Not fancy in appearance, Backwaters stood at the end of a line of businesses. Notified of a twenty-minute wait prompted Martha to begin another barrage of prattle before they were seated. Once inside, she was silenced by a quaint setting of wooden tables and chairs that gave the eatery a homier feel. Joe asked that they be seated on a rear deck overlooking Clearwater Harbor. Across the water lay the community of Belleair.

"This is beautiful, Joe." Martha gushed. "I imagine there are places like this up and down the coast."

"All kinds for all tastes."

Their server took their drink orders and handed out the menus.

"What are you going to have, Lionel?" Martha quizzed.

"Joe's recommendation, the ribeye platter."

"And you, Joe?"

"I'm not sure." He pored over the selections. "One of my favorites is—"

He was interrupted by the tone of his cell phone, and quickly stuffed his hand into his pants pocket.

Martha studied the menu.

Lionel studied Joe.

"Joe, it's Carly."

"Is anything wrong?"

"I just remembered something...something that happened in the townhouse."

"Uh, I'm just about to have supper with friends from out of town. Can I call you later?"

"Oh! I'm sorry! Sure! I'm not going anywhere."

Joe ended the call and stuffed the phone back into his pocket.

"Is everything okay?" Martha asked.

"A friend wanted to talk. She...had an accident yesterday. I thought she might need my help." Joe shifted his attention to Lionel, whose lips hinted at a smirk.

"Does your friend live in your condominium?"

"No, she lives in Dunedin."

Martha glanced at her husband, whose expression was definitely noticeable.

"Is there a chance we could meet her? Maybe the four of us could do something together while we're here."

Joe's eyes left Lionel and went straight to Martha. "It's not that kind of...I mean, it's more of a...what I mean is she's a cop."

"Oh!"

Lionel's glee promptly vanished.

"It's complicated."

In an attempt to remain cordial, Joe did his best to appease the talkative Martha and reserved Lionel. After an hour that felt like many, they returned to the Tropical Sunset Condominiums. Declining an offer for another cocktail, Joe said goodbye and started his toward journey home. Mandalay Avenue was sparsely littered with traffic, affording him the opportunity to think.

Carly had sounded excited when she called. What concerned him was whether her recollection would help or hurt her. Mounting evidence was compounding her situation. Too much supposition could drag her down further.

The left turn off Memorial Causeway onto Island Way was accomplished with a minimum of thought or effort. The same was true of locating his spot in the Crimson Conch parking lot.

Still engaged in mental gymnastics as he neared the entrance to the building, Joe decided to call Carly before going inside. He hadn't gotten his hand into his pocket when his phone rang.

"Joe."

Her voice surprised him.

"I was just about to call you." He studied her in the dim illumination emanating from the lobby.

"I...could I stay with you tonight? I'm still a bit shaky and..."

"What's wrong?"

"About a half-hour after I called you, I got a text message."

"Another video?"

"No, an actual message." She brought her phone up close to her face, tapped it several times then held it at arm's length for him to see.

Joe squinted as he read: You're next.

Chapter 9

Joe could sense Carly's trepidation as they rode the elevator to the fourth floor. He found it unusual that the strong woman he had encountered when they first met now revealed a vulnerable side. Was it the loss of confidence or a principal sign of guilt? Or maybe the wound she had suffered was more severe than originally diagnosed.

After they entered his condo, he pointed to the green and blue-striped sofa while making certain that every curtain was drawn before joining her. Drained and beaten down best described his young friend, which made Joe very sad. Several moments of silence ensued. Then Carly sighed.

"Joe, I don't know what's going on. I can't seem to keep my thoughts straight. And now I've been threatened."

"You've suffered a concussion. It'll take some time to get squared away."

"And the threat? What's that all about?"

"You weren't able to trace the phone number?"

"I tried. No luck. It's probably a burner."

"A what?"

"A phone with pre-paid minutes. When the amount of time is depleted, you either buy more or toss it. They can't be traced."

"Have you given any thought as to who might be responsible?"

"No one comes to mind. Of course, lately when something comes to mind, it vanishes soon after."

Joe attempted to mirror her feeble smile.

"When you called earlier you said you'd remembered something that happened when you were in the bedroom with Tim."

Carly pinched up her face.

"Take your time. It'll come to you."

In an instant, her eyes widened. "I remember! As I was trying to wake Tim up, I caught a whiff of cologne. Men's cologne. Right before I got hit, I guess."

"Can you recall the scent? Do you know what kind it was?"

"No, but I'm certain it wasn't the kind Tim wore. And the scent was strong."

"In what way?"

"Like when someone uses too much."

"And that's the only time you noticed it? Not when you first came through the front door?"

"I don't think so."

"We need to notify Kaczmarek and Ramsey. This is important to your defense."

"The detectives, you mean?"

"See, your memory's coming back."

"I wish I knew the brand of cologne I smelled."

"We'll visit some department stores tomorrow. You can test a variety of brands, and maybe we'll get lucky."

"Thanks, Joe. This has been so frustrating. I've never been so off-balance and unsure in my life."

A sharp rapping on the door interrupted their conversation.

Joe rose from the sofa, checking the peephole when he reached the door. Grinning, he unlocked it and allowed the visitor to enter.

"David!" Carly shouted.

She jumped to her feet, hurried to her partner, and embraced him.

Joe's grin widened at the bewildered expression on the young detective's face.

"Does this mean we're engaged?" David whispered.

Carly released him, and stepped back. "I am so glad to see you. We need your help."

"We?"

"Why don't we sit down," Joe said. "Then you can tell David all about it."

The detectives set their eyes on each other.

"I have to tell you that I'm relieved you're here," David said. "I got worried when I stopped by your apartment and it was dark."

"I'm sorry. I called Joe and, uh..."

"I wanted to tell you what I learned about Rogan Cavanaugh."

"Who?"

"Rogan Cavanaugh. His phone number showed up in Karen Bachmann's call log."

"Oh, right. Our case. What did you find out?"

David glanced at Joe then back to her. "Why don't you go first."

Carly began by relaying the series of events, admitting her confusion and fear. Only after showing Joe one of the videos and receiving the threatening text message had she been able to recall the strong odor of cologne in Tim's bedroom.

David arched his eyebrows when she was done. "We need to contact Ben and Ramsey right away."

"That's what Joe said." Carly looked relieved that he believed her. "Now what about your interview with, uh..."

"Rogan Cavanaugh."

"Right."

"Well, you remember his number appeared multiple times on Bachmann's phone."

Carly nodded, without grimacing.

"He said he was a good friend of hers. He was concerned about her recent attraction to Tim."

"Is that what he said...attraction?" Joe asked.

"Yes."

Looks like she was more than attracted, Joe thought.

"He admitted that he had tried to persuade her to end the relationship, but she would have no part of it. When he persisted, she stopped taking his calls."

"How long has he known her?" Carly asked.

"Six years."

"And he claims that he's just a good friend?"

"Right."

"Had they dated before?"

"On and off is what he said."

Joe grinned.

Carly noticed. "Is something funny?"

"You're acting like your old self again."

She blinked twice. "I guess I am."

"Do you remember the digital photos we found in Bachmann's apartment?" David asked.

"Kind of."

"Cavanaugh said they were taken at an exclusive resort when Bachmann and Tim vacationed in Punta Mita. That's in Mexico."

Carly shrugged. "Tim never mentioned anything to me about a vacation. Of course, he never mentioned that he was screwing her, either."

David looked at Joe for one long second. He faced his partner, and sighed. "Carly, I believe there's enough reasonable doubt working in your favor, but the—"

"Reasonable doubt? I didn't kill anybody!"

"I never said that you did. But you have to tell Ben and Ramsey about the videos and your knowledge of that photo. Once they combine them with the existing evidence, you're not going to be sitting in a favorable light. I think it's time you considered getting a lawyer."

Joe nodded in agreement. "I don't like saying this, Carly, but from where I sit, the only thing working in your favor is the death threat."

Chapter 10

David left Carly and Joe, knowing that he had to surrender what had been discovered in Karen Bachmann's apartment to the sheriff's office the next day. He wanted to believe that his partner would do the right thing as well.

Joe offered Carly his bed, but she refused, having grown accustomed to the sofa during her previous stay. He gave her a pillow and a blanket, and retired to his bedroom, exhausted from his eventful evening. Tomorrow they would see about getting her an attorney. He didn't know a single one in Clearwater or the Tampa Bay area. He hoped that Carly was better informed. Tonight he would rest—or try.

Joe opened his eyes to darkness, which always unnerved him a bit when first waking up. Feeling like he hadn't slept at all, he lingered for a time, waiting for the alarm clock to release its loathsome reveille. Before long he became lucid and his head filled with the thoughts that had plagued him since David had taken him to Karen's apartment. In one sense he enjoyed being back in the game again, especially dealing with a mystery such as this. It kept his mind active, made him feel useful, and what better reward than helping a friend? And yet, the game had worn him out, used up the best of his years, and corrupted his belief that not everyone possessed a dark side. The love and devotion of Joyce had saved him. When he'd retired, he'd relished the dream of the years they would spend together. As sometimes happens, fate had a different plan. Her untimely death was unforeseen. After that he'd drifted in purgatory, waiting to die, wanting to die, until Carly walked into his life, bringing meaning and purpose with her.

Joe rolled over, sat up, and reached for the alarm clock to relieve it of its duty. Next, he donned a pair of khaki trousers and a forest green polo shirt, skipping his socks and shoes.

Passing the sofa on his way to the kitchen, he glanced down at Carly. She was lying on her left side, wearing only yellow panties and a black T-shirt. She'd removed her blue jeans and hung them over the living room chair. Her sneakers sat side by side on the floor. He could tell that she'd had a fitful night. Part of the blanket lay across her legs. The rest was draped over the side of the sofa and crumpled on the floor.

Joe walked around to the front of the sofa, noticing her automatic on the coffee table, and picked up the blanket. Spreading his arms wide, he covered her with it then moved quietly to the kitchen to make coffee.

Moonlight pouring through the kitchen window yielded enough light for him to locate the coffeemaker. As he pressed the button to bring it to life, a litany of faces took shape in his mind: Carly and David, Kacmarek and Ramsey, Tim and Karen Bachmann, Karen and… He didn't know what Rogan Cavanaugh looked like. The faces began to fade. What was it about David's recounting of his interview with Bachmann's faceless friend that was bothersome?

By his own admission Cavanaugh had dated Bachmann on and off. But that wasn't the burr rankling Joe.

He tried to persuade her to end her relationship with Tim, but she wanted no part of it. "And that's when she stopped taking his calls," he whispered.

Allowing the words to settle a moment, he wondered if Cavanaugh was the killer. Cavanaugh probably had a key to

Bachmann's apartment after knowing her for six years—or he'd had one made. And she might have had a key to Tim's townhouse, since she and Tim had gotten real cozy. How simple it would be for Cavanaugh to find that key once he'd killed her. Overpowering Tim would have been easy, if Tim was already drunk. Putting a gun to his head and forcing him to drink and then to call Carly to come over wouldn't have been difficult, either. Once Tim passed out, Cavanaugh baited the trap, and waited. When Carly arrived, Cavanaugh knocked her out, noticed the back-up revolver strapped to her ankle, and used it, instead of his own gun, to kill Tim. Bachmann is already dead. Carly is framed for Tim's murder. Cavanaugh walks away clean. Game. Set. Match.

"The videos of Bachmann and Tim had been part of the trap. But how did Cavanaugh get them? And how did he get Carly's phone number before killing Tim?"

The aroma of coffee floated on the air as he mulled over the latest possibilities.

From out of the darkened living room, Carly appeared, yawning beneath drowsy eyes.

"Good morning, Joe. Coffee smells good."

Joe reached for a second mug and set it on the counter. "How did you sleep?"

"Not very well. I couldn't seem to shut my brain off."

It was when she yawned again and stretched that Joe made a startling discovery. He lowered his eyes to the floor.

"Shall I pour, Sir?"

He jerked his eyes up. "Uh, sure, but would you put your pants on first."

Carly looked down, then quickly back at him. "Oops! Guess I'm not awake yet." She spun around and disappeared into the darkness. A minute later she came back. "Sorry, Joe, I guess I wasn't thinking."

Joe had filled the mugs and slid one in her direction. "Sugar is on the counter. I don't have any milk."

"Thanks. Black is fine."

"We think alike."

He watched her carefully.

"I can really use this."

"I can't get going without it." Joe took a long drink.

"I could use a shower. How about I buy you breakfast after I get cleaned up."

"Sound good to me."

"I brought some extra clothes with me. I need to run down to my car."

Joe remembered the ominous text message and set his mug on the counter.

"You finish your coffee and jump in the shower. I'll go get your things."

"That's okay. I can do it."

"No, I insist."

He held out an opened hand.

She dug into the pocket of her blue jeans, pulled out her keys, and handed them to him.

"Let me go put my shoes on."

Joe ambled to his bedroom to throw on his favorite black running shoes. When he returned to the hallway, Carly was standing by the bathroom door.

"I'll be right back," he said.

Later that morning found them at Kohl's in the Men's Department examining the wide variety of cologne. Carly sighed, knowing the task of identifying a particular fragrance could be discouraging. She drew a breath, selected a sample bottle of Dolce & Gabbana Light Blue, and sprayed it on her hand.

"That's not it."

Kenneth Cole Signature came next.

"Nope."

She moved on to Mont Blanc Emblem.

"Not even close, but I would jump the bones of a guy who was wearing this."

Joe chuckled.

Five more samples failed the test.

"I don't know. This hit or miss method could take the rest of the day."

"Did you think it was going to be easy?"

"No, but I was hoping we might get lucky."

Joe eyed the bottles. "Now where have I heard that before?"

"You said it last night."

Joe shifted his gaze to his beleaguered friend. "Your memory is getting better. Now keep trying."

As Carly picked up another bottle, Joe heard the annoying tone of his cell phone. He retrieved it from his pants pocket, not bothering to check the caller I.D.

"Joe, it's David."

"How goes it?"

"I've been better. Say, is Carly with you?"

"Yes, do you need to speak with her?"

Carly stopped sniffing her hand and looked at him.

"Not really. I came by her apartment to check on her. When she wasn't here...well, anyway, I just got a call from Cliff Parton. He works in Homicide with Carly and me. He was called to the Tropical Sunset Condos on the north end of Clearwater Beach early this morning."

An all too familiar fear raced through Joe.

"A couple was found dead on the beach. When Parton was searching their rental, he came across a slip of paper with the phone number for the Crimson Conch and the name Joe on it. By any chance do you know some people from Pennsylvania named Berkshire?"

Joe winced, and shook his head. "They're friends of mine. I had supper with them last night."

"Would you mind driving over there and talking to Parton? I'm sure he would appreciate your help."

"Yeah...sure."
"I'll let him know you're coming. And I'm sorry, Joe."
Joe pushed his phone into his pocket and hung his head.
"What's wrong, Joe?" Carly asked.
"I'll tell you on the way."

Chapter 11

Guilt was an unusual emotion plaguing Joe of late. No important responsibility had been shirked or steadfast rule broken. His only sin had been dreading entertaining far-removed acquaintances. Yet, here he was, torturing himself for his failure to protect them. The Berkshires deserved better. He had failed them.

"Are you all right, Joe?" Carly asked.

"I'm managing."

"I'm sorry about your friends."

"They were Joyce's friends. I barely knew them."

"It still hurts though, doesn't it?"

"I feel like I let them down…let her down."

"You're being too hard on yourself."

Joe let her comment slide as he steered his Toyota onto Mandalay Avenue. In Philadelphia he had earned a reputation as an outstanding crime-solver. He hadn't enjoyed all the celebrity that came with it, but it was hard to let go. The "old itch" to solve a mystery came and went in his winter years, but to overlook an obvious possibility at any time was inexcusable in his book. He should have realized that the death threat to Carly would have affected him as well. As always, there were other possibilities. He could be wrong.

"This is difficult for you, I know, but you can't protect everyone."

Joe didn't answer.

"I got that one out of the rookie patrolman's handbook."

The hint of a smile creased his lips.

"I know that this is, most likely, a random killing," he said. "They were at the wrong place at the wrong time. But where we're heading is close to where Rusty Goodfellow was found. And you know me, I don't believe in coincidences."

"That's right. We never positively identified who killed him. David still thinks that Victoria Combes and her daughter, Cecily, tag-teamed him."

"I agree," Joe said, envisioning the mother-daughter serial killers.

"But, Joe—and I don't mean to dwell on the subject—Cecily is dead, and her mother is in jail. If ever there was an argument for coincidence, it's now."

Joe fell silent again. His reference to Rusty Goodfellow had been an intentional act of deceit to lead Carly away from what was really bothering him. Like the videos Carly had received, was the killing of Martha and Lionel an attempt to lure him into a trap? Was the mastermind one and the same? But how would he know about the couple from Pennsylvania? Unless...

Bohenia Circle North appeared, and Joe steered into the curving left turn. The short stretch of road was a section of a larger arch that bulged out east of Mandalay Avenue and circled back to Eldorado Avenue.

Police and Criminal Analysis Unit vehicles formed a barricade across the front of the beach access footbridge.

Joe parked a half-block away, then he and Carly left the car and began to walk in the direction of the access.

The patrolman standing guard on the sidewalk wore a wary expression as they neared.

Here we go again, Joe thought.

Once they stepped onto the sidewalk, the patrolman exhaled relief.

"Sergeant Truffant. It's been a while."

Carly smiled. "Yes, it has. Officer Wyman, this is Joe

Hampton."

The young man extended his right hand.

Joe shook it.

"We need to speak with Detective Parton."

"Down at the end on the right," Wyman said. He nodded, and moved from in front of the bridge.

This is too beautiful a day to be investigating a murder, Joe thought. *But what day is a good day*?

Criminal analysis technicians milled about in a section of beach populated with small sand dunes and scrub brush. Two men in plain clothes stood apart from the others.

Carly led Joe to the shortest of the pair, whose rumpled brown suit perfectly complemented his thinning, disheveled brown hair. He turned and nodded as they approached.

"Sergeant."

"How's it going, Parton?"

"Same shit, different day." He eyed Joe.

"This is Joe Hampton. He knew the victims."

"Oh, right, Sizemore said you'd be coming. Sorry for your loss."

Joe nodded, and looked beyond him at the Gulf. He tried to recall the first time he and Joyce had taken in the splendor of the blue-green gem and imagined the sensation the Berkshires must have felt at their first glimpse—Martha, anyway. Too bad their first glimpse turned out to be their last.

"How were they killed?" he asked.

"Both shot in the chest at close range. One round each."

"Witnesses?"

"None so far."

"Any clues?"

"We're still looking. Say, Mr. Hampton, outside of the usual information, what can you tell me about them?"

"It's Joe, and, unfortunately, not very much."

Joe passed along what little he knew about the couple, feeling their murder would be added to the list of unsolved cases involving other unfortunate visitors who never made it back home.

"We'll do our best to get the bastard who did this, Joe," Parton said. "And thanks, again, for your help."

Joe stared hard at the cordoned-off patch of sand where Martha and Lionel had been discovered.

"You can take a look inside their condo if you like," Parton added.

Joe turned around and started toward the footbridge.

"Thanks, Parton," Carly said, and trailed behind him.

She caught up to him in the middle of the bridge and matched his stride. She waited until they were a good distance away from Officer Wyman.

"Mind telling me what's bothering you, Joe?"

"I already did."

"That's part of it. Now tell me the rest."

She must be feeling better, he thought. He didn't answer until they got into his car.

"Tell me something, Carly. In your time on the force, have you ever had to deal with so many murders in such a short amount of time?"

"This is a first, but I've learned that just when I think I've seen it all, something unusual happens."

"Karen Bachmann, Tim, and now the Berkshires. All were shot in the chest."

Carly didn't answer.

"Are you with me?"

"Yes, uh…I…it just hit me that Tim is really dead."

Joe paused until after he'd turned onto Gardenia Street. "We can talk about this at another time."

Carly sniffed. "No, no, go ahead. I want to hear what you have to say."

Joe laid out his theory of how she was set up, adding that the death of the Berkshires was somehow connected.

"But, Joe," Carly began, "I still don't see how one has anything to do with the other."

"This may sound far-fetched, but it could be a message...like the last one you got."

Carly pinched up her face. "Threatening to kill you because you're my friend?"

"More like a warning not to get involved."

"Any idea who it might be?"

"I was counting on you for some names."

Silence rode with them down Mandalay Avenue, through the roundabout, and onto Memorial Causeway.

"It has to be someone who knows me fairly well," Carly finally said.

"Or knows how to find out about you."

"That would take some doing. Hacking into the police database isn't easy."

"I was leaning more toward it being on a personal level."

Carly's mouth fell open as she turned to him. "You can't mean David."

"How about Rogan Cavanaugh?"

"Karen Bachmann's friend?"

"Cavanaugh told David that he'd tried to persuade Karen to break it off with Tim."

"He doesn't know me...or you."

"Tim did. If Cavanaugh killed Tim, he could have gotten your number from Tim's phone. Just like he found out about me from your phone after he knocked you out. A little basic computer research would provide enough answers."

Joe made the easy left turn onto Island Way.

Carly drew a breath. "If it was Cavanaugh, how did he know where to find the Berkshires?"

"Maybe he's been stalking me...and you. I don't know what he looks like. Do you?"

Carly's pained expression led Joe to believe that his theory was not only viable, but troubling. He knew what she was thinking. She would contact David and get a complete description of Cavanaugh. Then she and her partner would have a chat with him.

Joe drove straight to his parking space in the lot of the Crimson Conch Condominiums, and together they slowly headed toward the entrance. Carly glanced over her shoulder several times, as did he, making certain they would not fall victim to being surprised.

Passing through the automatic glass doors, Joe veered off to the building manager's office.

"Let me check for messages before we head up."

About to slide his key into the lock, he froze. A slip of paper was jammed near the doorknob between the edge of the door and the frame. He removed the note, carefully unfolding and reading it, then looking at Carly.

"What does it say?" she asked.

He held out the paper between two fingers.

She removed it, and read: Keep your distance!

Chapter 12

Joe and Carly didn't say a word to each other for five minutes. For reasons unknown, reasons originating in someone's troubled mind, they were being stalked.

Her head much clearer now, Carly tried to rationalize why she had been drawn into the affairs of her soon-to-be ex-husband. And why was she being marked for death?

Aside from the mounting guilt over the murder of the Berkshires, Joe was struggling to piece together a plan to keep Carly alive. First, though, he knew he must contact David.

"You can stay here as long as you like," he finally said. "In fact, I insist on it."

"Thanks, Joe, but you've done enough. I can't allow you to get involved any further. Someone wants to kill me, and he'll kill you if you get in the way."

"Too late. I'm already involved. We need to contact Clearwater P.D. to get some protection for you. Then we need to bring David in on this."

"I'll call him right now and tell him to get over here."

Before she could retrieve her phone, a forceful knocking rattled the door.

Carly and Joe locked eyes for several seconds, curious and confused.

Joe stood up and went to the door and peered through the peephole.

"It's Kaczmarek and Ramsey."

He unlocked the door and opened it a quarter of the way.

"Joe, we're looking for Carly Truffant," Kaczmarek said. "Have you seen her?"

Joe peered over his shoulder. "Yes, she's here."

Carly got to her feet, unsure as to the purpose for their calling.

"May we come in?"

Joe opened the door wider, and the detectives stepped inside.

After a few awkward seconds, Ramsey said, "Carly Truffant, you're under arrest for the murder of Timothy Truffant."

Carly was stunned, glancing at Joe while being advised of her rights.

A solemn Ramsey then moved behind Carly, pulled her arms together behind her back, and locked the handcuffs around her wrists.

Joe's mind was already at work. He'd scrapped all plans to protect his friend, and started to devise a means to raise her bail—if bail was allowed. First, he would call David, tell him what had happened then go about finding a good lawyer. Once those needs were satisfied, he would go after Rogan Cavanaugh.

David moaned when Joe told him that Carly had been arrested.

"I figured this was going to happen the minute I told Ben about the photo in Bachmann's apartment. And when Carly showed him the videos she was sent, I knew that would cap it."

"She, uh, never showed him the videos."

"What!"

"She went with me to the other crime scene."

"Your friends?"

"There's been another development."

Joe made him aware of their search for a certain brand of cologne and the note he'd removed from the door to his office as business manager.

"From the tone of the note, it sounds as though someone

knows a lot about Carly...and you."

"It would seem so."

"But why would Carly remember something as nondescript as the aroma of smell-good?" David wondered aloud.

"She didn't say. She *did* say it wasn't anything that Tim wore."

"I guess some of the things we notice about women would seem odd to them, too."

"Was Cavanaugh wearing cologne when you interviewed him?"

"As a matter of fact he was...a lot of it."

"Do you know what kind?"

"I don't pay attention to colognes, Joe. I wear Aramis. That's all I know."

"But if you smelled it again, you *would* recognize it, right?"

"Probably, but I don't have time to—"

"David, give me a description of him."

Joe could hear him flipping through the pages of his notepad.

"He has wavy, auburn hair that sits close to his head, and green eyes. He's about six feet tall, fair-skinned, and weighs about two-thirty, two-forty, I'd say. You're not planning on paying him a visit, are you?"

"I think he's the one behind all of this. The murders, the videos, the messages. Everything."

"But we have no proof."

"Does he have an alibi?"

"No, he said he stays home a lot. I'm not so sure he needs one, anyway. Nothing about either murder points to him."

"What about jealousy as a motive?"

"I thought about that, but, as I said, we don't have any proof."

"I'm retired, David. I don't need any proof."

"Joe! I *can't* let you do it!"

"Let me do what? Talk to someone who inquired about residency at the Crimson Conch?"

"Joe, you know that's not true!"

"Find Carly a good lawyer."

He ended the call, and sat down on the sofa, pondering the steps he would need to take to locate Cavanaugh. There were plenty of search engines to choose from, and some of the websites listed were free. If he had to, a call to some old friends back home would get him the answers he needed.

Shifting in his seat as he debated whether to take a weapon with him when he confronted Cavanaugh, something poked him in the butt. Annoyed at the nuisance, he shifted again and tried to focus. When the object dug into him once again, he grumbled and shoved his hand between the cushion and padded back.

I don't believe it. He slowly removed the object. In his hand was a shiny, black Sig Sauer 226. *Must be Carly's service automatic. But why would she leave it here*? The answer was quick in coming. *Because she knew I might need it...especially if I went after Cavanaugh.*

Joe smiled as he slid the automatic back into its hiding place. His next stop would be his building manager's office to use the computer.

Chapter 13

Joe's search of the Tampa Bay area for anyone named Rogan Cavanaugh yielded three results: an eighty-four-year-old retiree living in Temple Terrace, a ten-year-old girl in Spring Hill, and a thirty-five-year-old mechanic in Clearwater. Barring the chance that the information was outdated, one of a block of houses on Satsuma Street would be his destination. The next question was when.

With no idea of where Cavanaugh worked or his working hours, Joe figured he wouldn't be home until later in the day or early evening. Scoping out the neighborhood might not be a bad idea. A leisurely drive-by to identify the house would attract less attention during the second go-round—nothing was more conspicuous than a house-hunter driving slowly. If, by chance, the man *was* home, then Joe would initiate a meeting right then and there.

Upon learning that Cavanaugh was a mechanic, Joe's analytical mind presented him with a puzzling question. Why would a person like Karen Bachmann, who possessed such an elegant, yet singularly-themed apartment, rub elbows with a roll-up-your-sleeves kind of guy like Cavanaugh? Did they happen to meet at some black-tie affair where the truth lay hidden under layers of sophistication? Was he the type to put on airs, or she the type to go slumming? And what *was* her occupation? David had told him, but he couldn't remember.

Curious, he thought. *But those couples only exist in the movies. Maybe they were childhood friends.*

He quickly dismissed the notion. Boys and girls that grew up together most often got married. Men and women being "just friends" were rare. An old sensation rose up as he shut down the office computer.

For someone who's retired, it certainly feels like I'm back in the game.

He found no humor in his observation. Getting back into the game was how he would exonerate Carly.

Joe left his condo a little before one p.m. Once on the mainland, he turned south on Fort Harrison and proceeded to Lakeview Road, a preferred alternative to the other arteries through Clearwater. He headed east at an easy pace, knowing there was no need for urgency. A procedure had to be followed regarding Carly's incarceration, and he wasn't quite certain when she would be brought before a judge. But he *was* certain that locating Cavanaugh's house was his first priority, and if a meeting didn't happen, he would drive to the county jail and request a visit with his friend.

For reasons unknown to him, the traffic was heavier today and slowed to below thirty miles an hour. The slower pace was actually a benefit, making it easier to turn onto Highlands Avenue. The bulk of the traffic behind him, Joe relaxed and focused on the road signs until he spied Satsuma Street.

Easing his Toyota around the corner, he took a deep breath.

If he's home, I'm going in, he thought.

A skinny, shirtless man mowing his yard glanced at Joe as he drove by. The rest of the homes were without activity, some without cars or trucks in the driveways. The corridor of houses seemed endless. Then he caught sight of an unremarkable, sun-bleached tan dwelling.

That's it!

He slowed his car to carefully study it. The garage door was down and the curtains in the picture window drawn.

At least I know where he lives.

The end of the block brought him to Lake Drive and led him back to Lakeview Road.

Instead of joining the mania of commuters in the race on U.S.19, Joe chose Keene Road as his route. He would then take East Bay Drive to 49th Street to pursue his desire to visit Carly at the county jail.

Lost in thought as he crossed Nursery Road, Joe didn't notice the dark blue sedan that had been following him for a block. When he finally glanced in his rearview mirror and saw the red and blue lights flashing from inside the sedan's grill, he turned onto the first street he came to, Faulds Road.

I don't know what this is all about.

He rolled down the window before bringing his car to a halt, sliding both hands to the top of the steering wheel. Glancing in the side-view mirror, he saw that the driver approaching him was not in uniform, and waited to be addressed.

"Joe, what the hell are you doing?"

Joe snapped his head around. "David! I...what're *you* doing here?"

"I asked you first."

"I was going to the county jail to see if they would allow me to visit with Carly."

David sighed, and looked to his left down the road. "Mind if I get in? I want to talk to you."

"Sure."

The detective rounded the rear of the car, opened the door, and slid into the passenger seat. He picked up staring down the road.

"I know where you've been, Joe, and I told you not to go there."

"Go where?"

David slowly brought his head around and narrowed his

steel-blue eyes. "Cut the shit! We're watching Cavanaugh's house! That's why I told you to stay away!"

"So you think he's the killer?"

"Of Bachmann and Truffant, anyway. I don't know about your friends."

"Why didn't you tell me?"

"Even a fool can see how you feel about Carly. And she feels the same way about you. You're too personally involved, Joe, and you need to stay out of it."

A slow burn began to consume Joe. He didn't appreciate someone dictating what he should do when it came to his friends—not even the police.

David's eyes softened. "Ben and I worked out a plan. We had Carly arrested to protect her...for her own good."

"Why the hell did you do that? She's smarter than both of you. She could have figured a way to draw out Cavanaugh."

"Come on, Joe, she's not herself and you know it. That crack on the head scrambled her brain."

"She was coming around. Any fool could see it."

David's eyes lit up. "So what was I supposed to do? Wait until she got back on track? You saw the text message! Cavanaugh wants to kill her!"

"We can protect her!"

"We? Are you listening to yourself, Joe? As you so often remind us, you're retired!

We *are* protecting her by locking her up!"

By now Joe was incensed. "Well, you're wrong!"

David snatched the handle and shoved the door open. "That's not your decision to make! Stay out of it, Joe!" He swung around, kicked his feet to the ground, and pulled himself out before slamming the door.

Still angry, Joe waited until the detective was out of sight before pointing his car back to Keene Road. He continued south to Belleair Road, making a turn to the west with the idea of returning to South Fort Harrison.

Why are you so angry, Joe?

This is not the time, Joyce.

He's right, isn't he?

No, he's not.

Carly would have forced that man's hand and you know it.

Joyce, please!

She's hardheaded...like you.

Joe was struggling with short, heavy breaths when he caught the red light at Missouri Avenue. He didn't like being wrong, had a hard time admitting it, and, sometimes, refused to admit it.

"I've got a wet-behind-the-ears punk trying to tell me what to do," he mumbled.

Something about the black Chevy Silverado that crossed the intersection in front of him caught his eye. That something was the red-haired driver with a tattoo sleeve covering his right arm, which was draped over the steering wheel.

Cavanaugh!

Joe checked for oncoming traffic then turned right in pursuit of the truck. Careful not to appear anxious by closing in too fast, he left a comfortable cushion between them.

The redhead surprised Joe when he jumped on the brakes and turned onto Bellevue Boulevard without using a directional light—an all-too-common practice among some drivers.

Motoring at an even pace on the quiet stretch of road brought them to a familiar sight—Lakeview Road. Joe waited ten counts before following the man, praying that the truck was heading straight for Satsuma Street.

A short time later, Joe eased to a halt in front of the house on Satsuma Street with a black Chevy Silverado in the driveway. He got out of his car and took his time getting to the front door, still doing his best to control his anger. He rapped hard on the blanched, cracked mahogany door three times, and backed up two steps on the walkway. A man with red hair, a freckled, pock-marked face, and a half-finished cigarette stuck in the right side of his mouth answered.

"Whadduh you want?"

"Rogan Cavanaugh! It is *so* nice to meet you."

"Who the hell are you?"

"I'm a friend of the woman you've been harassing."

The redhead's green eyes caught fire. "I don't know what you're talkin' about!"

"And I know what you did to Karen Bachmann and Tim Truffant."

"Go fuck yourself, asshole!"

Joe laughed, then slowly let his amusement fade to a frown. "Bother her again, and I guarantee you'll wish you'd died at birth, you son of a bitch!"

"You keep your distance, you old shithead!"

Joe paused, stared, and took a step forward. "First and last warning, Punk Boy."

Showing Cavanaugh his back, he strode to his car, knowing he'd gotten the best of the mechanic.

"Keep your distance," he whispered.

Chapter 14

Confronting a suspected murderer wasn't the smartest thing Joe had ever done, particularly at his age, but it was, by far, not the dumbest, either. He'd stood toe-to-toe with a few of them while on the force in Philadelphia. Ability, skill, and plain old luck had seen him through some tough scrapes—when he was younger. Now, as the pride of standing tall in a game of one-upmanship started to wear off, he knew he would have to take a smarter tack when Cavanaugh came calling. And the redhead *would* be calling. His kind couldn't control their rage—especially after being called out by an old man. But Carly was safe. That was the most important issue at the moment. He would deal with David later in a more relaxed and civilized manner.

Joe tried not to laugh when he neared the entrance to the Crimson Conch. "David will be furious when he finds out what I did," he whispered.

As the "swoosh" of the automatic doors closing sounded behind him, Joe noticed a man rounding the corner into the hall. A second later, the man stuck his head back into the lobby.

"Henry, were you looking for me?" Joe asked.

The bald-headed man clad in a white, short-sleeved Chambray shirt and pastel yellow shorts walked up to him.

"The Rec Room is locked. The boys and I need to set up the tables and chairs for bridge tonight."

"Sorry, it slipped my mind. I'll get the key from the office."

"Thanks, Joe."

Henry struggled around and headed to the hallway, the brown leather sandals strapped to his white-socked feet slapping against the linoleum floor.

Joe opened the office door and went inside, spying the ring of keys laying on the desk. When he reached down to grab them, he saw the missed-call light flashing on the desk phone.

Probably one of the contractors with some bad news, he thought.

He picked up the receiver and punched the button to listen to the message.

"Hi, Joe, it's Martha. I just wanted to tell you how much we enjoyed visiting with you. And the restaurant was simply marvelous. Even Lionel said he liked it, and for him that's saying a lot. It's such a beautiful night that we've decided to go for a walk on the beach later. I hope we can see you again before we leave. Goodbye, Joe."

Joe cradled the receiver and lowered his eyes to the desk. Goodbye was right. He'd never see the Berkshires again. The guilt about Carly's arrest, which had been displaced by the elation he was feeling over having enraged Rogan Cavanaugh, returned like a crippling blow from a sledge hammer.

He picked up the keys, looked one last time at the phone, and left the office for the Rec Room.

Two hours later, Joe was still despondent over hearing the message from Martha. Brief periods of anger distracted him from his sorrow. He knew that Rogan Cavanaugh was behind the murders—*all* of them. His inability to prove it was the reason for his torment.

"Come out of hiding and face me, you son of a bitch!" he whispered. "Face me so I can kill you!"

A knock on the door sent icy spurs tumbling down his spine. He reached under the sofa cushion and pulled out Carly's Sig

Sauer.

Ask and it will be given to you, he thought.

He got to his feet and moved quickly to the door, taking care to peer through the peephole.

Ben Kaczmarek and Kathleen Ramsey waited in the hall.

Joe hurried back to the sofa, shoved the automatic under a cushion, and returned to the door, fixing a smile on his face.

"Detective Kaczmarek...Detective Ramsey...to what do I owe the pleasure of your company?"

The detectives were not so cordial.

"May we come in?" Kaczmarek asked.

"Certainly."

Joe opened the door wider, and gestured into the room with his right hand. Another chill descended when both detectives took seats on his sofa, Ramsey the closest to where he'd stashed Carly's automatic.

"Joe," Ben began, "David told us about your going to see Rogan Cavanaugh earlier today. Both times. He's very upset with you."

"I imagine he is, but that's not the reason you stopped by, is it?"

"Hardly. What David told you is true. We *did* arrest Carly to protect her." Kaczmarek sighed. "But after looking at the videos she received, along with the evidence we have so far, we're going to be formally charging her soon."

"She showed you the videos? Does she have a lawyer?"

"She voluntarily surrendered them."

"We advised her of her right to counsel," Ramsey said. "The union representative who was present agreed that she should get a lawyer, but she refused."

Joe lowered his eyes to the floor, amazed that Carly had waived her right to legal assistance. If she had ever needed help, it was now.

"Wait here. There's something I want you to see."

Joe went to the dresser in his bedroom, pulled open the second drawer, and slid his hand under a stack of T-shirts. Locating the slip of paper he'd hidden there, he shut the drawer and returned to the living room. Before he sat down, he handed the paper to Kaczmarek.

"Keep your distance," Kaczmarek said, passing the note to Ramsey. "What does it mean?"

"It's warning from Cavanaugh."

"How do you know?"

"When I was at his house, I...advised him to stay away from Carly."

"How did he respond to your *advice*?"

"He said, quote, 'You keep your distance, you old shithead,' unquote."

"He said exactly those words."

"I'll swear to it under oath."

Kaczmarek paused, eyeing Joe for one long minute. "When did you receive this warning note?"

"This morning...before you took Carly away."

"Why didn't you mention it then?" Ramsey asked.

"I wasn't sure."

"That could be considered withholding evidence."

"I don't see how. The message was intended for me personally. I don't have anything to do with your case, or any case for that matter. Unless you believe it was Cavanaugh that killed Tim Truffant."

Kaczmarek grinned. "You're a pretty smart guy, Joe."

"Look, I know I overstepped my bounds by going to see Cavanaugh, but Carly didn't kill her husband, and she didn't kill Karen Bachmann."

Ramsey shifted on the sofa. Joe's eyes darted to her as he swallowed.

"We understand some friends of yours were murdered," she said. "Do you believe this note and their killing are connected?"

"I most certainly do."

"Can you prove it?" Kaczmarek asked.

“I have a plan that might work. You won’t like it. Carly and David won’t like it. And a smart lawyer might twist it in a different direction so it looks like entrapment.”

The detectives remained silent.

Joe leaned back in his chair. “A fellow I met when I first moved here told me that the only way to catch a shark is to use the right kind of chum.”

Chapter 15

The plan Joe relayed to the detectives was simple. He would ignore the warning to keep his distance and continue to pester Rogan Cavanaugh until his aggravating compelled the mechanic into an act of stupidity. The police would take care of the rest.

"You're right, Joe, I don't like it," Kaczmarek said.

"The same goes for me," Ramsey said.

"And I don't want to hear anymore," Kaczmarek added.

He nodded to Ramsey, and they rose from the sofa.

Ramsey handed Joe the slip of paper. "I have a feeling you're going to need this."

Joe took the note and saw them to the door.

Kaczmarek paused and faced him. "For the record, and for what it's worth, I'm asking you not to do follow through with your plan. Carly and David are quite fond of you. If anything were to happen, they would be devastated."

"I appreciate that, Ben, but Carly needs help *now*."

Ramsey stared at him a second before she and Kaczmarek started down the hall.

Joe closed the door and leaned against it.

And avenging Martha and Lionel needs to be swift, he thought.

Joe felt a pang of hunger. Admitting to Kaczmarek and Ramsey, and to himself, that he was going to take action had temporarily relieved him of all sorrow and guilt. After deciding what he wanted to eat, he headed for the condominium office to tie up a few loose ends. When finished, he decided to take a look at those new-fangled prepaid cell phones—"burners," Carly had called them. A smile spread across his face. Rogan Cavanaugh had no idea of the trouble that was coming his way.

Finding a telephone number for his nemesis proved easier than the first few steps out of bed each morning. Not having to involve his Pennsylvania friends in this undertaking brought him great pleasure.

Next in line was the purchase of a phone. Nothing fancy, he figured. No inordinate amount of minutes or the latest bells and whistles. For him, the function of sending and receiving text messages was the first and foremost requirement. Searching online, a low-priced model caught his attention right away: The Cendar PCS Mercury 7 was the ideal tool needed to carry out his plan. The strengths of the New Age gadget were its "lightning" 5G speed, and easy approach to messaging.

Everything today's grandparents need to stay in touch with their millennial grandchildren, he thought. "Cool!"

A trip to Best Buy in the morning was first on his to-do list. Right now, though, he needed to set up a secure position in the building as a sentry post.

He knew the Gentry's on the third floor were traveling, gone for at least a month they had told him, and being the building manager permitted him access to everyone's home. The balcony of their corner unit overlooked the parking lot. Not all of the property could be seen, but most of it was visible, including the white concrete roof over the walkway to the entrance. A strategically placed chair in the shadows at this level afforded the perfect cover to observe any and all late night or early morning trespassers.

Joe shut down the computer, grabbed the ring of keys, and locked the office. Nods and smiles were offered to all he met on his way to the elevator, and to kindly Ophelia Tellios in the third-floor hall.

A roost on a higher floor to avoid the risk of accidentally being seen was Joe's preference, but the third floor presented an opportunity to get to the parking lot much quicker should the need arise.

"And I hope it does," he whispered.

The Gentry's condo was not unlike his own—the tables and chairs and their location in the living room being the only difference—and the fragrance of cinnamon heavy in the air. He flipped the light switch, igniting a pair of floor lamps, and moved quietly to the ivory pinch-pleat curtains shielding the sliding glass door to the balcony. After peeking through the curtains, he returned to the entrance and switched off the lamps.

A thin veil of moonlight lay across the room, enough to guide Joe through the maze of furniture without mishap. He moved back to the balcony area, parted the curtains, unlocked the sliding glass door, and slid it open.

The usual absence of sound, save for the hissing of tires on asphalt emanating from Memorial Causeway, greeted him as he stepped onto the deck. He set his eyes on Island Way, lowering them across the parking lot to the space where his Toyota was sitting.

"Perfect," he whispered.

He looked over every inch of the deck, deciding that a seat in either corner provided the necessary line of sight. Twin, six-foot-tall Dracaena plants in terra cotta pots served as conventional outdoor garland, and offered thinly disguised camouflage.

After restoring the Gentrys' home to the condition in which he'd found it, Joe strode down the third-floor hallway to the elevator, pinching his face in disgust at the pink walls and maroon carpeting he so despised. When the doors opened, he stepped forward and stopped, surprised by the passenger in the elevator.

"David!"

"Joe." Entering the elevator, Joe stood beside his friend.

David didn't speak, his brow furrowed and jaw clinched.

"I take it you came to see me?"

"If you can spare the time."

Their ride to the fourth floor was short, the trip to Joe's condo even shorter. Joe unlocked the door and felt along the wall for the light switch. David followed him inside, waiting until the lights were on to close the door. His expression hadn't changed.

"David, would you care for some—"

"Do you want me to put you in jail, Joe? Because I will, you know."

"I guess you talked to Ben."

"I can't say it any plainer. Stay out of the investigation."

"Is Carly okay?"

"She's fine."

"Does she need anything?"

"Just stop it, Joe! Please! I know you were an outstanding detective in your day! I did the search on you, remember?"

"You know it's Rogan Cavanaugh, don't you? You know that he killed Karen Bachmann and Tim Truffant."

"What I know or don't know doesn't concern you! But sticking your nose into my investigation *does*!"

"And Detective Parton knows he killed the Berkshires."

"Dammit, Joe! Would you listen to me! Stay out of it, or I'll arrest you for interfering with an investigation!"

David didn't wait for Joe to respond. He threw open the door and stormed into the hall.

Joe wrapped his hand around the doorknob and eased it closed, lingering a few seconds at a standstill. He knew that David was right. He understood the position he'd put the young detective in, and the others as well. This time he *was* interfering more than helping. If any part of his plan were faulty, and he underestimated Rogan Cavanaugh in any way, he could wind up dead.

He shuffled to his sofa and sat down. Releasing a heavy sigh, he felt something poking him and shifted when he remembered

Carly's automatic hidden under the cushion.

"Sorry, David, but I'm going to be standing in front of Best Buy tomorrow morning the minute it opens."

Chapter 16

The next morning was like every morning, and Joe managed to sleepwalk his way through his routine of shave, shower, and breakfast. Surprised by an absence of anxiety, he relished the calmness, in no rush to pursue the one task he felt obligated to complete.

When it was time to go, he eased his car out of the Crimson Conch parking lot, not giving a second thought of the route to the Best Buy on U.S. 19. Brainless drivers in a hurry to get somewhere didn't annoy him. Red light after red light was no cause for exasperation. And, best of all, he came across a parking space near the entrance, where he joined the small group of shoppers waiting to be admitted.

At ten a.m., the doors opened and people were civil in their quest to locate the department they desired.

Joe had no trouble finding the aisle of cell phones, taking his time to pore over the many models on display. He located the Cendar PCS Mercury 7, studied its many mystifying options, and moved on to the more expensive models with accessories he couldn't begin to fathom. Perplexity filled him as he glanced at the Mercury 7.

I wonder if an upgrade might be better as a safety measure, he thought.

"Excuse me, sir, but you look baffled. May I help you?"

Joe turned to discover a blond with a smattering of freckles over her nose standing beside him.

"Is it that obvious?"

Her widening smile was the answer.

"I think the Cendar model, there, is all I need."

"Will you want to download apps, troll the WEB, and Skype your friends?"

"Young lady, you may as well be speaking a foreign language. All I want is a phone, and to send messages to my grandkids."

"Then the Mercury 7 is all you'll need."

"I have a question. On the phone I have now I sometimes get calls I don't want. I understand I can stop getting them with...what do they call it, road blocking?"

The blond chuckled. "Yes, sir, with call blocking you can stop those calls. Give me your phone and I'll show you how to do it."

Joe dug into his pocket and handed it to her.

"You've got a clamshell," she said. "This will be easy."

Joe shrugged. "Whatever you say."

She flipped open the phone and punched one of the buttons. "Scroll to Settings." She showed him the icon on the screen. "There are your options. Scroll down to Call Blocking, enter it, and punch in the numbers you want to block." She closed the phone and returned it to Joe.

"You'll have the same function on the Mercury 7 to block text messages...but you won't have to open it."

"Then that's the one for me. And thank you. You've been most helpful."

The blond pulled the phone encased in a box off the hook and passed it to him. "Anything else? A case for carrying your phone, perhaps?"

Joe wanted to verify that the phone was, indeed, untraceable, but thought better of it. The blond was smart. She understood the technology. Too many questions might arouse suspicion.

"I believe that's all."

He thanked her then wove his way through the aisles to the

front of the store to pay for his tool of revenge.

The serenity he had felt earlier had given way to excitement as he got into his car and started back home. The fun was about to begin.

Enjoying a light breeze blowing in from the west, Joe was stretched out on a blue chaise lounge, fiddling with his new toy. A heavy sigh preceded his laying down the phone and removing a small book from the box.

When all else fails, follow the instructions, he thought.

Thirty minutes later the phone was operable. He was ready to start playing a most dangerous game.

Glancing at the paper on which he'd written Rogan Cavanaugh's phone number, he punched it in and paused, considering what he wanted to say. He grinned when the answer came.

"Do your parents know that you're an asshole?" he typed, and pressed the send arrow.

He leaned back and gazed at the cotton-ball clouds drifting across a sky the color of the Best Buy blond's eyes.

Ten minutes passed without an answer.

"Then I'll make sure to tell them."

Joe laughed as he hit send again.

Seconds later a tone sounded. He peered at the screen.

"Jimmy if I find out this is u I'm gonna kick yer ass!"

"Guess again, dumb shit!" Joe had to wait until he stopped laughing before he could press the send button.

"Miguel?"

"You really are stupid!"

Joe shut off the phone and closed his eyes. He'd let Cavanaugh wallow in uncertainty for the rest of the day. Tomorrow—a little later or a little earlier, perhaps—he'd pick up where he'd left off with his antics. For now he would rest. Maybe take a nap. Bide his time until ten or eleven o'clock. Then he would station himself on the Gentry's balcony and wait for the mechanic.

Chapter 17

The night air wasn't chilly, damp more than cool, which persuaded Joe to wear his flannel shirt. Blending into the shadows covering one corner of the Gentry's balcony, he was perched three feet behind the Dracaena, hidden from those with inquisitive eyes. The hour was late, well past midnight, and Island Way was a ribbon at rest. Joe looked to the east, to Clearwater, and soaked in the street lights defining the avenues of office buildings and stores.

Why do some people feel the need to spoil the beauty? he thought. *Why do they inflict their selfish ways on the ideals the rest of us cherish?*

A lone car leaving Clearwater Beach on Memorial Causeway distracted him. He followed the headlights that became taillights that soon disappeared altogether. He set his eyes on the condo parking lot, watching and waiting for the least sign of movement. Periodic noises disturbed the tranquility—slamming, banging, and barking. Humans and mongrels. In the sum of all things most were respectful of others, but some, like the one he sought, were driven by their self-serving nature and disregard for decency.

Joe had come to hate stakeouts during his time on the force. The majority of them were unsuccessful, a colossal waste of time, not to mention loss of sleep. This stakeout felt different—was different. He knew his quarry. Had read the mechanic like a book during their brief encounter. The man couldn't resist retaliation. Especially when challenged by someone viewed as inferior. Joe wondered if Cavanaugh had figured out who was behind the text messages. He grinned at the notion.

He's as dumb as a red brick. I could be sending messages for days.

Joe pored over the scores of vehicles filling the parking lot, each one unique in its machinery.

Peace was the theme on this night, all quiet, everywhere quiet, quiet until another car announced its presence on the causeway. In seconds it was gone.

With no impetus or urging, Carly's face materialized in his mind. He missed her. Missed seeing her. Missed her smell. Missed their conversations. Jail was no place for a woman like her. Even if it was for her own good. She needed to be free from confinement. She needed to be doing what she did best—making a difference.

A door slamming caused Joe to jump, and with it, he realized that he'd dozed off. His eyes darted around the parking lot, straining to get a fix on the imagined intruder as his fingers tightened around the grip of Carly's automatic. He saw no one. He scoured the lot again, his heart pounding until he heard laughter. Lifting his eyes to the apartment building across the street, more laughter guided his focus to a pickup truck parked just off the sidewalk. He shifted in the chair and leaned forward.

That can't be him...can it? he thought.

A figure rounded the rear of the truck with difficulty, bouncing off the bed and staggering to the passenger-side door. Whoever was there got out immediately, dropped to the ground and started laughing—a woman judging from the pitch and tone of the voice. Her escort helped her to her feet, and, together, they wobbled and wove to the building.

Joe sat back, disgusted that he'd fallen asleep.

If Cavanaugh has been here, I missed him. Dammit!

He yawned and promised himself he would not be so careless again.

The hours dragged on, made longer by the drone of silence. Joe struggled to stay alert, shifting every few minutes, wanting to stand or walk around, but knowing he couldn't risk it. He considered creeping over to the other side of the balcony.

With my luck he'll show about the same time and see me. I'll just sit tight.

An aroma he hadn't smelled in years filled his nostrils—pancakes in the skillet, and bacon frying. Its scent was overpowering. Exactly the same as when Joyce used to make breakfast.

Get up, Joe! he heard her say. *You're going to be late for work*!

Joe slowly opened his eyes, seeing only the Dracaena and the ebony sky.

Dammit! *I did it again*!

His watch read four-fifteen. He grumbled as he ran a hand over his face.

"I missed him!" he whispered. "Dammit to hell, I missed him!"

He looked over the parking lot one last time, and got to his feet.

Locking the sliding glass door behind him, Joe tucked Carly's automatic into his waistband and draped the tail of his flannel shirt over it before ambling quietly through the Gentry's home. He cracked the entrance door, eased it open, and searched the hallway through bleary eyes. Seeing no one, he left.

As he entered the elevator, he decided he should check on his car. Cavanaugh had gotten a good look at it during his visit, and if the mechanic had slipped into the parking lot unnoticed, he may have left another message.

The first-floor hallway was still, the only sound being the swoosh of the entrance doors when he exited the lobby.

The early morning air was damper, cooler, and his flannel shirt lay warm against his T-shirt and skin. When he came within feet of his car, he slid his hand under the shirt and gripped the automatic. No sense taking chances. Circling the car was without incident. No message from Cavanaugh was attached, so he headed back to the building.

He was about to unlock his door when a wicked thought wormed its way into his mind. Once inside, he locked the door and strode through the darkness to his bedroom. He turned on the closet light, went to his dresser, and pulled open the second drawer. The Mercury 7 was right where he'd left it.

Let's see, what kind of message should I leave as a wakeup call, Cavanaugh?

He turned on the phone, still searching for the right words. The face of the phone glowed to life, and as he started to activate the text messaging function, three words derailed his mission. One Missed Call. He punched the first digits of his voicemail number then hesitated, his shirt unable to shield him from a chill. He cleared the digits and scrolled to Messages. The words were bold and strong.

"I'm coming after you old man."

There hadn't been many times in Joe's career, let alone in his life, when he'd found himself not knowing which way to turn. He'd ignored good judgment and David's warning not to interfere and initiated the mind game with Cavanaugh. Underestimating his adversary left him in the unenviable position of being alone to face the pending assault. Where or when it would come, he didn't know.

He considered his options, though they were few.

I should tell David the truth. He won't be happy, and he might arrest me, but at least he'll know what I did.

Joe sat down on the edge of his bed with a firm grip on the Mercury 7.

Or I can end the game now and hope that Cavanaugh is one for making idle threats.

He paused and thought of Carly.

But I know he isn't. He's killed two people. He would have killed Carly if she hadn't served a purpose.

The third option was the least desirable, the thought of

which had driven him to take action, the consequences seeming much less gratifying now.

Or I can call him out and kill him.

Even in his exhausted state, Joe knew that line of thinking was wrong. Murder was wrong. Self-defense was the only justification for killing a killer. Entrapment could lead him to being tried and prosecuted and sent to prison. And prison was no place for a cop.

He fell over on his side, rolled onto his back, rested his head on the pillow, and stretched out his legs.

"I'm going to call David and admit to what I've done," he whispered.

Minutes later, he was asleep.

Chapter 18

Dreamless, blissful sleep left Joe wondering how long he'd been out when the knocking woke him. Lingering to clear the uncertainty from his head, he heard a second round and swung his feet to the floor, realizing that he was still dressed. More knocking sounded as he reached the living room. Daylight was pouring in from every window. Peering through the peephole, he was relieved to see a friend waiting in the hall.

Joe opened the door. A yawn interrupted his greeting. "Oh, sorry, David, what has you out so early?"

"I'd like to talk to you...if it's convenient."

"Of course. Please come in. Would you like some coffee?"

"No, thanks, I've filled my quota."

"I'll put some on if you don't mind. I need a kick-start early in the morning."

"Joe, it's eleven-thirty."

"Really? I've lost half of the day. Have a seat." He waited until David was settled. "Now, what's on your mind?"

David pursed his lips and folded his hands. "I'm sorry for being so rough on you the other day. I'm still not happy with what you did, but you didn't deserve to be chewed out."

Joe studied the young detective.

He's really going to blow when I tell him what I did yesterday. "I appreciate that, David, but there's something you should know."

"Oh?"

Joe went on to explain his plan, and the dueling messages exchanged between him and Rogan Cavanaugh. Each revelation added to the anger building in David's eyes.

"If you want to retract your apology, I understand."

"Joe, what in the hell ever possessed you to do such a thing?"

"Joyce always said I was hardheaded."

"Well she was right!"

"He's going to come after me. His type has no control over their rage."

David shook his head. "You've set yourself up with no recourse, Joe."

"I know. And now you can get him."

"What if he kills you before we get him? What if he kills you and skips town? Carly will never forgive me."

"He won't."

"Oh, really? How can you be so sure?"

"He's not that smart."

"It didn't take him long to figure out that you were doing the texting."

"True, but I had confronted him the day before. Even a blind squirrel finds an acorn now and then."

"What the hell does that mean?"

"He guessed right. He had a fifty-fifty chance of knowing it was me. I don't think he has the intelligence to get out of Florida without being caught."

"You're willing to take that risk?"

"Yes."

"Why?"

"The reason is sitting in jail for her own protection."

David started to speak then hesitated. "She's not in jail. Her arrest was bogus. She's staying with Kathleen Ramsey."

"Why didn't you tell me?"

"Our plan was to keep it a secret. After we told her what we were doing, she made me promise not to tell anyone. And now

I've broken that promise."

An ache throbbed deep in Joe's insides.

"I thought she understood that she could trust me."

"She *does* understand. But she figured you'd go after Cavanaugh, and..."

"And what?"

"Never mind. I've said too much already."

"She's planning something, isn't she?"

"Joe, I'm telling you...asking you for the last time to let us do our job. I'll make sure a patrol car stays close by in case Cavanaugh pays you another visit."

"I'm sure he will. As I told you before, his type can't control the...wait a minute! What do you mean pays me another visit?"

"When I was in the parking lot I passed by your car. There's a deep scratch running the entire length of the driver's side."

Joe groaned and pinched up his face. *Dammit! I missed him!*

An hour after David left, Joe was still infuriated, more so at himself than at Cavanaugh for vandalizing his car.

How could I have missed the scratch when I checked my car? he thought. *I'm sure I checked every side. Did he come by later?*

He stewed a while longer before calming. Ham and cheese lathered with mustard between two slices of whole-wheat bread put an end to his sudden hunger.

His next stop would be the office to fulfill his responsibilities as building manager. Then, if time permitted, he would institute a computer search to locate the garage where Cavanaugh worked. He needed an oil change and an estimate to repair the damage done to his car, anyway.

Polite and courteous best defined Joe's attitude during his trek to the first floor, greeting all he met with a nod and a smile. Knowing that Carly wasn't in jail and Cavanaugh had taken the bait made for a wonderful day. All he needed to further elevate his spirits was a face-to-face with his nemesis.

Foregoing a phone call to a contractor, Joe clacked away on the computer keyboard until the object of his search was located.

"All-American Repairs on West Bay Drive," he whispered. "Employer of the biggest piece of shit in three states."

He checked his watch. He had plenty of time to get there. If they weren't too busy, he'd wait while they changed the oil. If not, he'd make an appointment. He would whatever was necessary to make contact with Cavanaugh again.

He locked the door to the office and strode out of the lobby to the parking lot. The afternoon sun felt warm against his face, which helped subdue the anger he felt upon seeing the ugly gouge that stretched all the way down the side of his car.

No worries, he thought, climbed inside, and steered the Toyota onto Island Way.

The face of Rogan Cavanaugh remained clear and unwavering in Joe's mind during the trip down Clearwater-Largo Road. From time to time he glanced in the rearview mirror to make certain he wasn't being followed, counting on David's being too busy to have set up a watchdog patrol car to keep tabs on him.

Unfamiliar with this part of the county, Joe remained alert, not wanting to miss his turn and be forced to backtrack. The green road signs kept him informed. He was getting close to West Bay Drive.

Flipping on the directional signal, he eased into the inside lane, and then the left turn lane, stopping for a full cycle of the traffic lights. Finally seeing the green arrow, he completed the turn.

A block later, on the southwest corner of West Bay Drive and Ridge Road, sat All-American Repairs.

Joe maneuvered his Toyota into the undersized parking lot of the washed-out red, white and blue dual-bay garage. The bay doors were open, and a pair of cars sat on lifts above the floor. A door marked "Office" caught his eye.

The inside of the office was cooled by a rattling air conditioner that had seen better days. A worn-out, padded folding chair flanked each side of a scuffed and chipped black cherry coffee table overflowing with car magazines.

Seconds later a rotund, round-faced man in dark blue work clothes entered from a side door. The forest of black hair on his burly arms made up for the few strands plastered to his bald head. Yellow-stained teeth defined his smile as he moved behind the counter.

"What can I do for ya?"

"I need my oil changed and an estimate on fixing the side of my car."

"What's wrong wid it?"

"Someone ran something sharp front to back."

The man winced. "Ouch! Is it deep?"

"I'd say."

"I can help ya wid duh oil change, but we don't do no body work. If it can't be buffed out, I mean."

"Know any good body shops?"

"Yeah." The man reached under the counter and brought out a brown clipboard with a work order attached. He reached under again, then handed Joe a business card. "These guys're good an' reasonable. They're right down duh street."

Joe eyed the card before sliding it into his pants pocket.

"Now lemme get'cha name an' address."

After Joe told him, the man laughed, close to a giggle.

"Yer a long way from home."

"I happened to see your garage and decided to stop in."

"What kinda car do ya got?"

"A 2012 Toyota Camry L-E."

The man looked up from his clipboard. "Well, we are All-*American* Repairs, but I think we can git the job done."

"That's a joke, right?"

"Some people might think so."

Joe smiled. "And a very funny one."

"Just an oil change?"

"Right."

"You gonna leave duh car?"

"I hadn't planned on it."

The man looked toward the garage bays. "It's gonna be thirty minutes or so before we kin git to it."

"I'll wait."

"I'd offer ya sum coffee, but we ran out. We got plenty of magazines, though."

"Thanks, but I'm trying to cut down."

The man stared a second before bursting into laughter. "Dat's a good one. I gotta remember dat one." He was still laughing when he disappeared through the side door.

Joe went outside and stretched. Shoving his hands into his pockets, he strolled to the first bay. The man replacing the wheel hub on a gray Ford Fusion sported a shaved head, handlebar moustache, and wore the same dark blue work clothes as the man in the office. He gave Joe a quick look and continued working.

Let's see who's working in Bay Number Two, Joe thought, and ambled to the next opening.

This man was wearing the same blue outfit, but had his back to Joe as he struggled to remove the front-end strut on a black Chevy Cavalier. His red hair gave him away.

Joe walked to within four feet of him, watching, waiting, until the mechanic yanked the strut free.

When Cavanaugh lowered his head to avoid running into the undercarriage, he glanced to his left and did a double take.

Joe offered a wide grin. "You don't hear too well, do you, Dumbass? Keep fuckin' around and I'll kill you."

He continued to grin as he turned and walked away.

Chapter 19

In the days that followed, Joe's new cell phone didn't ring once. Not receiving a single word from Cavanaugh confounded him, and uneasiness that he might have underestimated the man began to knot his stomach. He was expecting a knee-jerk act of stupidity. Instead, the mechanic was exhibiting an inordinate amount of restraint—unusual to Joe's way of thinking, considering the number of hardcore felons and sociopaths he'd dealt with while on the force.

Worse, the silence was eating at Joe, a taunting more difficult to ignore with each passing day. Word from David that little, if any, progress was being made in solving the cases of Karen Bachmann and Tim Truffant didn't help matters, but the estrangement from Carly bothered him the most. How the green-eyed, pixie-haired brunette managed to garner his adoration still amazed him at times. Yet, somehow, he knew the attraction was mutual—a father-daughter relationship born of strangers.

Another Thursday was nearing late afternoon, and Joe was glad to see the last of the paperwork on his desk. He affixed his signature to the bottom of the contract and slid it into a brown envelope. The yard maintenance company would be grateful for an additional year's worth of business. He pushed his chair away from the desk and stretched, happy to be caught up.

He could breathe easier for a while—or until the next resident cornered him with a problem.

People he met in the first-floor hallway acted cordial, never the same people, but the same pleasantness about them. With very few exceptions, the Crimson Conch was a good place to spend one's winter years. And those exceptions weren't viable enough to darken the ambience.

Leaving the elevator after it stopped on the fourth floor, Joe strolled down the well-lit corridor, ignoring the maroon carpeting and pink walls, though he still despised them. They didn't seem to matter anymore. At his door, he paused and floated an idea.

I think I'll go out to eat tonight. And I want seafood. Haven't had it in quite some time. "Yep, that's the ticket," he whispered.

Heading straight to his bedroom, he was considering which restaurant would best satisfy his desire and which clothes to wear when a thought foreign to the other subjects turned his attention to his dresser. Pulling open the second drawer down, he slid his hands under the dull array of socks and removed the Mercury 7. Seconds after bringing it to life, he grinned when he saw the words: Missed One Message.

Excited at the prospect of catching the one responsible for bringing so much suffering to his friends, Joe retrieved the message.

"Do you like the beach old man? Your friends did. They were thrilled to death. Midnight tonite. You know where. If you have the balls."

Joe could feel his cheeks flush with anger. So the punk wanted a showdown.

"Well, you're going to get it," he whispered.

He reached into the drawer and shoved his free hand under the socks. Carly's automatic felt secure in his grasp. An early supper at Backwaters in tribute to his friends the Berkshires would set the tone for the evening. At midnight, he would seek out Cavanaugh on the same stretch of beach where they had been murdered.

***

Joe sat in s chaise lounge on the balcony and stared at the half-moon carved into the onyx sky. In less than an hour he would face a killer. In less than a second, the killer would be dead—no subsequent thoughts, no hesitation, no last-minute calls for leniency. Tonight, justice would be served.

Joe checked his watch. Ten fifty-seven p.m.

Another fifteen minutes or so and he would leave for the beach access on Bohenia Circle. Arriving early might provide the edge he needed to surprise Cavanaugh before the mechanic could initiate his plan. Joe wasn't counting on it, though. Underestimating the man was not a mistake to be made again.

More than once he'd considered calling David to advise him of what was about to happen. Each time he hadn't. Entrapment was an act not held in high regard by law enforcement.

Self-defense was another story. Joe could manufacture a feasible excuse for bringing a gun to the rendezvous. Later on he would have to, considering the automatic belonged to Carly.

Joe rose from the chaise lounge and looked in the direction of Clearwater Beach one last time. No sense waiting any longer.

Memorial Causeway was deserted except for a small number of cars, unusual even for that time of night. Mandalay Avenue was quieter.

Joe parked on Eldorado Avenue and headed in the direction of the beach access. As he had done before, he stuffed the automatic into his waistband and hid it under the tail of his flannel shirt.

The wooden footbridge stretched before him, an ominous passageway in the absence of light. A multitude of shadows on either side hinted of danger, and possibly concealed the killer he sought.

Joe hadn't noticed the small stand of palm trees dotting the sand dunes on the left during his last visit. Shy in number and thickness, their presence among the sea oats and scrub brush still presented a model hiding place. He remained calm, glancing in their direction at times, and slid his right hand under his shirt to grip the automatic. As he neared the end of the bridge, he looked over his shoulder and stared hard at the darkness blanketing the trees.

"Don't move a muscle, Old Man!"

The voice came from the sand dunes behind him.

Joe let his right hand drop to his side.

The sound of thick foliage crackling underfoot and scratching the legs of Cavanaugh's pants grew louder.

"Now, turn around with your hands out to your sides—and make it slow."

Joe realized his mistake once he was facing Cavanaugh. A four-foot concrete wall edging the property line on the right of the access had shielded his nemesis.

"I knew you'd fall for it. Cops like you don't know when to quit."

"You know all about me, do you?"

"I know enough. If you know where to look, you can find out anything. That's how you found me, isn't it?"

"Then you must have guessed that I wouldn't come alone."

"Shove it up your ass, Old Man! It won't work! Nobody was with you when you came to my house, and nobody was with you when you came to the garage! Ain't nobody here to save you now!"

"Are you sure? I mean, are you *really* sure?"

Cavanaugh let go a smoker's chuckle as he pulled back the hammer on the revolver in his right hand.

"Drop the weapon and show me your hands!" someone shouted from the bridge.

Cavanaugh hesitated, his pistol leveled at Joe's face, then wheeled around and fired.

The figure on the bridge fired as Joe tore the automatic from his waistband and pumped two rounds into the mechanic's chest. Cavanaugh stumbled backward and collapsed into the sand.

Joe kept the automatic trained on the man as he inched

forward. A swift kick in the ribs proved that Cavanaugh was dead. Joe reached down and yanked the pistol from his lifeless hand.

"Don't move or you're dead!" a woman behind him yelled.

Joe carefully raised his arms and straightened up. "Don't shoot, Carly, it's me."

A lengthy second passed.

"Are you all right, Joe?"

"Yeah." He lowered his hands, turned, and faced her. "It's over." Looking toward the bridge, he saw the figure was crumpled over the railing. "We'd better check on him, though."

"Oh, my god! David!"

Carly took off running. Joe followed her as fast as he could. Two patrolmen waving flashlights sprinted onto the bridge from the street.

David let loose a groan as the group reached him.

Carly grabbed a hold of him. "Where are you hit, David?"

"Left shoulder...Joe...Joe okay?"

"I'm right here. Cavanaugh is dead. I'm...I'm sorry."

David groaned again.

"I'll radio for an ambulance and the Crime Analysis Unit," one of the patrolmen said. He looked at the second. "Let's get him back to my S-U-V."

"Better call the Medical Examiner, too," Carly said.

The patrolmen lifted David from the railing and struggled to help him across the bridge.

Carly and Joe began the slow trek back to the other end where Cavanaugh lay dead in the dunes. A faint siren wailed in the distance. Joe handed Carly her automatic and Cavanaugh's pistol.

"I'm glad you had more than two weapons in your arsenal," he said.

"I dug out my old automatic from when I first joined the force. I don't even know if it works."

"I'm really sorry about David. I guess I should have contacted him before I decided to come out here and—"

"Yes! You should have! This was a damn fool thing you did, Joe! You could have gotten yourself killed!"

Joe hung his head.

"That's why we put a tail on you. We figured you were planning to do something."

Carly couldn't see him grin in the darkness.

"I'm glad you did." Joe looked down at Cavanaugh. He heard Carly sniff. "What is it?"

Carly leaned over and inhaled. "That's it! That's the cologne I smelled the night Tim was killed!"

"Then you were right about Cavanaugh being there."

Carly put her arm around him. "We were right."

Chapter 20

Joe set his coffee cup on the folding TV table, clasped his hands over his chest, and closed his eyes. The cool breeze brushing his face did nothing to chase the sadness from his heart. In the time before and since he'd moved to the Crimson Conch Condominiums, his wife had passed away, several friends and acquaintances had been murdered or put in jail, and now, a young detective whom he respected lay in the hospital due to his unwillingness to leave well enough alone.

Joe sighed, opened his eyes, and gazed beyond the buildings, houses, and roads to the blue-green Gulf of Mexico that filled the distance to the horizon. Another cool breeze poured into the balcony only to steal away in an instant.

"You okay, Joe?"

Joe rolled his head over on the padded headrest of the other chaise lounge. "I'm fine. I was just thinking."

Clearly relaxed, Carly's drooping eyelids all but covered her emerald eyes. "Thinking good thoughts, I hope."

"Well...thinking." He rolled his head back and stared again at the expanse. "I'm glad it's all over. And glad it worked out for you."

"Kaczmarek and Ramsey are good cops. They cut me some slack during the investigation. But they would have nailed me if I'd been guilty."

"They determined that Cavanaugh was behind it all?"

"A partial print was found on the hammer of my backup snub nose. The medical examiner determined it belonged to him. It wouldn't have stood up in court, but it was good enough for them. And the fact that no residue was found on my hands."

"You allowed them to test you?"

"Against my better judgment. I was lucky."

"Did you mention the cologne?"

"At the station and at the shooting. They found a bottle of Havana Sunset when they searched his house. I never heard of it. They hadn't either."

"I guess a unique scent has its benefits sometimes."

"I'll never forget it, that's for sure."

"What about Karen Bachmann?"

"The striations on the bullet that killed her matched Cavanaugh's revolver."

"The same revolver he stuck in my face?"

Carly nodded. "And the one he used on your friends."

A vision of Martha and Lionel Berkshire flashed into Joe's mind.

"They didn't deserve to die."

"None of them deserved to die. Tim and I were finished, but I didn't hate him. I was really hoping we might..." She coughed then looked away for a second. "And Bachmann...Cavanaugh had a ton of her pictures plastered on the wall of his guest room. We found a video camera hidden in her bedroom that must have been installed without her knowledge. He was obviously obsessed with her, and you know that old story. Unrequited love leads to jealousy leads to murder."

Joe nodded in agreement. "Why do you think he came after me?"

Carly gave him a dubious look. "Other than the fact that you dared him, you mean?"

Joe winced.

"I think you scared him. I think he believed he had gotten away with it until you showed up. And when he went online to look for your address to deliver the threatening note, he discovered the success you had achieved in Philadelphia. At that point, he had no choice but to get rid of you. But the truth is we'll never know for certain."

"Do you remember what you called me shortly after we met?"

Carly chuckled. "You mean besides The Gray Detective? I said you were a nosey old goat whose time had come and gone."

"Yeah. Joyce always said I was hardheaded."

"A smart woman who knew her man."

Joe eased his head over. "Listen, young lady, when it comes to hard heads, an expert would have a difficult time deciding whose head is harder, yours or mine. Don't ever forget that."

"Yes, Sir," Carly said, grinning.

"I promised myself when I retired that I was going to put it all behind me. I was doing pretty good until Joyce died. After that I..."

Carly reached over and took his hand. "She was your reason, the best reason for letting go. Without her, it's hard for you not to slip back into doing something you've done for so long, especially when you're so good at it."

"Thanks, Carly. You're a true friend. What's really bothering me, though, is that I almost got David killed. I'm having trouble coming to terms with that."

"Have you been to the hospital to see him?"

"I haven't worked up the nerve."

"Go see him. It'll be good for both of you."

Joe squeezed her hand.

"Which brings me to an idea I've had for a while." Carly sat up and shifted her bare feet to the floor. "I want you to think about something."

"I don't think I'm going to like what you have to say."

"Since you don't seem to be able to keep your nose out of police business, I'd like you to consider becoming a consultant."

"A consultant? Carly, I'm retired. I don't want to punch a time clock again."

"Gimme a break, Joe. You start salivating every time David and I mention a case."

"But I already have a job as building manager."

"I don't mean as a full-time consultant. I'm talking about on an 'as needed' basis."

"I don't know."

"Joe, you're one of the best detectives I've ever known. Having you on the team would be a tremendous asset. David agrees with me."

"Really? Even after what happened?"

"Yes. I've already talked to the captain about it, and he's going to run it by the chief."

Joe lowered his eyes and pondered the idea. Being a detective and hunting down criminals was in his blood. Helping the Clearwater Police Department would be beneficial to the community.

Carly shook his arm. "Let's go see David. You can talk it over with him."

Joe's eyes brightened. "Sounds good to me."

"But I want you to promise me that you'll think long and hard about taking the job."

The old detective smiled at his young friend. "Okay, but no promises."

ACKNOWLEDGMENTS

Thanks to George Salter, Claire Kemp, Theresa R. Richardson, D.T. Bush, Sue Lloyd-Davies, Patricia Grayson, Heloise Jones, Tom Horrigan, Joyce Wagner, the Gulfport Fiction Writers, David Mather and the Gulfport Public Library, Technical Advisors Rod Steckel and Ken Beaudoin, Alex Cameron, Dia and the wonderful folks at the Neptune Bar and Grill, and Gini and Mike of the Beach Bazaar. Special thanks to Lynn Taylor, Steph Post, Jeffery Hess, and Johnnie M. Clark for their guidance, support, and friendship. Many thanks to my dear friends Mike O'Malley, John and Nancy Lamson, Al and Nancy Karnavicius, Rim Karnavicius and Michelle Rego, Charles Lyon, and Jim and Debby Herden. And most of all, I wish to express my grateful appreciation for my family.

Photo credit Sue Lloyd-Davies

STEPHEN BURDICK was born and raised in Florida. He is a retired civil servant currently living in the Tampa Bay area. He enjoys getting together with friends and attending various events.

On the following pages are a few more great titles from the Down & Out Books publishing family.

For a complete list of books and to sign up for our newsletter, go to DownAndOutBooks.com.

Hell to Pay
A Diggy and Stick Crime Novel
Andy Rausch

Down & Out Books
March 2022
978-1-64396-248-1

Dirty ex-cops Robert "Diggy" Diggs and Dwayne "Stick" Figgers have found themselves in a terrible situation. After Kansas city drug lord Benny Cordella discovers that they have wronged him, he devises an insane plan: he's going to force them to commit suicide. This, he believes, will send them to hell, where they will track down Dread Corbin, the man who killed his daughter. Of course, Diggy and Stick don't believe this is possible, but they will soon discover that hell is real.

Hell to Pay: Diggy and Stick Book One is unlike any crime novel you've ever read before. It's dark, dangerous, edgy, and laugh-out-loud hilarious. Buckle up for one hell of a ride!

Groovy Gumshoes
Private Eyes in the Psychedelic Sixties
Edited by Michael Bracken

Down & Out Books
April 2022
978-1-64396-252-8

From old-school private eyes with their flat-tops, off-the-rack suits, and well-worn brogues to the new breed of private eyes with their shoulder-length hair, bell-bottoms, and hemp sandals, the shamuses in Groovy Gumshoes take readers on a rollicking romp through the Sixties.

With stories by Jack Bates, C.W. Blackwell, Michael Bracken, N.M. Cedeño, Hugh Lessig, Steve Liskow, Adam Meyer, Tom Milani, Neil S. Plakcy, Stephen D. Rogers, Mark Thielman, Grant Tracey, Mark Troy, Andrew Welsh-Huggins, and Robb White.

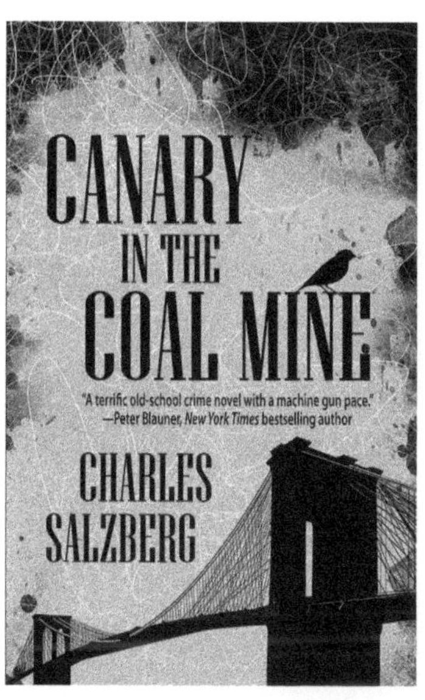

Canary in the Coal Mine
Charles Salzberg

Down & Out Books
April 2022
978-1-64396-251-1

Pete Fortunato, a NYC PI who suffers from anger management issues and insomnia, is hired by a beautiful woman to find her husband.

When he finds him shot dead in the apartment of her young boyfriend, this is the beginning of a nightmare as he's chased by the Albanian mob sending him half-way across the country in an attempt to find missing money which can save his life.

Breaking Character
Mark T. Conard

Down & Out Books
May 2022
978-1-64396-254-2

A small-time actor is accused of murdering his girlfriend's abusive ex, and he escapes the heat when he accepts the bizarre role of an eccentric billionaire's long-lost friend, allowing him to hide in plain sight while he searches for the real killer.

The actor must risk losing his identity, his freedom, even his life to end the drama he's been unwittingly cast in.

www.ingramcontent.com/pod-product-compliance
Lightning Source LLC
Chambersburg PA
CBHW032101040426
42336CB00040B/632

* 9 7 8 1 6 4 3 9 6 2 8 1 8 *